A TREASURY OF

RELIGIOUS

HUMOR

Edited by

James E. Myers

THE LINCOLN-HERNDON PRESS, INC.

818 S. Dirksen Parkway

Springfield, Illinois 62703

A Treasury of Religious Humor

Published by
    Lincoln-Herndon Press, Inc.
    818 S. Dirksen Parkway
    Springfield, Illinois 62703
    (217) 522-2732

Printed in the United States of America

LIBRARY OF CONGRESS CATALOGUING-IN-PUBLICATION DATA

    ISBN 0-942936-24-8 $10.95
    Library of Congress Catalogue Card Number 94-075864
    Second Printing

Typography by
    Spiro Affordable Graphic Services
    Springfield, Illinois

TABLE OF CONTENTS

INTRODUCTION

Humor in church? In religion? And laughter, too? To say "yes" seems a contradiction in terms. Yet there **is** humor in the Bible, and why not! The Bible reflects life today as well as thousands of years ago. For example, in Psalm 2, we read: "When the people, kings, rulers take counsel against the Lord and His anointed, what does the Lord do? He that sitteth in the heavens shall laugh." [At the colossal effrontery of the 'big shots' who presume to go against His will.]

The great philosophical tome, ECCLESIASTES, says in verse 3, "To everything there is a season, a time to weep and a time to laugh." This collection of humor is geared to the latter half -- laughter time.

Again, in Psalm 216:2, written after the return to Zion from the Babylonian captivity, the Jews sang, "Then was our mouth filled with laughter and our tongue with singing."

There are at least thirty-seven references to laughter in the Bible.

And so, with such superb examples of the place and value of laughter in our religious lives, a book of religious laughter seems altogether appropriate because, given the shortness of our lives, we might as well laugh with our contemporaries, and those who preceded us. And why not leave a little laughter for those who follow us?

We think this collection reveals the fun, virtue and joy in religion and its practice. Today we use religious humor for the purpose of drawing attention to God, His ways and our ways of coping with His ways.

It is the editor's hope that ministers, priests, rabbis, and their congregations will find here sources for laughter that will illuminate their own feelings about the basic goodness of God and of man, as revealed in religion.

As we hope that parishioners, congregants and even those who affiliate with no church, will find in these stories and cartoons, a solid proof and substance to sustain their own various beliefs.

Another reason for compiling these good stories and cartoons is simply to provide amusement, laughter and the relief from daily heaviness and concerns. Laughter does lighten the soul. And -- to quote the ancient proverb -- "Laughter is the best medicine." (And might we add after "medicine," that laughter can **doctor** a sermon, and make it more easily understood and acceptable.)

Most of all, we offer these words simply for the enjoyment of humor. That, alone, is enough. For as Reverend Henry Ward Beecher (1818-1887) said: "A person without a sense of humor is like a wagon without springs, jolted by every pebble in the road."

And, as our great American poet said:

> The best preacher is the heart,
>   say the Jews of faith.
> The best teacher is time.
> The best book is the world.
> The best friend is God.
>   WE, THE PEOPLE.
>   Carl Sandburg

So, at last, ENJOY!

1
PREACHER HUMOR

"Souls Burning in Hell" will be the subject of Thomas Q. Potter, Pastor of the United Baptist Church, next Sunday evening. *"Tell Mother I'll Be There"* will be sung as a quartet by four ladies.

✳ ✳ ✳ ✳ ✳

A couple of fellows, never able to hold a job for long, met on the street. "What ya been doin' lately, John?" the one asked.

"I got the best derned job I ever had. It's great. Got over 500 people under me." His friend was surprised. "Gee, that's great. What ya doin' now?"

"Like I said, it's a very responsible job. I'm mowing grass at the cemetery."

✳ ✳ ✳ ✳ ✳

A preacher must know that his sermon,
That points to the heavenly portal,
Need not be totally eternal,
Just to be eternally immortal.

✳ ✳ ✳ ✳ ✳

A woman flees from temptation, but a man just crawls away from it in the cheerful hope that it may overtake him! (Still true?)

✳ ✳ ✳ ✳ ✳

A minister walked up to a member of his congregation, and he was furious! "I'm told that you said I stole the sermon I gave last week. I insist on an apology."

"Well, Pastor, I guess I ought to apologize because I did say I thought you'd stolen the sermon. But after church last week, when I got home, I found it still in the same book from which I thought you'd stolen it."

✳ ✳ ✳ ✳ ✳

America still has more marriages than divorces, which proves that preachers can still outtalk lawyers.

The minister of the Christ Episcopal Church in New Salem says that he has stopped telling the members of his congregation that they should pay their pledges with a smile because too many of them are doing just that.

* * * * *

"Daddy," asked the little boy who had just awakened in church during the sermon, "has the preacher finished?"
"Yep! He's finished, but he hasn't stopped!"

* * * * *

Here's a story that proves it is of great value to regularly turn to the Bible.
The preacher called on a little old lady who was supposed to study the Bible every day. But she showed no evidence of doing so. He showed up at her door one day, demanding that she spend an hour with him reading the good book.
Grumbling, she went to the closet and dug out a dusty old Bible -- which she handed to the preacher. When he opened it, out fell a pair of spectacles. "Heck fire," the old woman yelled, "I been huntin' fer them specks for near to a year!"

* * * * *

Most people who fly from temptation usually leave a forwarding address.

* * * * *

A Quaker from Pennsylvania moved down south to try his hand at farming with mules. He'd never worked with mules before and knew not how unmanageable and stubborn they can be. He hitched a mule to the plow, and yelled "Giddiyap!" but the mule never moved. The Quaker got madder and madder, of course. At last, he walked around to face the mule, grabbed the bridle and looked directly in the animal's eye, saying, "Thou knowest full well I may not strike thee. Thou knowest that because I am a Quaker, I cannot curse thee. But thou knowest not that I can sell thee to a Baptist deacon who will beat the ---- out of thee!"

Rep. G. Ellit Hagen, Georgia.

* * * * *

There is a real speculation when resisting temptation. Just suppose that it might never come again.

2

"BROTHER JULIUS SEEMS TO GET MORE THAN HIS SHARE OF DAILY BREAD!"

＊＊＊＊＊

It was a very long sermon and the preacher motioned to one of the ushers to come forward, which he did. "Would you please open a couple of windows, Larry?" the preacher asked.

"I really hate to do it, Pastor. It's zero weather outside."

"I know that," said the minister. "But medical authority states that it is not healthy to sleep with the windows closed."

＊＊＊＊＊

There was once a preacher who called another one on the long-distance telephone. It was a parson-to-parson call.

＊＊＊＊＊

Whenever a minister haz preached a sermon that pleazes the whole congregation, he probably haz preached one that the Lord won't endorse.

Josh Billings

3

A minister was scheduled to perform a special wedding immediately following the Sunday morning service. He planned to do the ceremony before the entire congregation but, for the life of him, he could not recall the names of the two members whom he was to marry. He got around his dilemma this way: "Will those who want to get married now, please come stand before me."

At once, six single ladies, four widows and five single men stood, went to the aisle and walked to the front.

✳ ✳ ✳ ✳ ✳

An elderly Minnesota preacher was telling a protege of his -- a man recently ordained and due to occupy his first pulpit -- a few experiences of his long life in the hope that it would provide meaningful, if vicarious, experience for the younger man.

"It is essential that you preserve your dignity, come what may. Sometimes the smallest error can bring great embarrassment and you don't need that. For example, I was invited to have dinner with a member of my congregation in Pyote, Texas. When the host asked me if I would like some corn, I made the mistake of passing my glass instead of my plate."

✳ ✳ ✳ ✳ ✳

The most satisfying way to resist temptation is publicly.

✳ ✳ ✳ ✳ ✳

Pastor Timothy Brown did not get along well with his congregation. But they all turned out for his very last service and, in his last sermon, he quoted, "In my Father's house are many mansions. . .I go to prepare a place for you." That ended the sermon and the service. It was not until several days later that the congregation learned that Pastor Brown was going to be pastor at the state penitentiary.

✳ ✳ ✳ ✳ ✳

Question: Iz a reveng a viktory?
Answer: Kill a hornet after she haz stung yu, and see if the wound heals enny quicker.

Josh Billings

✳ ✳ ✳ ✳ ✳

A well-known comedian once remarked: "I'm torn between vice and versa."

4

In an upscale Manhattan church, the pastor saw a rich, dignified old lady having difficulty trying to get up the steps to attend services, so he hurried down to take her arm and help her up the steps. Reaching the top, the old lady asked, "Who is preaching this morning?"

"The last minister you had is here for the day and he'll be preaching."

"Oh, Sir," she said, "could I ask you one more favor?"

"Of course."

"Will you help me down the steps again?"

✳ ✳ ✳ ✳ ✳

Two parishioners stood beside the casket of the Reverend Edmond Talcott. They crossed themselves, turned and walked out. Once outside, they began to reminisce on the life of the deceased minister. "I went fishing with him once," said the one, "and you never heard such swearin'."

"Swearin'? Pastor Talcott swear? I find that impossible to believe."

"I know it sounds awful, but it's true. Y'see, there were just the two of us in the boat and Reverend Talcott hooked a huge muskie. He battled it ... musta been ten minutes ... finally got it up to the side and just as I was about to haul his fish into the boat, that derned fish flipped a time or two, got off the hook and away he went!

'That's too damned bad, Reverend Talcott,' I said. 'Just too damned bad!'

'It certainly is,' the Reverend said. 'And y'know ... that's the only time I ever heard him use such strong language!'"

✳ ✳ ✳ ✳ ✳

A retiring Methodist minister happily announced the name of his first permanent home as "Dunmovin'."

✳ ✳ ✳ ✳ ✳

A minister met a new member of the congregation named Hummick. He tried to fix her name in his memory by associating it with a similar evocative word. So he chose "stummick." The next time he met her he said, "How do you do, Mrs. Kelly."

✳ ✳ ✳ ✳ ✳

When a man gits tew talking about himself he seldum fails tew be eloquent, and frequently reaches the sublime.

Josh Billings

5

A preacher loved riding horses and had three of them. He had ordered a load of hay from one of his parishioners.

About noon, the little son of the parishioner came running into the house and told the minister, "The load of hay tipped over in the street, Pastor, and I'm sure sorry."

"Don't worry about it. Come eat dinner with us and we'll go out after we eat and make things right."

"Pa wouldn't like it."

"Sure he would. Come on."

After dinner, the minister asked the boy if he wasn't glad he'd had dinner with them.

"Sure," the boy said. "But Pa sure won't like it."

"Why do you keep bringing your Pa into this?" he asked.

"Pa's under the hay," the boy replied.

✳ ✳ ✳ ✳ ✳

"THIS IS HIS ANSWERING-SERVICE."

Did you hear about the saint who taught her dog to heal?

＊ ＊ ＊ ＊ ＊

"I feel so sorry for Rev. Smith," a man told his neighbor. "He bought a used car, but doesn't have the vocabulary to drive it."

＊ ＊ ＊ ＊ ＊

Just after two o'clock on a bitter winter morning, a physician drove six miles to answer a desperate phone call from a dying man.

The physician picked up a minister to administer last rites, just in case. After the two of them had entered the dying man's house, the doctor asked, "Where is your pain? What hurts most?"

"No pain. I just feel death is near."

The doctor took his pulse, examined his eyes, listened to his heart, then asked, "Have you made your will?"

"No, Doctor, I never thought . . ."

"Who's your lawyer?"

"Michael Myers. . .but. . ."

"Who's your bank trust officer? Better send for him, too."

"Oh, Doctor, do you really think I'm going to die?"

"No, I don't," he replied. "There's not a damned thing wrong with you. But I'd hate to have the Reverend here and myself be the only ones you've made a fool of on a night like this."

＊ ＊ ＊ ＊ ＊

From a church bulletin: "We regret to report that our minister does not plan to be away over any Sunday this summer."

＊ ＊ ＊ ＊ ＊

Mr. Smith had recently become the father of triplets. The minister stopped him on the street to congratulate him.

"Well, Smith, I hear the Lord smiled on you," the minister beamed.

"Smiled on me," exploded Smith. "He just purely laughed out loud at me!"

＊ ＊ ＊ ＊ ＊

When it comes to giving to charity. . .some folks stop at nothing.

A minister had been invited to address the congregation of a small church deep in the Cajun Country. He went to the hotel and noticed that the beds were not prepared with mosquito netting. He asked the hotel clerk why they didn't provide mosquito netting for guests, and the lad replied, "Well, Suh, mos' everybody gets kinda drunk before bedtime and so they don't feel no mosquitoes atall. In the mornin', the skeets is ginrally so 'toxicated, dey don't pay no 'ttention to de people."

✳ ✳ ✳ ✳ ✳

Question: "Which du you kount the happyest time in a man's life?"
Answer: "Immediately after he haz did a square thing."
Josh Billings

✳ ✳ ✳ ✳ ✳

AN INEFFECTIVE PRAYER
I always enjoy having Mr. R. S. Eckles of Black Mountain drop in to see me because he always has a good story to pass on.

During the course of his last visit, he told us about Uncle Pres Watkins who was quite a hunter and guide up in the mountain country many years ago.

There was a meeting of Presbyterian preachers at Montreat and they wanted to take a trip to the top of Mount Mitchell. The services of Uncle Pres were engaged with the understanding that he would act as a guide on the journey.

At the present time, there's a paved road up to the top of the mountain, but when this little incident took place, there was only a narrow dirt road. Inasmuch as there were a number of branch roads emanating from it, a person could get lost very easily. That's why a guide was essential.

The party made the top of the mountain in safety. While there, a terrific electrical storm broke out, and the preachers were scared to death. They offered up individual prayers for their safety. One of them turned to Uncle Pres and said: "Brother Watkins, wouldn't you like to join us in prayer?"

Uncle Pres shifted his cud of tobacco around a little bit, hesitated slightly and finally spoke up: "Well, to tell the truth, preacher, I only know one little prayer and I don't think that would be worth a damn in a storm like this."

Excerpts from *"Just For The Fun Of It."* 1954.
Written by *Carl Goerch,*
used with the permission of the
Estate of Carl Goerch

The sermon went on and on and the preacher asked, "What more, my friends, can I say?" and a voice from the back of the church said, "Amen."

＊ ＊ ＊ ＊ ＊

Returning from her ministrations at a nursing home, the nun ran out of gas. A passing motorist stopped and asked if he could help.

"I'm out of gas," the nun told him.

"I've got gas for you, but I haven't got anything to siphon it into."

The nun went to the rear and opened the trunk compartment, then removed a bedpan from it, closed the door and handed the bedpan to the kind man. He filled it, siphoning gas from his own tank.

The motorist left after handing the bedpan, filled with gasoline, to the nun.

The sister walked to the rear of her car, unscrewed the lid to her gas tank and, ever so carefully, began to pour the gas into her car.

While she was slowly, slowly pouring, a motorist passed by, observed what she was doing, turned to his companion and said, "Genuine faith!"

＊ ＊ ＊ ＊ ＊

"REVEREND, YOUR 'CROSS MY HEART AND HOPE TO DIE' HARDLY CONSTITUTES ADEQUATE COLLATERAL."

The minister's secretary: A lady who looks like a woman, thinks like a man, acts like a lady and works like a dog.

✳ ✳ ✳ ✳ ✳

The minister had pounded hard on the virtues of the born-again Christian. From that, he went on to the matter of punishment as opposed to reward for the righteous.

"I'm sayin' to y'all heah and now and forevah, that Hell ain't no easy place 'cause there ain't no messin' around an' laughin' an' sech down theah. No Suh! Down theah, they got molten iron abubblin' and aboilin' in them 'normous furnaces. An' now, brether'n and sister'n, let me make it cleah. . .down where I'm talkin' about, they use dat stuff fer ice cream!"

✳ ✳ ✳ ✳ ✳

A minister looked out over his sparse congregation on Sunday morning and said, "Looks like too many members of our congregation are sack-religious."

✳ ✳ ✳ ✳ ✳

A pious friend was telling a Quaker of the misfortunes suffered by a poor relation. "I certainly did feel sorry for him," said the man sadly.

"Yes, friend," replied the Quaker, "but did thee feel in the right place -- in thy pocket?"

✳ ✳ ✳ ✳ ✳

Be a peacemaker. . .always remember that it's hard to shake hands with a clenched fist.

✳ ✳ ✳ ✳ ✳

A visiting minister was the guest of a family, all of whom were members of the church where he was to preach. He had declined lunch with the family saying that he did not preach well after a big meal and would abstain.

After services, when the host returned home, his wife asked how their guest had performed at church.

"He might as well have et," said the husband.

✳ ✳ ✳ ✳ ✳

One ov the most reliable phrophets I kno ov iz an old hen. They don't phrophesy enny egg untill after the egg haz happened.

Josh Billings

Too many of us are willing to accept God in an advisory capacity only.

✳ ✳ ✳ ✳ ✳

At a church in Iowa City, where the town was caught in one of those terribly hot summer spells, the minister said he would preach the shortest sermon of his career. It was just too hot to do a longer one. He sermonized: "If you think it's hot here in Iowa City...just you wait!"

✳ ✳ ✳ ✳ ✳

The Lord loveth a cheerful giver...but He also accepts from a grouch.

✳ ✳ ✳ ✳ ✳

The minister told the congregation that, on the following Sunday, he would preach on Noah and the Ark and he hoped all would read the section before next Sunday. He gave them the chapter and verse. Two lads slipped into the church and pasted two pages of the pulpit Bible together. The next Sunday, the preacher began to read the announced text.

"Noah took unto himself a wife," he read, "and she was. . ." He turned the page and continued: ". . .300 cubits long, 50 cubits wide, 30 cubits wide."

He seemed startled, then turned the page and re-read the lines to himself. Then he looked up at the congregation and said, "Y'know, it's a marvelous thing that's just happened. I've been reading the Bible close on to forty years, and I still find there are some things hard to believe."

✳ ✳ ✳ ✳ ✳

Do you give to the Lord's work weekly...or weakly?

✳ ✳ ✳ ✳ ✳

The minister of a church that had come on hard times wrote to the richest member of the congregation asking for a donation. In return, he got only a $1.00 check. Vastly disappointed, the minister said, "I don't know whether to cash it or frame it!"

✳ ✳ ✳ ✳ ✳

It was a wise preacher who said, "I have learned that it does not make a sermon immortal to make it everlasting."

A minister was awakened at night by an intruder, a burglar who, when he saw the minister awake, said, "You make one move, mister, and you are dead, dead, dead! I'm lookin' for money."

"Let me get up and turn on a light," said the minister, "and I'll hunt with you."

* * * * *

If you are stupid enough to make money your god, it'll bother you like the devil!

* * * * *

"Is it your considered opinion, Sir, that a missionary goes to Heaven and a cannibal, an eater of man, goes to Hell?"

"Sure. It's a fact. Missionaries go to Heaven."

"But then what happens...just supposin', if the minister is in the cannibal?"

* * * * *

A church member, describing her minister, said, "Six days of the week he's invisible and one day of the week he's incomprehensible."

* * * * *

A minister had been unusually successful in every church he had served. When asked to explain his astonishing success, he said, "Every time I walk up to the pulpit, I say a little prayer like this: 'Lord, fill my mouth with real good, worthwhile stuff -- and shut my mouth when I've said enough!'"

* * * * *

Note on a small town preacher's door: "Bring your troubles to us and tell us about them. If not, come in anyway and tell us how you do it."

* * * * *

The man who wrote: "I would not liv always. I ask not tew sta," probably never had been urged sufficiently.

Josh Billings

A minister walked in the fish market and he was quite upset. "I want you to throw me four big fish," he said to the proprietor. "Just toss 'em to me."

"But why toss them to you?" the salesman asked. "Can't I just wrap them and give them to you like everyone else?"

"No, Sir!" yelled the preacher. "You do just as I say. So if anyone asks me if I caught any fish today, I can truthfully say: 'Sure did. Caught four big ones!'"

✳ ✳ ✳ ✳ ✳

"DON'T CALL ANYONE SINNERS UNTIL AFTER THE COLLECTION."

✳ ✳ ✳ ✳ ✳

One morning, the Reverend Jenkins went to his front door to get the newspaper, looked out and saw a dead mule in the street in front of his house! He quickly called the city health department, told them who he was and asked to have the mule disposed of. The man on duty was a smart aleck and said, "Hey, Reverend, I always heard that you preachers buried your own dead."

"Yes, we do. But not in all cases. As in this one, we like to offer the blessing first to the next of kin!"

✳ ✳ ✳ ✳ ✳

He was said to be a great preacher -- at the close of every sermon, there was a great awakening.

A clergyman took a well-earned vacation and decided to go to a golfing resort where Arnold Palmer frequently played.

As the clergyman approached the toughest hole on the course, the caddie said: "When Arnold Palmer plays this hole, he uses a No. 3 iron and says a prayer."

"I'll certainly give it a try," the clergyman remarked. But, when the ball landed in the water, he said, "I guess the Lord didn't hear me."

"He probably heard you," the caddie said, "but when Arnold Palmer says his prayers, he keeps his head down."

* * * * *

It's been suggested that the Internal Revenue Service should hang the following sign in all their offices: IN GOD WE TRUST; EVERYBODY ELSE WE AUDIT.

* * * * *

There were two banquets at the large hotel...one was for the liquor dealers and distributors and the other was for a group of clergymen. There was to be a special dessert for the liquor people, a sweet having watermelon spiked with rum, brandy and Benedictine. By mistake, the whisky-soaked watermelon went to the ministers' table. The man in charge reported this to the hotel manager. "What was the result?" the manager asked. "Did they say anything?"

"Not a word," the banquet hall manager said. "They were just too darned busy putting watermelon seeds in their pockets."

* * * * *

Everyone should try to spend their lives doing things that will outlast it.

* * * * *

The revival meeting had come to the time of baptism and the elders stood in the water performing one ceremony after another. One old man was brought out and the usual questions were asked, as to whether there was any reason why the baptism should not be done. One fellow in the crowd stood up. "I sure don't want to mess things up, Elder, but one dip ain't agonna do that old son-of-a-gun of a sinner much good. You'll have to anchor him out in deep, deep water overnight!"

Benjamin Franklin said: "None preaches better than the ant, and she says nothing."

* * * * *

A real tough guy strides into the saloon and orders a drink: "I want a milk punch and make it strong with forty-rod whiskey," he says. Then he went to the bathroom. About that time, a man came in wearing a black, worn-out coat. He walked to the bar and said: "Bartender, I'm a pore travelin' preacher and I've been travelin' the desert for a week, often without water and very little food. I only got a dime. Would you sell me that glass of foamy milk fer a dime?"

"Take the milk and welcome. And you owe me nothin'. You deserve it fer nothin'."

The preacher drank slowly and acted like it was a mighty good drink. When he'd drained the glass, he wiped his lips and said, "Lordy...Lord...Lord! What a cow!"

* * * * *

The worst part of being an atheist is that when things go really well for you, there's no one to thank.

* * * * *

There once was a preacher named Kind,
Who preached parishioners out of mind,
His hearers quite slack,
Got pains in their back,
And put pillows behind their behinds.

* * * * *

We should all give both freely and generously and in strict compliance with what we reported on our income tax.

* * * * *

Woodrow Wilson loved to tell the story of the time he went on a visit, a parish call, with his minister father. They had gone to visit a neighbor and, as was customary, had taken the horse and buggy. The neighbor/parishioner took a look at the horse and asked, "Reverend Wilson, why are you so thin and gaunt while your horse is fat and sleek?"

The Reverend Wilson was a bit slow in replying, so young Woodrow took over: "Probably because my father feeds the horse and the congregation feeds my father."

There was this elderly Presbyterian minister who was beloved by his congregation. He devoted himself to the needs of the congregation almost completely, except that, every now and then, he needed to go fishing. But he thought himself too old to go alone and so he would call on the town's ne'er-do-well, Bill Leefers, who was known as a "go-getter." By that the town meant that when his wife got off work, Bill would "go get her."

So Bill and the Pastor went fishing. Old go-getter hooked a good one and fought him for half an hour until, just before he got him to shore, the fish flipped over and was gone. Old Bill cut loose with a flow of profanity lasting several minutes.

About half an hour later, the preacher hooked a good one and played him for many minutes, until, just before he reached down to pull the fish on shore, his fish, just like Bill's, flipped off and was gone.

Flabbergasted, the preacher stood clenching his teeth and shaking his head furiously. "Bill," he said, "could you say a few words to that fish, please?"

＊ ＊ ＊ ＊ ＊

People usually consider it a good Sunday sermon when they feel that the minister didn't refer directly to them!

＊ ＊ ＊ ＊ ＊

A man wrapped up in himself makes a very small bundle.
Benjamin Franklin

＊ ＊ ＊ ＊ ＊

Bone orchard: A cemetery.

＊ ＊ ＊ ＊ ＊

In Alabama, there are hardy folks who can take or leave the ghosts said to frequent several small towns. There, a visiting preacher in one of those ghostly, small towns came down to breakfast one morning to announce that the town ghost had visited him shortly after he had retired the night before. "But I got rid of him easily," the preacher announced.

"How!" exclaimed the family with whom he was staying.

"I simply asked him for a donation."

＊ ＊ ＊ ＊ ＊

Anxious seat: Seat at the front of the revival meeting indicating the occupant's anxiety to be saved.

Passing through the garment factory at the Joliet State Prison one morning, a pastor noticed a prisoner sitting cross-legged, sewing a burlap bag on a bale of cotton pants. "Good morning, good friend, sewing, eh?"

"No, Chaplain," the prisoner said with a wry grin. "Reaping."

✳ ✳ ✳ ✳ ✳

In Oklahoma City, it got so hot and dry a few years back that they swear the Baptists were sprinkling, the Presbyterians were using a damp cloth and the Episcopalians were giving rain checks.

✳ ✳ ✳ ✳ ✳

Bible Two: Second Bible of the Texas Rangers containing the most wanted men! Said to have been read more avidly than Bible One!

✳ ✳ ✳ ✳ ✳

Billy Sunday said: "Try praising your wife, even if it does frighten her at first!"

✳ ✳ ✳ ✳ ✳

A Southern gospel pounder began his sermon by saying: "Brethren and sisters, Ah don' understan' you folks all comin' heah to pray fo' rain! Your lack of faith ain't <u>good</u>! Thar ain't a single one of yuh done brought an umbrella!"

✳ ✳ ✳ ✳ ✳

If only Americans spent as much on religion as on alcohol.

✳ ✳ ✳ ✳ ✳

An Episcopal minister applied for membership in the local Kiwanis Club only to be told, "Sorry, Pastor, but we have one fellow in your line of work. We got a preacher and we only take one from each profession. In fact, now we only have room for one other category, a hog caller."

"OK, I'll accept that," said the minister. "I'm usually called the shepherd of my <u>flock</u>, but then, you know your membership better than I do."

✳ ✳ ✳ ✳ ✳

Rafters: What a slambang, rousing hymn should make ring!

17

"HOW COME YOU NEVER CHANGE WATER INTO WHISKEY?"

* * * * *

"Brother Edwards," said Irv Thompkins to a rival minister. "Why don't you put more hell and damnation into your sermons? Is it too much push on your imagination to tell them about the terrors of hell?"

"No, it ain't that atall," Brother Edwards explained. "But it simply disrupts the service and I can't have that."

"Really? And just how does it disrupt the service?"

"Well, when I cut loose about hell, I got to declare a recess just about every five minutes because the congregation makes so much noise fanning themselves!"

* * * * *

Bible Puncher: A preacher, ordained or not, but also an ordinary, religious man who can quote biblical texts.

* * * * *

Henry Jenks, pastor of the rural Irish Grove Presbyterian Church, had just married a young farm couple. "God bless you both," Parson Jenks told them, "you're at the end of your troubles."

A year later, the groom ran into the minister in the Wal-Mart store, stopped him, pulled him aside and said, "It's been a terrible year since my marriage, Parson Jenks. And you told me we'd be at the end of our troubles."

"Yes, I did, son," the preacher said. "But I sure didn't tell you which end."

A first-rate definition of religion:
Religion Is Goodness
With Its Sleeves Rolled Up.

✵ ✵ ✵ ✵ ✵

Two ministers were discussing the art of the sermon. "I always try, when I preach a sermon, to make people laugh. And then, when their mouths are open with laughter, I try to put something in for them to chew."

✵ ✵ ✵ ✵ ✵

If you want proof that appearances can sometimes be deceiving, consider the dollar bill in a collection plate that looks exactly as it did thirty years ago.

✵ ✵ ✵ ✵ ✵

A Southern minister was visiting a service in Superior, WI, and was astonished to hear the minister explain hell as a region of ice and snow and eternal cold. Later, he asked the resident preacher to explain.

"Your description of hell, Reverend, was excellent but very unorthodox. Could you explain?"

"Well, Pastor, I'm glad you came to our service. But you see, in the summertime, it's mighty nice around here. Folks come to vacation and to fish and have a very good time. But when frost and snow and winter sets in and your house leaks cold and your clothes aren't heavy enough and you could use another blanket on your bed and even church on Sunday isn't warm enough, if I tell this congregation how warm hell is...why most of 'em would develop a powerful liking for the place."

✵ ✵ ✵ ✵ ✵

Parson John Beecher bought a new boat and named it, well, what do you think? He named it "Holy Scow."

✵ ✵ ✵ ✵ ✵

A preacher was concerned about the spiritual welfare of a pretty, shapely and quite frivolous widow in his congregation. He ran into her on the street, one day, stopped and said, "Last night, I prayed for you for a solid hour, dear girl!" "Why, Pastor, you didn't have to do that. If you'd just gone to the phone and called me, I'd have come right over."

19

Too often, by the time a man arrives at those famed "green pastures," he's too darned old to climb the fence!

* * * * *

The minister took one look at the tiny sum in the collection plate and turned to the congregation to say, "The sum in the collection plate reminds me of the fellow who approached the druggist one Sunday morning, just before church services and asked for change for a dime. 'Glad to oblige,' the druggist said, 'and I do hope you enjoy the sermon.'"

* * * * *

Question: Which do yu konsider the most general pashun ov the human heart?
Answer: The luv ov applauze, it sticks tew evrybody during life, and repeats itself on the tumestun.

Josh Billings

* * * * *

Pastor William Hendricks was known for his long sermons. But this particular Sunday morning, his sermon went on and on, far longer than usual. Pastor Hendricks realized it, ending the sermon by saying, "Dear people, I apologize for the long sermon. But I had so much, so very much to tell you."

A voice from the congregation said, "It's all right, Pastor. You sure did a lot to shorten the winter."

* * * * *

Tew bring up a child in the wa he should go -- travel that wa yourself.

Josh Billings

* * * * *

Pastor Henry Elkins had a prodigious memory that endowed him with amazing knowledge on most every subject. He was asked how he was able to know so much about so many things.

"Well, I learned a bit here, picked up a bit there and I was just too lazy to forget all of it."

* * * * *

Solitude: A good place to visit but a poor place to stay.

Josh Billings

20

Elmer Jenkins, a well-to-do businessman, died and, surprising went to heaven! There he met St. Peter who took him on a personally conducted tour. They visited the elegant tennis courts, golf courses, country clubs, the lovely forests and gardens and then returned to the Pearly Gates, where St. Peter told Elmer that he could have his choice...to live eternally in heaven or hell. Then St. Peter took Elmer back to the Gate where he could catch an escalator to hell to compare things!

Once in hell, Satan took over, showing Elmer fine-looking men, lovely women gadding about elegant swimming pools with servants supplying their every need. The people were being fed delicious-looking food with all kinds of drinks available. Elmer, really impressed, went back to heaven and said to St. Peter..."I'm selecting hell as my everlasting home."

Back to the escalator went Elmer, but when he got to the bottom, all he saw was fire and men sweating and utter chaos all around him. He turned to the Devil and said, "Hey! This ain't nothin' like you showed me before. What's going on here?"

The Devil grinned, saying, "Yesterday when you were here you came as a prospect. But today you're a client. Got that? Get to work!"

Nothing tests your faith quite so much as being caught with only a fifty dollar bill when the collection plate is passed.

* * * * *

A minister in Iowa City usually placed his sermon on the pulpit about an hour before he was to deliver it to the congregation. A young lad, mischievous as can be, knew this and, one morning, sneaked to the pulpit and removed the last page.

The minister gave a wonderful sermon and came to the final line of the last page, still there, saying, "So Adam said to Eve..." Then he looked for the last page, cleared his throat, turned to the congregation and said, once again, "So, Adam said to Eve...there seems to be a leaf missing."

* * * * *

Bible (according to the cowboy) -- A cowhand's cigarette papers.

* * * * *

Back in the beatnik days, one of them wandered into church with his beard, long hair, tattered clothes, and sat quietly throughout the service. He joined the crowd waiting to greet the pastor at the end of services and, when he reached the pastor, he said, "You were really with it, Daddy-o. You were way, way out wing-dingin' it."

"What did you say? Please repeat," said the Reverend.

"I mean, I really dig that jive. You laid it on me, Jocko. I read you so good I put ten fish in that collection plate."

"Well," beamed the minister, grabbing the beatnik's hand. "That was cool of you, man, real cool."

* * * * *

The minister's wife in a small Missouri town was a wonder at conserving food and rarely had to throw away a bit of it. At one meal, she served the pastor nothing but left-overs that the parson viewed with considerable disdain. He began to pick at the food when his wife said, "Dear, you forgot the blessing."

"Listen, sweetheart, if you can show me one item on this plate that hasn't been blessed at least two times, I'll see what a prayer can do for it."

* * * * *

Sign on a church bulletin board: "Support your church. You can't take your money with you, but you can send it ahead."

A Protestant minister, Rev. Lawrence Phillips, was dangerously ill and would see no visitors. But when the town agnostic, Elmer Sanches, heard about the bad condition of the minister, he insisted on seeing him and was admitted to the sick room. "I'm most grateful, Pastor Phillips, that you allowed me to come while denying others that joy. Why did you do this?"

"Because, my friend, I feel sure of seeing my other friends in the next world. But you, Sir, this may be the last chance I have to see you."

* * * * *

"I allus advise short sermons, espeshily on hot Sundays. If a preacher can't strike ile in boring 40 minutes, he has either got a pore gimblet, or else he iz boring in the rong place."

* * * * *

"Frank, I don't like getting up early on Sundays for church, either; but, after all, you are the minister."

Cowboy dinner blessing: We'll come to table
As long as we are able
An' eat ever' goddam thing
That seems sorta stable.

✻ ✻ ✻ ✻ ✻

Pastor Blake saw the old battle axe, Mrs. Peterson, coming toward his house and made his way up to his study. After an hour or so, he stepped to the head of the stairs and called, "Is that troublemaker gone now?" His wife, a born diplomat, said, "Yes, she has. She went some time ago. Mrs. Peterson is here now!"

✻ ✻ ✻ ✻ ✻

The deacon was called up to the pulpit to make the offertory prayer and he offered it this way. "Dear Lord, above, how come it is that a ten-dollar bill looks enormous in the offering plate and absolutely tiny at the supermarket?"

✻ ✻ ✻ ✻ ✻

Cowboy dinner blessing: Eat the meat an' leave the skin,
Throw back your ears and all pitch in.

✻ ✻ ✻ ✻ ✻

The minister's car wouldn't start and he called the garage to come and tow it in for repair. When the truck driver appeared at his house to get the car, the minister said, "I hope you'll go easy on me when you charge me. You know, I'm only a poor preacher."
"I know," said the trucker, "I've heard you preach!"

✻ ✻ ✻ ✻ ✻

Sometimes a joke can reveal the truth better than a direct command to do the right thing. Here's an example. A minister was kneeling in church, deep in prayer, saying, "God in heaven above, give us a peaceful world, give us freedom from hunger, stop hatred and mistrust. Make certain that we love one another. Keep our population from exploding beyond sense and clean up the dirt, the smog in our cities and end war." Suddenly a big voice boomed out, "Do it yourself, you lazy bum! Go...do...it!"

✻ ✻ ✻ ✻ ✻

Announcements: The pastor will preach his farewell message, after which the choir will sing "Break Forth Into Joy."

Mice kan liv enny whare furst rate except in a church -- they fat very slow in a church. This shows that they kant liv on religion enny more than a minister kan.

Josh Billings

✳ ✳ ✳ ✳ ✳

A cute item was published by a California church in its bulletin. It read: "This ... is ... the ... way ... the ... church ... sometimes ... looks ... to... the ... pastor ... when ... he ... goes ... into ... the ... pulpit ..." "Wouldlooklikethisifeverybodybroughtsomebodyelseto church."

✳ ✳ ✳ ✳ ✳

This particular preacher and his congregation didn't get along at all. Each despised the other and arguments were the order of the day. So, at the end of the year, the preacher packed his bags and moved out, going down to the railroad station to catch a train to ... anywhere!

Soon a car drove up and two of his parishioners came up to him and said, "We want you back for another year, Pastor."

"Why?" asked the Pastor. "You can't stand me and I can't stand you, so why would you want me back for another year of fighting and arguments?"

"Well, we argued that question almost the entire day. Then we decided that we didn't want any preacher at all and that you were the next best thing to that we could think of."

✳ ✳ ✳ ✳ ✳

Billy Graham told of receiving a letter that declared, "I admire you a lot. And I want to help you in your exemplary crusade; and so you'll find enclosed, my check for $500. The reason it is not signed is that I prefer to remain anonymous."

✳ ✳ ✳ ✳ ✳

Bulletin: Due to the Rector's illness, Wednesday's healing services will be discontinued until further notice.

✳ ✳ ✳ ✳ ✳

Bulletin: The eighth-graders will be presenting Shakespeare's HAMLET in the church basement on Friday at 7 p.m. The congregation is invited to attend this tragedy.

Pastor Johnson concluded his Sunday morning service by asking his Board of Directors to remain and meet with him after services. But a stranger in the congregation came forward and sat with the deacons and elders. The minister walked up to him and said, "Sir, I guess you misunderstood me. I asked that only the Board remain."

"That's me, Pastor. I've never been so bored in all my life!"

* * * * *

Question: What iz the best religious kreed to hav?
Answer: Charity. If a man will swop off all the religious kreed he haz got on hand, and invest the proceeds in charity, he will allwus be proud ov the job.

Josh Billings

* * * * *

The Baptist minister was exhorting his congregation: "And now, my dear parishioners, don't you want your sins washed away?"

A visitor from the nearby Episcopal Church said, "Mine have done been washed away over at my own church, Pastor."

"They ain't been washed away over there, friend. They've only been dry-cleaned!" said the minister.

* * * * *

The pastor had received a gift of a pair of trousers that fit him perfectly except that they were two inches too long. His wife claimed to be too busy to cut them off that Saturday night, since she had too much to do before Sunday. The parson couldn't sleep that night so he got up and whacked off the two inches of excess trouser leg. Then, feeling guilty, his wife got out of bed and cut off two more inches. Then his daughter got up out of bed and surgically shortened her father's trousers. And there's really no need to discuss the rest of the story.

* * * * *

Lots of people spend six days sowing wild oats and one day, Sunday, praying for crop failure.

* * * * *

Carl Goerch once saw this sign in front of the First Baptist Church in Lenoir, N.C.: "Religion is Goodness -- With Its Sleeves Rolled Up." Carl remarked: "And you know, the more you study that, the more it grows on you."

He who casts the first stone --
Better have some more rocks ready.

✳ ✳ ✳ ✳ ✳

The minister repeated the old and true (if trite) saying, "It is better to give than to receive." Then he added, "Beside that, there is an added blessing...you don't have to write all those 'thank you' notes!"

✳ ✳ ✳ ✳ ✳

The Rev. Francis spoke briefly, much to the delight of the audience.

✳ ✳ ✳ ✳ ✳

It is not always easy for the clergy to come up with nice, kindly eulogies for some at whose funerals they officiate. Take the case of Elmer, a very nasty guy, with whom nobody in town could get along. What to say at his funeral. Well, the minister did all right, saying, "Elmer wasn't always as mean as he usually was."

✳ ✳ ✳ ✳ ✳

Seen in a church bulletin: Don't expect a thousand-dollar answer to a ten-cent prayer.

✳ ✳ ✳ ✳ ✳

A clergyman made a pilgrimage to Israel and his first visit was to the Sea of Galilee. He found a boatman to take him out to where Jesus is thought to have walked. "How much to take me to the precise spot?" the clergyman asked.
"Nothing. It's free," responded the boatman.
So they went to the prescribed area and the clergyman was overcome with emotion. When he'd recovered sufficiently to speak, he said, "Let us go back to shore, now."
"Very good," replied the boatman. "But going back will cost you $35."
"But you told me the trip cost nothing, that it was free!"
"But that was only for the trip out. The trip back costs $35."
"No wonder Jesus got out and walked." the pastor said.

✳ ✳ ✳ ✳ ✳

Church bulletin: "For those of you who have children and don't know it, we have a nursery downstairs."

Some churches don't say so, but this is what they want in a new minister:

> The strength of an eagle.
> The grace of a swan.
> The quiet beauty of a dove.
> The keen eyesight of a hawk.
> The night hours of an owl.
> The friendliness of a sparrow.
> The industry of a woodpecker.
> The beauty of a gander.
> The attractiveness of a peacock.

And when they manage to get the bird they want, yes, and with all the above qualities, they want him to live on the food of a canary!

* * * * *

The only folks you should try to get even with are the ones who have helped you.

* * * * *

An itinerant minister was invited by a mountain man, member of the congregation, to his house for dinner. As they sat by the fireplace, the minister noticed three holes at the bottom of the door, and asked why they were there.

"For my three cats to get out," was the reply.

"But why wouldn't one be enough for all three cats to go through?"

"Pastor, when I say, 'SCAT!' I mean 'Scat!'"

* * * * *

Church bulletin: Potluck supper: prayer and medication to follow.

* * * * *

Some unredeemed rogue once said that there are four stages to the average minister's life: less tired, tired, tiresome, retired.

* * * * *

A divinity student named Tweedle
    Refused to accept his degree;
He didn't object to the "Tweedle,"
    He hated the "Tweedle D.D."

Piety iz like beans, it seems tew do the best on a poor sile.
Josh Billings

* * * * *

There are many ways to grease the pockets of congregants so that they will give as they should. One of the best techniques that we've heard about was employed by a backwoods minister. One Sunday morning, just before passing the collection plate, he said: "Our church is in a bad state of anemia. It is sick with need for a new roof and the organ needs surgery. To help meet these emergencies, I have figured out a new collection plate. Whenever one or more half dollars drop, they land in a fur-lined pocket. A penny or a nickel will strike a bell, clearly audible to all. And a button, my dear congregants, will trip a device that'll fire a pistol. So govern yourselves accordingly and let us pray."

* * * * *

"I TOO AM IN FAVOR OF STREAMLINING RELIGION, HAWKINS, BUT ISN'T THIS GOING A LITTLE *TOO FAR?*"

* * * * *

Seen on a church bulletin board: Ask about our pray-as-you-go plan.

The minister of a small Chicago church believed some practical joker was joshing him as I.O.U.'s began to appear in the collection plate. But one Sunday night weeks later, the collection included an envelope containing bills equal to the total of the I.O.U.'s.

After that, the parson could hardly wait to see what amount the anonymous donor had promised. The range in contributions was from $5 to $15 -- apparently based on what the donor thought the sermon to be worth. For there came a Sunday when the collection plate brought a note reading: "U.O.Me $5."

✲ ✲ ✲ ✲ ✲

Be mersiphull to all the dum animals -- no man can ride into heaven on a sore-backed horse.

Josh Billings

✲ ✲ ✲ ✲ ✲

The minister was preaching on the evils of John Barleycorn and all the troubles that whiskey had brought on the world. "Who's the richest fellow in town? The bar keeper! And who wears the best clothes and drives the most expensive car? The bar keep! That's who. And who pays for all this? You, my friends, you pay for it all."

A few days later, one of the congregants known for his penchant for alcohol stopped the preacher on the street and thanked him for the great sermon.

"George," the minister said, "I hope you've given up drinking as a result of that sermon."

The man said, "Well, not exactly, Reverend Abel. Not exactly. But I did buy a saloon."

✲ ✲ ✲ ✲ ✲

Seen on a church bulletin board: Come in and have your faith lifted.

✲ ✲ ✲ ✲ ✲

"I'm afraid I'll disagree with you," said Jonah as the whale swallowed him.

"Could be," said the whale, "but that'll be nothing compared with the disagreements of the theologians when they argue about the incident in the future."

✲ ✲ ✲ ✲ ✲

Some give their mite; and some give with all their might; and some who might, and ought, don't!

Perhaps one of the frankest, cruelest assessment of the ministerial profession came from the mouth of a farmer who had attended a ministerial conference as a lay delegate. He grew impatient at the haranguing and debating that took place. When he got home, he remarked: "Preachers are like manure. Put them together in one big pile and they are a nuisance and useless. But spread them out all over the fields and they sure do a world of good."

❋ ❋ ❋ ❋ ❋

Church bulletin board: We hold sit-in demonstrations every Sunday morning.

❋ ❋ ❋ ❋ ❋

"It'll turn out OK, grandmother," the pastor said after finishing his farewell sermon. "The conference will send you a better preacher."
"That's what they promised to do last time," sobbed the old lady.

❋ ❋ ❋ ❋ ❋

The Lord does not detract from man's allotted time those hours spent in fishing.

❋ ❋ ❋ ❋ ❋

On an Illinois church bulletin board: Even moderation ought not to be practiced in excess!

❋ ❋ ❋ ❋ ❋

The clergyman was called to the bed of a multi-millionaire, the richest member of his congregation. The man was dying and could just manage to say: "I think I'll leave two million dollars to the church. If I do, am I assured of salvation?"
The minister replied, "Well, Sir, I can't be positive about this, but I think it's well worth a try."

❋ ❋ ❋ ❋ ❋

Hell: God's penitentiary.

❋ ❋ ❋ ❋ ❋

Did you ever hear of Wheelbarrow Religion? It describes people who only go to church when they are shoved.

I was so impressed with the pastor's sermon that I went up to him after services and told him so. "Pastor," I said, "I have but praise for you."

"I noticed that this morning...after collection," he replied.

✳ ✳ ✳ ✳ ✳

A congregant went to speak with the pastor immediately after the service: "I truly benefited from your sermon, Pastor," she said.

"Thank you. That's very kind of you to say so. But I do hope it won't benefit you as much as the last sermon you heard me preach."

"I don't understand, Pastor."

"Well," the Pastor said, "that last sermon you heard lasted you two months."

✳ ✳ ✳ ✳ ✳

A sign was mounted on the door of a Nebraska church:
TRESPASSERS WELCOME

✳ ✳ ✳ ✳ ✳

"There must be a lot of sick folks in the congregation," the new minister said to the deacon after his first appearance in the new church. "There was coughing like I never heard before, especially during my sermon."

"Sir, them wasn't signs of sickness," the deacon replied. "Them was time signals."

✳ ✳ ✳ ✳ ✳

Certainly liberalism has a conspicuous place in church and synagogue -- especially if you demonstrate yours in the collection plate and fund-raising campaigns.

✳ ✳ ✳ ✳ ✳

The big church at the county seat had called the rising young star, Pastor Emmet Groggins, from his tiny country church to be their pastor. He asked for a week to think about this momentous move to ask the Lord for guidance.

A few days later, one of the deacons of the big church happened to be passing by the country church and saw the pastor's son playing in the yard. "Has your Pa come to a decision about coming to town to be our Pastor?" the deacon asked the boy.

"No, Sir! Not yet. But Mama is upstairs packin'."

Found on a church bulletin board: "Daily Services. Come Early If You Want A Back Seat."

A group was loudly talking -- between slugs of whiskey -- about why they left home and came to Texas. All gave their reasons except one man, a professional gambler, whose clerical look had given him the name, "Parson."

"Tell us, Parson, why you came here, after livin' most of your life in Tennessee?"

"I'd rather not tell ya. Don't think y'all would believe me if'n I did."

"Now, ah never shot nobody. But if'n ah got to tell, so be it. Ah left Tennessee 'cause ah didn't build a church!"

"What kinda answer is that! What d'ya mean, ya didn't build a church?"

"That's what ah said. Y'see, the Methodist congregation raised one thousand dollars fo' me to build a church. And ah didn't!"

$$* * * * *$$

Definition of a clergyman: A man who works to beat hell.

* * * * *

An atheist asked the pastor of the Baptist Church if he truly believed that Jonah was swallowed by a whale.

"I'm sure he was," said the pastor, "but to be absolutely positive, when I get to heaven, I'll ask him."

"But just supposing he isn't there?"

"In that case, you ask him."

* * * * *

You may not like the Ten Commandments but, when you stop to think of them, it's good to recall that there are only ten of them.

* * * * *

Where you go in the "hereafter" depends on what you "go after" down here.

* * * * *

Talk about your tall tales! Pastor Edward Norfolk tells the "lie" of his family garden that grew enormous potatoes. It seems the neighbor's cow wandered into Pastor Norfolk's garden one evening and started to eat a potation. But in the morning, the cow was found dead. Part of the potato was found beside her. The Pastor reports that the other potatoes had to be taken to a nearby sawmill for slicing.

Pastor Norfolk also has a cornfield that yields mighty well. In fact, it takes so much time and money to harvest the field that he built a roof over the entire field as being cheaper than harvesting it. He says the grains of his wheat crop are so large that they are to be used for building blocks. He says they are more attractive than bricks and last longer.

* * * * *

Clergyman: A man who preaches that the best way to rise to the heights is to stay on the level.

* * * * *

Poster placed outside the church: Come in and let us prepare you for your finals.

A Bishop of the Anglican Communion was on his way to take over the job as the executive officer. He was asked how he felt about assuming this enormously increased responsibility. "I tell you exactly how I feel...sort of like a mosquito at a nudist colony. I know what I ought to be doing, but I'm not quite sure where to begin!"

✳ ✳ ✳ ✳ ✳

A minister called upon a sick parishioner whose entire crop had been lost in the floods of 1993. Even his house had been all but destroyed. The only remaining room was the one where the minister found the farmer in bed with a terrible cold.

"Whom the Lord loveth, he chasteneth," quoted the minister.

"Mebbe so, Preacher...mebbe so. But damned if He didn't overdo it this time!"

✳ ✳ ✳ ✳ ✳

"Not only are children a great comfort in old age," declared the Rev. Bill Vogel, "but they help you get there sooner."

✳ ✳ ✳ ✳ ✳

Don't lose your temper and never quarrel with an angry person. Just give him a soft answer. That'll make him madder than anything else you could say and besides that, Holy Writ commands it!

Some folks only attend church three times in their lives: when they're hatched, when they're matched and when they're dispatched.

✳ ✳ ✳ ✳ ✳

Pastor John Winokur was almost two hours late getting home for dinner. His wife, quite rightly, was furious. "John!" she exploded when he finally came in the door. "Where on earth have you been!"

"Well, I met Edna Smith on the street and asked her how she was feeling," sighed the exhausted pastor.

✳ ✳ ✳ ✳ ✳

Some folks use religion like a bus...used only when it is bound their way.

✳ ✳ ✳ ✳ ✳

On charity: You can't take it with you, but you can send it on ahead.

One minister made a ridiculous, critical error. His sermon was: "A Fool and His Money Are Soon Parted," just before they passed the collection plate.

* * * * *

Jason, the town barber, kept sober most of the week but on weekends, he cut loose.

On this particular Monday morning, his preacher came in for a shave. With shaky hands and the smell of a brewery, the barber lathered and shaved the minister. But, in the process, he happened to cut the preacher's chin. "That's what happens, Jason, when a man drinks too much!" the minister berated him.

"Thet sho 'nuff is true," replied Jason. "Drinkin' sure does make the skin tender, don't it!"

* * * * *

Self-confidence: A human taking lessons on the harp.
El Paso Times, 1929

* * * * *

Mark Twain was in the middle of a tough debate on the question of polygamy and his opponent was a Mormon. It was a hard debate and finally, the Mormon said, "Can you inform me in sacred scripture where it says that polygamy is not allowed?"

"No man can serve two masters!"

* * * * *

If there is no hell, a good many preachers are obtaining money under false pretenses.

* * * * *

Several years ago, the members of the Petersburg Methodist Church were having a picnic in the town park. It was quite a way from the church so they boarded a bus, and was it crowded! Whew! There seemed to be no room for one little lad who tried to get on with his picnic basket, but couldn't. Finally, the minister squinched over and made room for the boy and his basket. "Let me put the basket overhead in the rack up there, Sonny," the preacher said. He took the basket from the boy and placed it on the rack.

A few minutes later, the minister felt some drops trickling down his face and neck. "Son, I think the pickles you've got in your basket up there are leaking."

"Them ain't pickles," the boy said. "Them's puppies."

Blessed are the meek and lowly (and very lucky, too, if they don't git their noze pulled).

Josh Billings

If you kicked the person most responsible for your troubles, you wouldn't sit down for a week!

✳ ✳ ✳ ✳ ✳

"Is it possible for me to lead a Christian life in New York on a salary of $50 a week?" asked a young man of a famous minister.

"Young man," said the minister. "In New York with only $50 a week? It's the only kind of life you *can* live!"

✳ ✳ ✳ ✳ ✳

"GIVE 'EM HEAVEN, DEAR!"

The rare individual who unselfishly tries to serve others has an enormous advantage. He has little competition.

Dale Carnegie

* * * * *

Kneeling will keep you in good standing.

William L. Nies, "Detroit News"

* * * * *

The pastor of the Melody Ecumenical Church had just finished counting the Sunday morning contributions. He turned to the deacon and said, "When I see all those well-dressed men and gussied-up women in the congregation, I wonder where all the poor people went. Then I take a look at the collection and wonder where all the rich members went."

* * * * *

Generally speaking, preachers are.

* * * * *

It's good to have money and the things that money can buy: but it's good, too, to check up once in a while and make sure that you haven't lost the things that money can't buy.

George Horace Lorimer

* * * * *

A certain man, a bad citizen all his life, had yet grown enormously rich. Late in that life, he wanted to clear a path to heaven, so he gave a great sum to a local church, after which he met with the minister of that church to discuss his chances for making it to heaven.

Now the minister was an honest man and couldn't truly assure the man that he'd make it to heaven. Still, he didn't want to be too conscientious about it and lose the pledged amount. So he evaluated the rich, evil guy's chance like this: "Mr. Soule, you are about to embark on the heavenly railroad. There, I suggest that you consider yourself on standby."

* * * * *

Go to church this Sunday...avoid the Christmas rush!

Good 'Lige Suggests A Second Marriage

Having been a bit under the weather for several days, I missed my weekly visit to the Devil's Apron, but I felt better on Sunday, and, the afternoon being perfect although a little chilly, I drove over to Brandy Bill's home. A number of the boys were also visiting Brandy Bill.

"We heerd ye was sorty puny," said Little 'Bijie as I entered the select circle.

"And you heard right," I replied, forcing a cough to indicate how ill I had been.

"We kinda figgered ye'd be over today, so me an' Brandy Bill we fixed ye some hot ginger-stew. It's a-steamin' on the stove in the kitchen, an' it ort to be good fer whut ails ye."

"Gittin' purty clost to 'lection,"observed Good 'Lige, stroking his patriarchal beard thoughtfully. "Is it gittin' hot over in town?"

"I've seen them hotter," I declared, "but not in recent years."

"Same way over here," asserted Business Bill. "We figger to git out the biggest vote we ever had, an' it's goin' to be might clost."

"An' we shore aim to have us a clean 'lection this year," put in Little 'Bijie. "We've got Good 'Lige named as a 'lection jedge, an' we air a-goin' to vote in the meetin'-house. Ef'n they have one of them con-tests ag'in this year we figger we won't be in it."

We were all silent for several minutes, and then someone called attention to a car that was being parked on the road in front of Brandy Bill's house.

"Wonder who that is?" queried Brandy Bill. "I don't know as I've ever seed that cyar afore."

A tall, broad-shouldered young man, wearing overalls and a denim jacket, got out of the dilapidated vehicle, followed by a young woman. The man didn't offer to assist her, but stalked through the open gate toward us with the girl at his heels. We stood motionless awaiting them.

The visitor halted a few steps away, and the young giant eyed us questiongly.

"I'm Big Jim Potter frum over on Skin Fork," he announced, "an' I'm a-lookin' fer a preacher named Good 'Lige Cantwell."

Good 'Lige came slowly to his feet.

"I guess I'm the man ye're a-lookin' fer," he said quietly. "Whut can I do fer ye?"

"Me an' Melissy Maggard hyer, we was kinda a-figgerin' on gittin' hitched up, an' seein' as how ye married Melissy's maw an' paw some thu'tty years ago, she is shorely sot on the idee of gittin' ye to marry us."

"That's so?" murmured Good' Lige. "Wall, I reckon that can be fixed up. Have yet got yore license?"

"'Shore have, an' the blood-test papers, too. They told me at that store on the river that I might find ye hyer."

"I never thought to fetch my Bible a-long with me today," said Good 'Lige apologetically, "but I reckon I know e-nought of it to make it stick good an' tight."

"That's good e-nough fer us," said Big Jim with a wide grin. "Go ahead an' shoot the works."

The couple stood before Good 'Lige at the foot of the kitchen steps, and the old preacher intoned the marriage ceremony in a manner that bespoke long practice. All of us stood around in a semi-circle and when the wedding was over we all passed by them in a line, wishing them much happiness.

Big Jim kissed his blushing bride, and then strode off in the direction of his car.

Good 'Lige stood motionless for a minute, and then he took a couple of steps toward the newlyweds.

"Hold on, Potter!" he called. "Ain't ye a-fergittin' somethin'?"

"Whut?" demanded Big Jim non-plussed.

"Wall, folks gin'rilly pay me somethin' fer hitchin' 'em up thataway."

"That's the way of ye blamed preachers, allus a-tryin' to git somethin' fer nothin'," snarled Big Jim. "The law don't say as how I've got to pay ye fer marryin' us, an' I ain't goin' to give ye a single copper-cent."

"Wall, that's all right, brother," said Good 'Lige softly, but I could see from the glint in his eyes, and the manner in which is beard stiffened, that he was as mad as a hornet.

"Would ye do me a favor?" he asked in a deceptively mild tone.

"De-pends," replied Big Jim surily.

"I want ye to tell yore mammy an' pappy to come up to my church next Sunday."

"I'll tell 'em but whut do ye want 'em to come all the way up hyer fer?"

"I sorty figgered that they ort to git married, too."

And I don't believe that Big Jim has figured that one out yet.

Excerpts from "Carolina Chats. 1944," written by Carl Goerch, used with the permission of the Estate of Carl Goerch.

✳ ✳ ✳ ✳ ✳

Did you hear about the preacher in Central Illinois who recently compiled a list of 448 sins? He has been deluged by requests from his congregation for the list because many are afraid they have missed something.

In the midst of a revival, the evangelist announced, "All who want to go to heaven, please stand up." All stood but one old sinner who was sound asleep. After all the rest of the congregation had taken their seats, the preacher said in a loud voice, "All who want to go to hell, stand up." The old reprobate heard only the last command, to "stand up." As he arose and looked around, he said, "Parson, I don't know exactly what we are votin' on, but me and you are a powerful minority."

✳ ✳ ✳ ✳ ✳

My preacher's sermons are about as graceful as a pregnant woman skipping rope!

✳ ✳ ✳ ✳ ✳

A newcomer to his community called the Reverend Jackson to the telephone. "Pastor," she began in response to his query as to what she wanted of him, "Pastor, the strangest thing is happening just outside the kitchen window. There's an elephant in my garden."

"Really! There's a circus in town and I suspect one of their elephants has gotten loose and wandered over your way. I'll call the police for you. But tell me...is the elephant doing harm?"

"It's the strangest thing, Pastor, and I don't like it one bit. He's pulling up my cabbages with his <u>tail!</u>"

"Really? With his tail. How odd. And where does he put the cabbage?"

"Oh, Pastor, Jackson, it is just too embarrassing to say!"

✳ ✳ ✳ ✳ ✳

Enny man who kan swop horses or ketch fish and not lie about it is just about as pious az men ever git to be in this world.

✳ ✳ ✳ ✳ ✳

I wish they wouldn't put "In God We Trust" on our money. I'm always afraid that someday I'll be praying: Our Father who art in Chapter 11!

✳ ✳ ✳ ✳ ✳

It must be terrible to be an atheist. Just think how lost, how utterly hopeless he must be when he feels overwhelmingly grateful for a burst of good fortune and has nobody to thank.

The Internal Revenue Service called the pastor of a church and said, "I am going over the tax return of one of your members and he states in the return that he gave the church $2,000. Did he, in fact, give that sum to the church?"

"I have my records here at the office," the minister replied, "but I can assure you, Sir, that if he didn't he will."

✳ ✳ ✳ ✳ ✳

A perfect example of an arrogant, I'm-never-wrong parishioner is seen in the story of the minister who answered his telephone only to hear a parishioner say, "I need two cases of vodka sent to my house and charge it."

The minister recognized the domineering voice as a woman from his parish. He replied, "I am your minister, Madam."

He expected at least a hurried apology, explanation, something. But all he got was, "Pastor! What are you doing at that liquor store!"

✳ ✳ ✳ ✳ ✳

" I'M AFRAID YOU'LL HAVE TO LEARN NEVER TO LOOK UP, REVEREND. "

A-Men Sorter -- Preacher.

✳ ✳ ✳ ✳ ✳

The pioneers used to say: "Watch your tongue, Mister, 'cause it's seldom you'll find horse sense hitched to a *waggin'* tongue."

✳ ✳ ✳ ✳ ✳

The Chaplain appeared in church one Sunday morning with a finger swathed in a huge bandage. A G.I. whispered to his buddy: "What's wrong with the sky pilot's hand?"

"I heard that when he was shaving this morning, he had his mind on his sermon and cut his finger."

"It'd sure been better if he'd kept his mind on his finger and cut his sermon!"

✳ ✳ ✳ ✳ ✳

The other guy's failings, his sins, are kind of like his headlight...lots more glaring than your own.

✳ ✳ ✳ ✳ ✳

As the collection plate passed around and it was held in front of Tad Evans, he looked up at the holder and said, "Do you have change for a fifteen-dollar bill?"

The holder of the collection plate didn't bat an eye, saying, "Tell me, Sir, how do you want it...in five threes or a seven and eight?"

✳ ✳ ✳ ✳ ✳

America has become so tense and nervous it has been years since I've seen anyone asleep in church -- and that is a sad situation.

Norman Vincent Peale, "Sangamo Farmer," May 1990

✳ ✳ ✳ ✳ ✳

There was a faith-healer of Keel
Who said, "Although pain isn't real,
    If I sit on a pin
    And it punctures my skin,
I dislike what I fancy I feel."

43

A minister, commenting on today's fashions, remarked, "Women's clothes were never funnier...that is, if brevity is the soul of wit."

* * * * *

Self-made man: One who worships his creator.

* * * * *

Pastor Thomas and a member of his church were playing golf and it was a mighty close match. At the final hole, the pastor teed up, steadied himself, then swung with enormous force. But the ball merely dribbled off the tee and stopped ten feet away.

The pastor said nothing, merely gritted his teeth, scowled fiercely and bit his lip. Observing all this, his partner remarked, "Pastor, that is, without doubt, the most profane silence I have ever heard!"

* * * * *

Pay strict attention to what your conscience says...not what your neighbors say.

* * * * *

Opportunity knocks only once but temptation bangs on the door time after time after time.

* * * * *

There's one thing a preacher
    Should remember, for certain!
The mind won't absorb much
    When the bottom starts hurtin'.

* * * * *

The preacher's Sunday morning prayer was fervent: "O Lord, grant us a pure soul, a clean heart and mind, and please, Lord, give us gentle, sweet hearts." And do you know that every unmarried girl responded with the most soul-felt "Ah-men!" ever heard in that congregation.

* * * * *

When our preacher at last finishes his sermon, there is enormous awakening.

44

At a funeral, the minister seemed to preach an endless requiem and the funeral director became concerned about the lateness of the hour. He walked over to a member of the church and asked, "Does your Pastor always preach this long at a funeral oration?"

"Nearly always," responded the member. The funeral director stepped back, but continued to look at his watch and worry about the lateness of the hour.

Soon the church member he had spoken to came to him and asked, "Don't you believe in the resurrection, Sir?"

"Yes, I sure do," the director replied, "but I worry about whether we'll get this man buried in time for it."

✳ ✳ ✳ ✳ ✳

Why preach against modern dress when there's not all that much to talk about.

"The Ram's Horn"

✳ ✳ ✳ ✳ ✳

CRENSHAW

"HOW MANY APOSTLES ARE THERE UNDER THE METRIC SYSTEM?"

At Fort Sam Houston, Texas, during World War II, a chaplain organized a bowling team. He named it: *"The Holy Rollers."*

* * * * *

An Internal Revenue agent went back to his office laughing like crazy. His fellow workers were amazed and asked what he was laughing at. "I heard a great story," he told them, "the one about the Internal Revenue agent and two ministers. When they went to heaven, St. Peter asked each of them: "What have you done on earth to deserve this Sanctuary?"

"Well," said the Baptist preacher, "I've been a preacher in my denomination for 35 years."

"OK," said Peter, "move on over to the side there. And you, number two, step forward and declare what you've done."

"I've been a Methodist minister for over forty years."

"Okay, step aside by the Baptist over there. And you?" he said to the Internal Revenue agent.

"I've been an examiner for the Internal Revenue Service for twenty years."

"Pass through the gates," the angel said to the federal agent.

"St. Peter," screamed one of the preachers, "why have you allowed...this...this...this usurper of our money to go ahead of us?"

"Because," said St. Peter, "in his twenty years, he has scared the hell out of more people than both of you have in seventy-five!"

* * * * *

Gospel Pusher -- Minister.

* * * * *

The men's club of a big city Presbyterian church had a very well-attended dance for members. The parking lot was jammed except for one space in which several drivers turned, then turned away. There was a sign that read: THOU SHALT NOT PARK IN THIS SPACE! RESERVED FOR THE MINISTER.

* * * * *

Every church and synagogue has too many members who are willing to give the Lord credit but reluctant to give cash.

* * * * *

Don't worry! Swallowing your pride will **not** give you indigestion.

46

A missionary in Africa was making his first visit to a heathen, cannibal tribe saying: "You are contradicting the law of God. Don't you know anything at all about religion?"

"Well," replied the chief, "we did get a little taste of it when the last missionary visited us."

* * * * *

"We are prepared to say a prayer for the shortcomings of members of this congregation," the minister told his seated listeners. "Is there anyone who would like us to do that for them?"

"Me," said the wealthiest member. "I'm a spendthrift and I throw money around like crazy."

"So be it," said the minister. "We will pray fervently for our brother...but we'll wait until after the collection plate is passed."

* * * * *

They used to say that circuit-riding preachers were so poor that if they didn't fast twice a week, they'd starve to death.

* * * * *

Headed for an interfaith conference, a priest and a Methodist minister were driving down the road when the priest ran over a rabbit. He stopped the car and went to the dead animal, sprinkling the poor creature with holy water. "Last rites," he explained. "It's the least I can do."

The Methodist minister then took a bottle out of his topcoat and went to the rabbit to sprinkle its contents on the dead animal. Immediately it sprang to life and ran off.

The priest was absolutely confounded. "My gracious," he said. "I didn't know you Methodists used such powerful holy water."

"We don't," responded the minister. "That was hare restorer."

* * * * *

Good advice from a minister: "So live that you would not be ashamed to sell your parrot to the neighborhood gossip."

* * * * *

Hypocrite: One who prays on his knees Sundays, and on his neighbors the rest of the week.

Pastor George Patrick announced the following conditions about his sermon to the congregation assembled one Sunday morning: "I offer three sermons and I ask that you select the one for today. The first sermon is worth a ten dollar donation and lasts ten minutes. Your second choice is a five dollar job that lasts thirty minutes. The third and last choice is a two dollar delivery that lasts one hour. We will now offer the collection basket and you will judge which sermon you wish me to deliver."

* * * * *

Zero: The last row at back of the church.

* * * * *

How's this for a promotion of church attendance:
Hold this sheet of paper to your face. Then blow on it. If it turns:
    Green -- Call your doctor.
    Brown -- As soon as possible, see your dentist.
    Purple -- Consult the nearest psychiatrist.
    Yellow -- See your banker.
    Red -- Call your lawyer and instruct him to make a will.
Should the paper remain the same without changing color, you can be sure you are in good health and realize that there is no good reason why you should not be in church this week.

* * * * *

A hearse in Norwich, CT, has this gentle reminder as a license number plate: U-2.

* * * * *

At the community ministerial meeting, Pastor Bob Evans told the gathering about the most disconcerting experience he'd ever had. It seems that an elderly parishioner sat in the front row for the morning service. She sat quietly for a time, listening to the sermon, then took a hearing aid and affixed it in her ear. That was fine. But about ten minutes later, she reached up, took the hearing aid out of her ear, put it back in her pocketbook and sat quietly for the rest of the sermon.

* * * * *

When the outlook seems awful, try the uplook.

After Eve and Adam were exiled from the garden of Eden, Adam was talking to his two kids, Cain and Abel. As they walked past the ancestral home, Eden, one of the lads asked, "What's that?"

Adam said, "Kids, that's the place we lived before your mother ate us out of house and home."

* * * * *

If ignorance is bliss, as the saying goes, how do you explain why there aren't more happy folks?

* * * * *

The minister was appraising the search committee of the First Baptist Church of Roanoke. He asked: "Are the parishioners of this church bibulous?"

The chairman of the committee replied: "You bet we are. There ain't any members I know of that don't own a Bible."

* * * * *

Prayer: A declaration of dependence.

* * * * *

Parson Lowell Pittman was in Jacksonville, Illinois, as a visiting preacher. He had some time to waste so he thought he'd go to the post office and mail a letter. He stopped in front of an ancient house where an old man sat swinging on the porch. "Sir, I'm new in town. Could you tell me how to get to the post office?"

The old fellow gave explicit directions and Parson Pittman thanked him, then added, "Sir, I'm preaching tomorrow at the Congregational Church and I'd like to see you sitting in the congregation. I promise to show you the way to heaven. Do come."

"Thanks, Mr. Preacher, but if you don't know the way to the post office, how in hell can you direct me to that other place!"

* * * * *

When the Lord gave us the Ten Commandments, He didn't mention amendments.

* * * * *

"When I preach, advise, counsel, my congregants say nothing but 'Yes, but...yes, but...yes, but.' Honestly, I think they're heading straight for hell on their 'butts.'"

Slander is like a tin kettle tied tu a dog's tail -- a very good kind of kettle so long as it ain't tied to our dog's tail.

Josh Billings

* * * * *

Noticing that he had already preached for over an hour, and that the congregation was unusually restless, the pastor asked, "Does anyone in the congregation have a watch?"

A voice in the back row yelled, "Don't think so, Pastor, but there's a calendar on the wall behind you."

* * * * *

"Your estimate runneth over."

* * * * *

I hav known men so pious that when they went fishing on Sunday, they allus prayed fer good luck.

Josh Billings

Ministers take a terrific beating in most church stories, here's one where he comes out on top.

It seems that a minister had worked diligently on his first congregational sermon and all seemed to be going well. But, nearly finished, he noticed that he'd lost most of the congregation.

When he stated his last paragraph, he ended with, "I fervently and joyously wish that it's true."

The congregation was startled to attention by that and the minister continued, saying, "I hope it's true because if it is -- and you learn while you sleep -- I'll have the best-informed, most knowledgeable congregation in the entire state."

* * * * *

I suppose the reason why the "road to ruin" is broad is to accommodate the great amount of travel going in that direction.

Josh Billings

* * * * *

While saying good-by to his congregation filing out of church, the preacher saw a fellow he hadn't seen in church for many months. "Good morning to you, Brother Clark," the minister said. "I'd sure like to see you here in church a bit more often."

"What do you mean more often?" the fellow said angrily. "Why I haven't missed an Easter in fifteen years."

* * * * *

"Resurrection is proven every day at our church," the pastor observed, "and if you want to experience it, just come back at quitting time and see how our staff comes back to life."

* * * * *

A well-balanced life is one which fails to give you what you ask for about as often as it fails to give you what you deserve.

* * * * *

The monuments of wit survive the monuments of power.

Francis Bacon

* * * * *

A good sense of humor helps us in many ways. It helps us understand the orthodox, tolerate the unpleasant, overcome the unexpected, and survive the unbearable.

Gene Brown

51

Now that newspapers have statistically proven that most people still believe in God, it might not be bad journalism to see if God still believes in us.

Life Magazine, 1929

Among those enterprises that depend for success on implicit faith are democracy, religion and hash.

Life Magazine, 1929

The only possible good result of the terrible number of automobile fatalities that occur every Sunday is that we may have to go to church for safety's sake.

Life Magazine, 1929

The latest style in wedding rings shows a very thin and narrow item. Understandable when you consider that the old-fashioned, cumbersome styles of the past were meant to last a lifetime.

Life Magazine, 1929

✻ ✻ ✻ ✻ ✻

Once a question was put to a Senate chaplain, Edward Everett Hale. "Doctor, when you pray, do you look at the tragic condition of the country and then pray that the Almighty will give the Senators the wisdom to find solutions?" The chaplain replied, "No, I do not. I look at the Senators and pray for the country."

✻ ✻ ✻ ✻ ✻

Our preacher preaches indefinite ideas with infinite words.

✻ ✻ ✻ ✻ ✻

I once knew this preacher back home who liked to use words that he sometimes didn't quite understand. One time he brought in a visiting preacher, and after introducing him to the congregation, he told him to preach loud, "because the agnostics in this church are not very good."

✻ ✻ ✻ ✻ ✻

Earl Wilson observes that there's so much good in the worst of us, and so much bad in the best of us, that it's hard to tell which of us ought to reform the rest of us.

A city evangelist was holding a meeting in a farm community that had been stricken with drought. It had been weeks since a rain. Crops were abut done for so the visiting pastor decided to illustrate the power of prayer and faith by devoting his full sermon to prayer for rain. Sure enough, that night the rain came...in a horrendous downpour, a real gully-washer. Fields were badly gullied, roads overrun, meadows washed out.

A couple of farmers were standing in their former fields of corn, completely washed out by the torrential rain of the night before.

"Man, that city preacher sure knows how to pray. Just look what he's gone and done for us."

"Yeah, he sure knows how to pray, all right, but he sure don't know a damned thing about farmin'."

✳ ✳ ✳ ✳ ✳

It is simply amazing how so many people cast a wormy piece of old bread upon the waters and hope to get back a piece of strawberry pie.

✳ ✳ ✳ ✳ ✳

Rev. Boyer delivered a wonderfully eloquent speech to the Rotary Club. His subject was the debt men owed their wives and how the passage of time should increase and enhance man's devotion to his spouse.

Member George Simpkins was impressed and couldn't get the idea out of his mind. All day he was preoccupied with it. So, on his way home from work, he bought a dozen roses, a chocolate cake, a set of earrings and a cookbook for his wife.

After he gave the presents to her, she burst into tears. "Oh, my goodness, this is just too much," she moaned. "What an awful day I've had. Johnny broke his leg, the maid burnt our dinner and now you come home drunk. It's just too much!"

✳ ✳ ✳ ✳ ✳

One minister told his assistant that at his last church in Kentucky, there were so many shotgun weddings that they named the church the Winchester Cathedral!

✳ ✳ ✳ ✳ ✳

Sign on a St. Louis church: "What on earth are you doing for heaven's sake?"

53

Edward Deacon was sent to his new job as a missionary in Africa. For his first sermon to a huge group of prospects, he began: "My friends, you must love your fellow man." The crowd nodded, shouting "Moaboola Samati!" He continued with: "White and black must cooperate, must be as brothers!" Again the crowd nodded vigorously and shouted "Moaboola Samati!" Encouraged, Pastor Deacon lectured on with a vigorous sermon, frequently interrupted by that enthusiastic "Moaboola Samati!"

Leaving town later, quite pleased with the enthusiasm of the congregation, they passed by huge herds of cattle maintained by the people of the village. His guide cautioned him to watch his step, saying, "Sir, be careful where you step. Watch out for the moaboola samati!"

* * * * *

A minister, in the course of his sermon, said: "God does not strike people dead for telling lies in modern times like these. And, if He did, where would all you folks be?"

The congregation smiled at the thought. But the preacher hadn't finished making his point: "Well, I can tell you where I'd be. I'd be right where I am now, preaching to a mighty empty church!"

* * * * *

You can be sure somebody will always be there to lend a hand whenever you have trouble opening your pocketbook.

* * * * *

Following the Sunday service, a farm family invited the preacher to dinner. He arrived for the dinner to find a huge family of husband, wife and twelve children. They sat at the dinner table and the minister preached a long, long, long prayer. Finished at last, the lady of the house asked: "Now, Parson, what will you have for dessert?"

* * * * *

If you want to know how truly rich you are, figure out what'd be left of you tomorrow once you'd lost every nickel you own today.

* * * * *

Life for some people is to sow wild oats during the week and then go to church on Sunday and pray for a crop failure.

Susie Wilkins, now ninety years old, was the favorite resident in the retirement home visited weekly by Pastor Emil Jenks. But when he entered her room during a pastoral visit, she was not there. He decided to wait for her return, meanwhile snacking on some peanuts in a bowl beside his chair.

When Susie returned to the room, the minister brushed off her apologies and said, "Don't give it another thought, Susie. I had a good time munching on your peanuts. Unfortunately, my dear, I ate them all and I'm sorry about that." She stilled his protests saying, "Oh, Pastor, forget that. I can't eat the things anyway because my teeth are so bad. I just suck the chocolate off them and put them back in the bowl."

✳ ✳ ✳ ✳ ✳

Money can't buy friends. But it does give you a better class of enemy.

✳ ✳ ✳ ✳ ✳

'EVER THOUGHT OF DOING A LITTLE MAGIC
TO PUNCH UP YOUR ACT?"

An Episcopal minister in a small Missouri town had a huge litter of pups to dispose of, so he advertised in the local weekly paper: "Presbyterian pups for sale." A customer came by, looked the pups over but bought none because he thought they were priced too high. Then he had a change of mind and returned. "I guess, after all, I'll take one of those Presbyterian pups even though the price is high," he told the minister.

"Fine. But they're Episcopalian pups now," the preacher said.

"How could that be when you said before that they were Presbyterian?"

"Well, you see, now they've got their eyes open!"

✲ ✲ ✲ ✲ ✲

The minister was paying his annual visit to the home of Sarah and Paul Tick. "You do have a lovely home here, Mrs. Tick," the minister said, walking about admiring the furniture. "And that vase on top of the piano is absolutely exquisite. What is that I see in it?"

"My husband's ashes," Sarah replied.

"Oh, my goodness," the preacher exclaimed. "I didn't know that Mr. Tick had passed away."

"He didn't," she replied. "It's just that he's too darned lazy to find the ash tray!"

✲ ✲ ✲ ✲ ✲

A reformer is the kind of guy who would have you believe that he gave Eve back her apple.

✲ ✲ ✲ ✲ ✲

Bob Smith had been a preacher for all of his long life. Now, approaching eighty years of age, he found that his memory simply wasn't up to the preaching job in which, as a younger man, he had excelled. He simply could not remember names. So, to counteract his deficiency, he kept cards pinned on the lining inside his coat pocket. As he needed a name, he would flip open his coat, look inside, find the name, use it and continue his sermon. This worked just fine until one time, he forgot to pin the cards inside his coat. His sermon, that day, was on Noah and he got to the part where he needed the names of Noah's sons -- Ham, Shem and...and...he simply couldn't remember. So he looked quickly inside his coat and pronounced the third son's name: J.C. Penney!

✲ ✲ ✲ ✲ ✲

"We will proceed to read from the Book of Numbers," said the vicar as he opened the telephone directory.

Everybody's Weekly

Three men of the cloth went to an ecumenical conference on "Religion In America." After the first session, the three men, a priest, a rabbi and a Protestant minister, went for supper together. During the meal, the Protestant minister admitted to one terrible sin. "I love to fight. A good, tough brawl is just my style. It is a besetting sin but I can't control myself when I get a chance to mix it up with someone."

"Since we are all confessing, let me say that it is not brawling that bothers me," said the priest. "Rather, it is this impulse I have for women. I fight it night and day. Sometimes I lose and then I feel a terrible remorse."

Both men turned to the rabbi. "You, Rabbi. What is your overwhelming sin? We've confessed. Now do your own soul good and let us hear from you."

The Rabbi paused, as if unable to speak, so terrible was his sin. Then he said, "Gentlemen...I...I must tell you. I have this awful, irresistible, uncontrollable impulse to...oh...dear!...to, to, to gossip!"

✱ ✱ ✱ ✱ ✱

Sin -- a natural distemper for which virtew haz bin discovered to be an antidote.

Josh Billings

✱ ✱ ✱ ✱ ✱

Edward Ellis was a minister and had been unemployed so long that he thought it best to seek another type of work. So he decided to apply to the fire department. After a thorough physical examination and hours of questioning, the interrogation officer asked one final question: "Suppose you were trying to get to a raging fire but couldn't get through a huge crowd of spectators who blocked your way. What would you do to disperse the crowd?"

"Sir, that's quite simple. I'd take up a collection."

✱ ✱ ✱ ✱ ✱

I sometimes think that God, in creating man, somewhat over-estimated His ability.

Oscar Wilde, 1899

✱ ✱ ✱ ✱ ✱

Most people repent ov their sins by thanking God they ain't so wicked as their neighbors.

Josh Billings

The minister of a country church was taken ill and, unable to perform services on this particular Sunday, he asked the assistant pastor of the church in a nearby town to conduct services in his place. The assistant was happy to oblige his friend. And so, on the Sunday morning he was due at the country church, the assistant pastor started early and headed out into the country, driving along a country road.

After traveling for an hour or so, the city pastor realized that he was lost. So he stopped alongside a field where a young strapping country lad was pulling weeds out of soybeans. "Hello, there," he called to the boy who looked up and replied, "Hello, yourself."

"Could you tell me where this road goes?"

"I ain't never seen it go nowhere. Stays right there where you see it."

"Could you tell me how far it is to the Irish Grove Church?"

"Don't know. I ain't never measured it."

And now the preacher lost patience. "You don't know anything! You are the stupidest, dumbest, biggest fool I ever did see."

"Mebbe so. Mebbe so," said the farm boy. "But I ain't lost."

✶ ✶ ✶ ✶ ✶

Death is the greatest kick of all -- that's why they save it till the last.

✶ ✶ ✶ ✶ ✶

Proof Positive

If virtue is its own reward
(And please do not jest)
Does not a preacher's salary
Show this off best?

✶ ✶ ✶ ✶ ✶

While shopping in Springfield, Missouri, during the hottest day of the year, the pastor of the Baptist Church met a woman he had not seen for several years. "And how have you been during all this time?" the preacher asked.

"Just dandy," the lady replied.

"And your husband...how is he standing the heat?"

"Pastor!" the woman said, shocked. "My husband's been dead two years!"

✶ ✶ ✶ ✶ ✶

Sign on a Memphis church: "Come in and have your faith lifted."

Probably no man ever got so much conversation out of a ⸱ operation as Adam did.

Arkansas Gaᴢ

✳ ✳ ✳ ✳ ✳

The story is told about a small church in rural Alabama where the preacher posted the following notice on the bulletin board: "If absence makes the heart grow fonder, then we must have many who love this church."

✳ ✳ ✳ ✳ ✳

It's a good idea for a man to live in such a way that, when he dies, and people speak evil of him, no one will believe them.

✳ ✳ ✳ ✳ ✳

The Reverend Timothy Elder had been called to a church that paid an unbelievably poor harvest for all the care that Rev. Timothy gave to his congregation. One day, his long-suffering wife asked him, "Timmy, what made you enter the ministry?"

"I was called, simply called to do so," he replied.

"Timmy, I wonder if you could possibly have misunderstood and that it might have been some other sound that you heard?"

✳ ✳ ✳ ✳ ✳

Pastor Edward Sudbury spent one day a week preaching to the residents of a home for the mentally disturbed. He noticed a newcomer one day and was quite flattered that the man seemed to hang onto every word that he said. He simply never took his gaze away from the preacher's face. It was the most satisfying experience that Rev. Sudbury had ever had in all his days of preaching to these disturbed people.

After the service, the pastor noticed that the very man so interested in his sermon, was talking vigorously to the superintendent and, as soon as he could, he walked up to the superintendent and asked, "I noticed that the new resident here was talking to you. Did he discuss my sermon? And what did he think of it?"

The superintendent grinned, seemed to want to change the subject, but the pastor was adamant. "Please tell me the gist of your conversation with him," Pastor Elder demanded.

"Well," the superintendent said slowly, "the one thing that sticks in my mind that he said was, 'How come he's out there and I'm in here!'"

gets for nothing, he iz very apt to value at just abut

Josh Billings

* * * * *

... large distributor of merchandise had made a shipment of various goods to a general store in a very small midwestern town. The merchant rejected the shipment and the jobber wrote saying they were going to sue for damages unless the merchant could give them a satisfactory reason for rejecting the shipment. His answer to the challenge was as follows:

"I received your important letter today and hasten to reply. In the first place, I am the railroad agent in this town and, as such, I must consider your letter. Secondly, I am also the president of our sole bank, so you can assume I am financially sound. Thirdly, I am the mayor of this town, too. Fourthly, I am the only member of the law association in this town. And if it were not for the fact that I serve as pastor of the town's church, I would tell you earnestly just where the hell you can go!"

* * * * *

The main difference between a gossip and a Texas buzzard is that the buzzard waits till the person is dead before he tears him apart.

* * * * *

Pastor Jerry Jenkins was asked to substitute as chaplain of a prison for just this one Sunday service. He accepted, but only if they would hold services Sunday afternoon. They agreed.

The service went very well and after it, the preacher went to the door to greet and chat with the men as they returned to their cells. One young man, handsome and innocent-looking, interested the minister, who asked, "Tell me, young man, how did you come to be in this closed world?"

"It was like this, Sir," the prisoner answered. "I was the victim of an unlucky number -- number 13."

"Oh," the Pastor was puzzled. "I don't quite understand."

"Well, Pastor, you see, there were twelve jurymen and one judge."

* * * * *

There was once an old mountain woman who named her triplets Surely, Goodness and Mercy, so they would follow her all the days of her life.

"ANYONE FOR GOODMINTON?"

* * * * *

The driver of a stalled car was trying to put it off the street, and swearing like crazy in the process. A minister heard him and suggested that he was going about it all wrong, "You really must think of some other remedy other than your profanity; that will do you no good and only harm. Try prayer. It can't hurt."

"Are you nuts!" the motorist shouted. "What the hell good will praying do! You try it yourself, wise guy, and see if it works."

Well, the poor preacher had no alternative but to accept the challenge. And he did: "Dear God, kindly start the engine of this car, owned by the poor sinner next to me. He needs it and can push no more."

The minister then stepped on the starter and...lo and behold...the engine started! Both men listened in a state of semi-shock until the pastor murmured, "Well, I'll be damned!"

* * * * *

When you go to church, leave your grouch outside.

Sara Jane Ransome's husband was beginning to worry her with his increasing drunkenness and she went to see her minister for help. He agreed to talk with her husband, Sam, and see if he could help the guy break this terrible habit.

On the appointed day and hour, Sam Ransome came into the minister's office, sat down and the preacher began to talk. "Sam, you really must quit your excessive drinking. Whiskey is not only bad, it is the terrible enemy of mankind...the most terrible enemy of all."

"I know it's bad, Parson, and I know I ought to quit. But, doesn't the Bible -- and you're always preaching from it -- doesn't it tell us to love our enemies?"

"Ye! It certainly does, Sam, but it says nothing about us swallowing them!"

✷ ✷ ✷ ✷ ✷

Judicious benevolence -- The brains of the heart.

✷ ✷ ✷ ✷ ✷

The minister's message was concerned with the meaning of faith and fact. "You are seated before me in this church," he began, "and that is fact. Also, you see me standing before you and that, too, is fact. But it is faith alone that leads me to believe that any of you are listening."

✷ ✷ ✷ ✷ ✷

Epitaph for Clive Brook: "Excuse me for not rising."

✷ ✷ ✷ ✷ ✷

It was a wealthy community and the church represented a good part of that wealth. But it so happened that the stock market had taken a bad fall and many in the congregation were glum. The preacher, thinking to cheer them up, concluded his sermon with these words.

"You all know that the Bible tells us that all of us came into this world poor, with nothing tangible, without riches. And we all know that when we pass on, we shall take no wealth with us to the next world. So, in a very real sense, my friends, your stockbroker is merely doing the Lord's work!"

✷ ✷ ✷ ✷ ✷

There are epitaphs that should read: "Died at thirty -- buried at seventy."

A committed church member decided to take it upon himself to convert a nasty old man. Both lived in a small Tennessee town. Now, the old man, named Pete Sudduth, was stubborn, profane, and never came to church. Although numerous church members tried their best, they got nowhere with this sinful old fellow.

"Pete," he preacher said, "just before I give you back to the Devil, ain't you even tetched a leetle bit by the Lord's dyin' to save yer soul?"

"Hey'll no! An' don't try to tell me that He died tryin' to save me when he ain't never even knowed me er see'd me."

"Pete, let me put it this way: You got a better chance fer the Lord to die to save ya jest because He ain't never seen ya or knowed ya like the rest of us folks in thiseyer town does!"

✻ ✻ ✻ ✻ ✻

Epitaph for Ilka Chase: "I've finally gotten to the bottom of things."

✻ ✻ ✻ ✻ ✻

A clergyman had always wanted a parrot. With a gift from his congregation, he decided he could now afford one. So he went to the store to acquire a new household pet...a parrot. But the storekeeper wouldn't sell him one, saying, "The only one I've got swears all the time, Pastor. But I'll have a new one in three weeks. I'll hold it for you. He comes from Mexico so I know he won't swear."

Sure enough, after three weeks, the Pastor found a new bird at the store. The bird was perched with a string tied to each claw. When the storekeeper pulled one string, the parrot recited the Lord's Prayer perfectly. When he pulled the other string, the parrot recited, "What A Friend I Have in Jesus."

"Wonderful," said the minister. "I wonder what would happen if you pulled both strings at the same time?"

Before the storekeeper could respond, the parrot screamed, "Ya damned fool, I'd fall flat on my ass!"

✻ ✻ ✻ ✻ ✻

Reformer: Someone who wants his conscience to be your guide.

Who tells better tales than a minister? Nobody, that's who! An illustration of this well-known fact comes from a story about a Wisconsin preacher who was discussing the best laying mash for chickens. "I always combine a little sawdust with the laying mash," he said, "because it's cheaper and gives a firmer texture to the egg white. However, I overdid it one time, fed too much sawdust and the result was that I had baby chicks each with a wooden leg and one hatched me a woodpecker!"

✳ ✳ ✳ ✳ ✳

"CHEER UP, REVEREND. WE'LL HAVE YOU UP AND BACK ON YOUR KNEES AGAIN IN NO TIME."

2
KIDS

A little girl in Sunday School was asked to write her impression of King Solomon. Here is her essay: "King Solomon had seven hundred wives and three hundred porcupines."

* * * * *

"...and I sure don't want to go to heaven if my piano teacher is going to be there."

* * * * *

"I've come for my allowance, Dad!"

* * * * *

Do your kids a favor...don't have any.

Robert Orben

A lad was reading a plaque on the wall of the church's entry hall. He asked the minister what it was. "That's a plaque honoring the men who died in service," said the minister.

"Which one?" the lad asked, "the ten o'clock or the eleven o'clock?"

* * * * *

Eddie, tell me...can you name three characters in the first Bible?

"Well, I'll try," responded Eddie: "First, I think of David. Then I think of Jonathan. Then I think of Howard."

"Howard? That's a new one. I never heard of him."

"Oh, you know. You recite him most every Sunday. You know, The Lord's Prayer, don't you?"

"Sure, but what's that got to do with Howard?"

"Think! It says, 'Our Father who art in heaven, *Howard* be they name!' Remember?"

* * * * *

If you must hold yourself up to your children as an object lesson -- hold yourself up as a warning and not as an example.

George Bernard Shaw

* * * * *

The minister and his deacon really disliked one another, but both hid their mutual animosity for the benefit of the church. Still, they took a dig at one another now and then.

One Sunday, the minister, a right-wing prohibitionist, spoke on the perils, evils of drink. "And I say unto you," he hollered, "if I was in total command in these United States, I'd dump every drop of liquor in the Potomac River. If I was head of things in Mississippi, I'd pour every drop of whiskey, wine and gin in the Mississippi River. And if I was Governor in Ohio, why I'd pour every last drop of alcoholic beverages into the Ohio River." Thus ended his sermon. He turned to Deacon Jones. "And now our brother, Deacon Jones, will lead us in song..."

It was a great opportunity for Deacon Jones and he took it! "Turn to page 88 in the hymnal, everybody. Sing it with might and main: 'Shall We Gather at the River!'"

* * * * *

"I ain't praying for anything for myself -- but a new bike for my brother, one we can both ride, would be just fine."

Down South, there are still a few places where they plow with mules. On one of these farms, a minister noticed a boy yelling and cussing profanely at his mule, trying to get him moving. The preacher got down from his car, walked up to the boy and said, "That's no way to handle that mule, son. Let me show you how to drive him without cussin' like that!"

The minister took over the reins and said, "Move on, you lovely creature. Just move ever-so-sweetly down the row, you sweet, gentle, wise and stately soul and we'll get this land plowed." The mule did fine and after one row, the preacher turned back the mule to the boy. "Now, you heard just how I did it. Go ahead."

The boy said, "You sure didn't use no cussin', but you sure told a lot of lies."

✳ ✳ ✳ ✳ ✳

Little Robert was attending his Sabbath School and was asked to give his regular evening prayers as an example for the entire class.

Robert got down on his knees and said, "Dear God, I want a new eight-speed bike, a baseball, a football and a new suit. And, dear God, these requests are non-negotiable!"

✳ ✳ ✳ ✳ ✳

Amos was kneeling beside his bed, saying his bedtime prayers. His Mother said, "Amos! I can't hear you."

Amos responded: "I wasn't talking to you."

✳ ✳ ✳ ✳ ✳

The little boy accompanied his parents to church one Sunday morning, his first time ever in church. After services, his folks asked him how he had liked it. "Well," said the lad, "the music was just fine, but I figured he coulda shortened the commercial a whole lot."

✳ ✳ ✳ ✳ ✳

The fifth-grade Sunday School teacher was telling the father of one of her pupils about his child. "You know that each Sunday, every child must donate to the collection box." The father nodded. "Well, I think that your Tommy doesn't quite understand it."

"What do you mean?" father asked.

"Well, when I asked for his collection, he gave nothing! And he said, 'a fool and his money are soon parted.'"

Sunday School: A child was asked to tell what he knew about the Last Supper. The lad answered, "I was away for that. I had Chicken Pox."

✳ ✳ ✳ ✳ ✳

The teacher of the first year Sunday School class was having trouble getting his pupils to identify certain biblical personages. "Can anyone tell me who St. Matthew was?" Nobody could! "Well, how about St. Mark?" The class did no better...not a hand raised. Finally the teacher said, "Surely, one of you can identify Peter for me?"

A youngster raised his hand. "Good!" said the teacher. "Tell us." "Wasn't he a wabbit, teacher?"

✳ ✳ ✳ ✳ ✳

What goes ho, ho, ha, ha, hee, hee?
Santa Claus laughing like crazy.

✳ ✳ ✳ ✳ ✳

"WHY NOT? WE HAFTA PUT SOMETHING IN HIS WHEN WE GO TO HIS PLACE!"

In church for her first time, four-year-old Janie whispered to her mother, "Mama, what are those people doing now?"

"They're praying dear. Praying," was the reply.

"Do you mean to tell me that they...pray...with their clothes on?"

✳ ✳ ✳ ✳ ✳

In answer to the question as to the meaning of FAITH, the Sunday School student said, "Faith lets us believe what we know ain't so."

✳ ✳ ✳ ✳ ✳

A lad who usually accompanied his father on fishing trips was forced to attend Sunday School this particular Sunday. When the teacher asked him to recite the 23rd Psalm, he did so, perfectly, until he came to the fourth line and recited it as: "Thy rod and thy reel, they comfort me."

✳ ✳ ✳ ✳ ✳

"...and, please, God, make Stewart stop hitting me. By the way, God, I've mentioned this before."

✳ ✳ ✳ ✳ ✳

The teacher asked the Sunday School class if they had any notions as to why churches and synagogues no longer sacrifice burnt offerings.

One lad raised his hand, was recognized, and said, "I think it was because we have laws against air pollution."

✳ ✳ ✳ ✳ ✳

The best way to keep children at home is to make the home atmosphere pleasant, and let the air out of the tires.

Dorothy Parker

✳ ✳ ✳ ✳ ✳

The little boy told his parents that he was going to the backyard to play ball with God.

"Tell us, Joey, how do you play ball with God?" his father asked.

"Easy," said their son. "I just throw the ball up in the air and God throws it back to me."

"And God bless Mommy, Daddy, Aunt Martha, Uncle Stanley, Grandma and Grandpa, but not my brother Stewart, because he socked me again today."

$$* * * * *$$

A man and his son went to church and, afterwards, the man told his son that he thought the sermon was too long, the preacher worthless and the singing just gosh awful! The little boy looked up at him curiously, then said, "But, Daddy, what did you expect for a dime?"

$$* * * * *$$

The minister patted little Johnnie on the head, saying, "So you tell me your mother says your prayers for you at night. What does she say?"

"She says, 'Thank God, he's in bed.'"

$$* * * * *$$

"Tell me, Jacob," asked the grandfather of his ten-year-old grandson, "what you learned in Sabbath School today."

"Well, Grandpa, we learned all about the Jews and Exodus. Man, did they have a hard old time. Teacher told us how the Jews got chased all the way to the Red Sea by Egyptian soldiers in chariots and how Moses ordered a dozen big boats and just made it across before the soldiers came up to destroy them. Those Egyptian soldiers started to cross the Red Sea, but a huge wave came up and drowned them all. But the Jews were saved."

"What!" shouted Grandpa. "Your teacher told you **that**?"

"Not exactly that, Grandpa," the lad said, "but if I told you what he really told us, you'd never believe it in a million years!"

$$* * * * *$$

These little supplicants usually call up God at bedtime when the rates are lower.

$$* * * * *$$

The little boy was asked to give his understanding of the word, "Lie." "A lie," he said, "is an awful sin most times but a heckuva help when in trouble."

Pastor Paul Brown, his wife and five-year-old daughter were traveling by train from Chicago to Los Angeles. When it came time to put daughter Ruthie to bed, Mrs. Brown told the little girl, "Don't be afraid or frightened, Honey. God will watch over you."

A little later, Ruthie called from her upper bunk, "Mama, are you there?"

"Yes, my dear, I'm here."

"Papa, are you there?"

"I'm right beside you, Honey."

Another patron in a nearby sleep yelled, "Everyone's here, your Ma and Pa, your sister and brothers, uncles, aunts, all of us are here. Now shut up!"

After a pause, Ruthie's whispered voice asked, "Mama?"

"Yes, Dear?"

"Was that God?"

✳ ✳ ✳ ✳ ✳

"DO YOU KNOW WHERE LITTLE BOYS GO WHO DON'T PUT THEIR SUNDAY SCHOOL MONEY IN THE PLATE?"

"YEAH, TO THE MOVIES."

✳ ✳ ✳ ✳ ✳

"Remember what I asked for last night, dear Lord? Well, it's ditto tonight."

Two kids, Norm and Aaron, were sitting with their black friend, Pete, and talking about nothing in particular, when a rabbi and a priest came toward them, both ministers on their way to an interfaith meeting.

The priest noticed little Norm and knew him to be of his parish. "Why hello, Norman," the priest said. "Tell us what it is you love best in the world."

Norm knew that his priest was trying to impress the rabbi with how much little Catholic boys knew. Dutifully he replied: "I love our church more than anything, Father."

The rabbi recognized Aaron, one of the boys, as a son of a member of his congregation and not to be outdone, asked: "Aaron, what do you treasure most of all in your life?"

Aaron knowing what was expected of him, replied: "I like my synagogue best of all, Rabbi."

The ministers both smiled, nodded and moved on. It was then that little Pete said, "Ain't you cats ever heard of girls?"

✳ ✳ ✳ ✳ ✳

The minister was waiting for dinner to be served while on a visit to one of his parishioners. The young son was entertaining him while the boy's dad and mom were in the kitchen preparing dinner. "What's for dinner, young fellow?" the preacher asked.

"Goat," the boy replied.

"Goat? Now that is unusual. Are you quite sure it's goat?"

"Positive!" the lad replied. "Last night, I heard my dad say to my mom, 'Might as well have the old goat for dinner tomorrow and get it over with.'"

✳ ✳ ✳ ✳ ✳

The little boy came home from Sunday School quite disturbed. "Papa," he asked, "the Bible is always talking abut the children of Israel. Don't the grown-ups ever do anything?"

✳ ✳ ✳ ✳ ✳

A Sunday School teacher decided that she would have to do some serious correcting of the ideas of kids in her class. One kid had said, "Howard by thy name." Another youngster prayed: "Lead us not into Penn Station." And a third had surprised everyone by saying, "Our Father, who art in heaven, how'd you know my name?"

The real menace in dealing with a five-year-old is that in no time at all, you begin to sound like a five-year-old.   *Jean Kerr*

＊ ＊ ＊ ＊ ＊

The Sunday School teacher had just finished her story about Lot and his wife, fleeing Sodom and Gomorrah, saying, "Lot was warned to get his wife and flee out of the city that was going to be destroyed. You know they made it just fine, but Lot's wife looked back and turned into a pillar of salt. Do you have any questions?"

"I got one," a little girl asked, raising her hand. "Could you tell all of us what happened to the flea?"

＊ ＊ ＊ ＊ ＊

"What are you giving your brother for Christmas?"

"I'm not sure. But last year I gave him chicken pox."

＊ ＊ ＊ ＊ ＊

Seven-year-old Seth Brown jumped out of bed one winter morning and rushed to the window. He looked out and said, "Darn it, I hoped I'd see rain. And I prayed mighty hard for it, too."

His mother said, "But, Seth, just think about it...some other boy has probably prayed that it wouldn't rain!"

Seth thought that over for a bit, then said, "By gosh, God sure has it hard, hasn't He!"

＊ ＊ ＊ ＊ ＊

"Peter, what is a skeleton?"

"Bones with people scraped off of them."

＊ ＊ ＊ ＊ ＊

A little girl, daughter of a Baptist minister, was sitting on her father's lap, holding a mirror and using it to admire her face and then her father's face.

"Papa," the little one asked, "did God make you?"

"Sure did, Honey. Why do you ask?"

"Oh, I don't know. It seems to me he's doin' better work lately."

＊ ＊ ＊ ＊ ＊

In Sunday School, the lad answered a question on marriage by saying, "In Christianity, people can have only one wife or husband and they call it monotony."

"MY MOTHER SAID HE WAS SENT FROM HEAVEN.
THEY MUST'VE WANTED SOME PEACE AND QUIET."

* * * * *

Little Eddie came several minutes late to Sunday School and the teacher demanded to know why he was tardy. "Well, teacher, I wanted to go fishing, but my father wouldn't let me and we argued and that's why I'm late."

"Good for your Father! On Sunday, one is not allowed to fish rather than attend Sunday School. Did your father explain why you couldn't go fishing this Sunday morning?"

"Yes, Ma'am. He said there wasn't enough worms for both of us."

* * * * *

What do ghosts eat for breakfast?
Dreaded wheat.

* * * * *

Georgie Newton climbed into bed, said his prayers and called out: "Mama, Papa, I'm all ready to say my prayers. Do you want anything?"

"And who can tell me which is the most important sacrament?" a Sunday School teacher asked her class.

"Marriage," was the quick response of one student.

"No, my dear, not marriage but baptism is first and foremost...the most important sacrament."

"Well, it's not in our family," sniffed the student. "We, Ma'am, are respectable."

* * * * *

The Sunday School teacher asked, "Where is God?"

Six-year-old Abe said, "In our bathroom."

"Bathroom?" said the puzzled teacher. "How do you know that?"

"Every morning when my Daddy wants to get in the bathroom, he says, 'Good God! Are you still in there?'"

* * * * *

Why did they put a fence around the graveyard?

Because people were dying to get in.

* * * * *

A student was an extreme disciplinary problem and was failing in school. At a conference the school held with his parents, it was decided that the lad might be better off in a parochial school. The parents agreed to try one and did. Well, it turns out that the kid was a model student in every way. When the parents asked the lad why this school seemed so much more agreeable to him, he replied, "When I first walked into the school, I saw some guy nailed to a cross and I figured that **this** school really meant business!"

* * * * *

"What did you learn in Sunday School, today?" the mother asked her six-year-old.

"We were studying Adam and Eve, Mama," the little girl replied. "How God made the first man. But the man was lonely and so God made the man fall asleep and while he was snoring away, God took out his brains and made a woman from them for him."

* * * * *

Mother: "Now, dear, tell the minister what Mama's little baby girl did at the Sunday School party today."

Little girl: "I frowed up."

"In all that time that Noah was alone on the ark, how do you think he spent his time?" the Sunday School teacher asked her pupils. One lad raised his hand saying, "I think he musta done a lot of fishin'."

Another lad shook his head. "Couldn't," the boy said. "Couldn't spend much time fishin' when all he had was two worms!"

＊ ＊ ＊ ＊ ＊

"Johnny, why did you hit your sister? That's terrible!"

"Well, Mama, she was supposed to tempt me with the apple, wasn't she? Well, instead of that, she ate it!"

＊ ＊ ＊ ＊ ＊

Father to his eight-year-old son: "Laddie, I want you to give up something for Lent...to make a sacrifice...such as candy. Both your mother and I are giving up liquor."

"But you were sure drinking something just before dinner," the boy said.

"That was merely sherry," the father replied. "We quit drinking hard liquor for Lent."

"Well, Papa," the boy said, "I'll give up hard candy."

＊ ＊ ＊ ＊ ＊

First child: "Did you know that all the animals came on the ark in pairs?"

Second child: "Yep! But not true of the worms! They came in an apple."

＊ ＊ ＊ ＊ ＊

"A Psalmist is a feller who tells your fortune by reading your palm," said the youngster in Sunday School.

＊ ＊ ＊ ＊ ＊

Little Emma started out that morning on her way to Sunday School. She carried two dimes, one for the collection and one for a candy bar on her way home. Half way there, one of the dimes slipped from her fingers and rolled into a drain. "Golly gee," she murmured. "There goes the Lord's dime."

76

Teacher: "Where is the River Jordan?"
Pupil: "You're the teacher, you tell us."

* * * * *

A well-known radio announcer took his daughter to a church dinner. The minister invited the young girl to say grace and she agreed. She bowed her head and said, "This good food, all you folks should know, is coming to you through the courtesy of our great God above."

* * * * *

A boy asked his minister: "How does it happen that if there wasn't any world and God created it, what in heck did he have to stand on to do it?"

* * * * *

Mother stood by her daughter's bedside, trying to understand what her kneeling child was saying. But she couldn' understand and asked, "Darling, just who are you praying to?"
The answer: "Winkin', Blinkin' and God!"

* * * * *

Teacher: "What shall I talk to you about today?"
Pupil: "About five minutes, Ma'am."

* * * * *

The preacher finished his biblical story of David and Jonathan. "Now, children, if you've any questions, please ask."
Elmer raised his hand. "I'd like to know, Pastor, just how do you manage to get that narrow collar over your head?"

* * * * *

"Do you go to Sunday School?" Susan was asked.
"I don't go, I'm sent!" she replied.

* * * * *

A little boy knelt to say his prayers, but before beginning, looked up at his mother and said, "Mom, do you suppose it'd be OK if I put in a commercial about a new bike?"

The minister was provoked to see an old man, a regular attendant, always fall asleep during the sermon. He called the old man's grandson aside and said, "It upsets me to see your grandfather sleeping during my sermons. I'll give you a quarter to keep him awake." The lad accepted.

For several weeks, the old man stayed awake. Then four or five weeks after the agreement with the boy, the old man started to fall asleep again.

The minister talked to the boy after a service, saying, "I thought the money I gave you obligated you to keep the old man awake, my Son. Why haven't you done it?"

"Because Grandpa gave me fifty cents to let him sleep," the lad replied.

* * * * *

"Is God home?"

* * * * *

A five-year-old had been to church that afternoon with his parents, and when he knelt to say his bedtime prayers, he said, "Dear Lord, we sure did have a good time at church today. I wish you'd been there."

"Now that you've made it to Sunday School, what would you like to do?"
"Go home."

* * * * *

Friend: "Johnny, do you say your prayers every night?"
Johnny: "Not every night. Because some nights I don't want anything."

* * * * *

One of the examination questions at the fourth-grade Sunday School was, "Who brought gifts to the infant Jesus?"
One pupil raised his hand. "I know, I know!" he exclaimed.
"Very good," the teacher said, smiling. "Please tell us."
"Mr. Frankincense and Mr. Myrrh."

* * * * *

Raymond Thomas got home from Sunday School and said to his mother: "Our teacher said some real nice things about me today."
"Really! Tell me what it was."
"He said, 'Oh, Lord, we thank Thee for our food and Raymond!'"

* * * * *

"Is the minister ugly?"
"I wouldn't quite say that. But he does have a perfect face for radio."

* * * * *

"I've told you the story of Jonah and the whale," the teacher said to his class. "Now, children, can you tell me the true meaning of the biblical tale?"
Paul Edgar raised his hand and the teacher nodded to him. He stood, saying, "It means to me something real important! It teaches us that you can't keep a good man down."

* * * * *

"Johnny, I told you to draw a donkey and a cart, like one of Jesus's time."
"I know. I drew the donkey. It'll draw the cart."

The teacher had assigned the Ten Commandments to his third grade class and, the following Sunday, asked, "Class, can you give me a Commandment that has only four words?"

James Petefish raised his hand. "Yes, Jimmy?"

"Keep off the grass."

* * * * *

Teacher: "Class...can you tell me what a land flowing with milk and honey would be like?"

Frankie: "I guess it'd be mighty sticky!"

* * * * *

The minister accepted the money that Jimmy Jones handed him during the collection. "Next time I see your mother, Jimmy, I'll thank her for the dollar and a half."

"Sir," Jimmy pleaded, "would you mind thanking her for two dollars?"

* * * * *

"Mrs. Randy, would you punish a kid for something he didn't do?"

"Of course not."

"Good, I didn't do my Sunday School assignment."

* * * * *

The engaged G.I. had been overseas on U.S. Army duty for almost a year. He was married to his sweetheart soon after arrival back home. The time came to kiss the bride in the marriage service and the groom and bride engaged in a sustained kiss. A little boy asked his mother a question so loudly that all in the church heard it: "Mommy...is he spreading the pollen on her now?"

* * * * *

Teacher: "Don't us 'a' before a plural. Don't say 'a horses.'"

Pupil: "But teacher, the minister always says, 'A-men!'"

* * * * *

"How were the Sunday School exam questions?"

"Easy. It was the answers that were tough."

*"If everybody's responsible for it, how can it be an **original** sin?"*

✳ ✳ ✳ ✳ ✳

Edith Barton was coaching her eight-year-old daughter, Emily, on how to address their new preacher, coming to call on them for the first time.

"Emily," Edith told her daughter, "when the preacher gets here, you be respectful at all times. If he asks your name, just say, 'It's Emily.' If he asks how old you are, just say, 'I'm eight.' And if he asks who created you, just say, 'God did.'"

Oddly enough, the clergyman did ask those very same questions and Emily did fine on the first two. But when the preacher asked her who had been her Creator, Emily turned to her mother and said, "Mama. I've gone and forgotten the man's name."

✳ ✳ ✳ ✳ ✳

Mary Thomas was expecting the Pastor for dinner and asked her daughter to set the table while she busied herself preparing the food. Soon the Pastor arrived, was seated at the table, said prayers and then noticed that he had no silverware. Embarrassed at the oversight, Mary asked her little girl why she had not set silverware for the Pastor. "Because, Mother, Papa says that he eats like a horse!"

Teacher: "Jack, why are you wearing cotton in your left ear? An infection?"

Pupil: "No. Last Sunday, you said everything you told me went in one ear and out the other. I'm trying to block things in."

* * * * *

Adlai Stevenson loved to tell the following story.

It seems that the young daughter of a renowned clergyman was busy with her colored pencils when the Pastor happened by and asked whose picture she was drawing. "I'm almost done," she said, "with a picture of God."

"But, dear daughter, nobody knows what our God looks like!"

"Just wait till I'm finished. *Then*, they'll know!"

* * * * *

Walking across the classroom floor, in Sunday School, Billy Joe stubbed his toe, then cussed a blue streak! The Sunday School teacher took him upstairs to the preacher. There she told the minister what terrible things Billy Joe had said.

"Billy Joe," the preacher began to scold him, "using words like that, cussin' and swearin' and such, will bring the Devil's bogeyman onto you."

"The bogeyman? Where is he?"

"You can't avoid him if you cuss like you did. He's everywhere."

"He is? Even in Uncle Joe's basement?"

"Yes! Even in Uncle Joe's basement."

"Now I know that's a goldarned lie 'cause Uncle Joe ain't got no basement."

* * * * *

"And what," inquired the kindly Sunday School teacher, "do we learn from the story of Jonah and the whale?"

"We learn," maintained little Ronald, "that people make whales sick."

* * * * *

During the Sabbath Saturday Hebrew School, little Oscar was asked if he knew what religion Abraham's father practiced. He nodded: "I don't recall the exact name of it, but it was a real lazy kind of religion. He believed in Idle worship."

82

It was a Sunday morning in July and, as usual, hot and stuffy and almost unbearable in the Sunday School classroom. The minister came in to see how things were progressing and the teacher asked him to say a few words to her class.

"Well," the minister began, smiling benignly, "dear class, I hadn't expected to talk to you and I hardly know what to say..."

A small voice spoke up. "Why don't ya just say 'Amen' and sit down!"

* * * * *

Preacher: "You must start at the bottom and work up to the top."

Student" "What about just swimming, Pastor?"

* * * * *

"Tell me about Good Friday."
"He worked for Robinson Crusoe."

* * * * *

"MOM, DAD, HIDE THE ASHTRAYS, IT'S PASTOR FEGAN."

In Sunday School, a little lad was asked if he know what the Israelites did right after they emerged from the crossing of the Red Sea. He replied, "I guess they dried themselves, didn't they?"

* * * * *

"Where do mummies swim?"
"In the Dead Sea."

* * * * *

It was an enthusiastic, deeply serious and loud prayer meeting after which seven-year-old Joshua, said to his father, "Gosh, Daddy, they wouldn't have to pray half that loud if they were a little closer to Him."

* * * * *

"What do you know about the Dead Sea?"
"I didn't know it was sick, Ma'am."

* * * * *

The rains of 1994 were horrendous, so bad that a little girl said to her father that she didn't believe heaven was a good place.
"Why not, Sally?"
"It looks to me," said Sally, "like everything up there is full of holes with water comin' through every darned one of those holes,. I sure don't want to go up there!"

* * * * *

"God bless my sister, God bless Mommy and God help Daddy."

* * * * *

The Sunday School teacher was discussing Creation. "Now, children, who can tell me what makes the flowers spring from the seed and then grow and grow and grow?"
One little girl held up her hand. "God does it," she replied, "but fertilizer sure helps."

* * * * *

"...And dear God, I do want to go to heaven very much, but only if my kindergarten teacher ain't there."

Invited for dinner at the Rogers home, the preacher made a very brief, succinct prayer before dinner. Peter, the six-year-old son, remarked, "Gee, Pastor, you sure don't pray long when you're hungry."

* * * * *

"Class," the Sunday School teacher asked, "can you tell me about the Philistine, Goliath?"

"I can, teacher," Jane responded. "Goliath was the guy that David rocked to sleep."

* * * * *

KIDS SAY THE DARNDEST THINGS

"Dear God...please make Jimmy stop bangin' on me. And, by the way, this isn't the first time I've talked to you about this."

* * *

"Dear God, remember what I asked for last night? Do you? Well, it's the same derned thing tonight!"

* * *

"Dear God, tonight I'm saying prayers for my little sister, Becky, because she's too little to pray for herself. Why, she ain't even toilet-trained."

* * *

The Sunday School teacher asked her class: "How many of you children expect to go to heaven and want to?"

All raised their hands, except for a new kid in class.

"Do I understand that you don't want to go to heaven, Peter?"

"Can't. It's impossible. Y'see, my Dad said I got to get right home after Sunday School."

* * *

Little Jeremiah listened to the concluding statement of his teacher in Sunday School: "And that, class, means that all men are brothers!"

Jeremiah held up his hand: "No, they ain't. Some of us are sisters."

"Dear God, please put vitamins in candy, 'stead of spinach."

* * *

Two little girls were discussing a family marriage of the day before. "I heard the strangest thing from the preacher yesterday, the one who married my brother to Sadie. That preacher said a man can have as many as sixteen wives. Isn't that something!"

Her little playmate looked puzzled. "Come on, now," she said, "that can't be right!"

"He said so..he said, 'four better, four worse, four rich and four poor.' And that makes sixteen...right?"

* * *

A child's prayer: "Dear God, help me be a good kid and, if it don't work out at first, I'll keep tryin."

* * *

"Dear Lord, I ask only for one thing. Make my brother, Albert, stop hitting me. Please remember that 'cause I've mentioned it before."

"From Art Linkletter's books about kids saying, writing or doing the Darndest Things."

"HOW COME I GOTTA GO THROUGH THIS EVERY SUNDAY WHEN ALL 'HE' CARES ABOUT IS THAT I'M CLEAN INSIDE?"

SPITBALLING FATHER
WHILE HE WAS PREACHING

There is one episode in my life that sets me apart.

So far as I can discover I am the only minister's son who ever threw spitballs at his father while the latter was preaching a sermon.

I don't want to be misunderstood. Ordinarily I do not object at all to going to church. It is a pleasant, quiet, relaxing environment. A person can sit and plan his program for the coming week; he can review his accomplishments of the past. Or he can just sit.

It was a hot, sultry July Sunday in 1911, when I was ten years old. The Hancock Congregational Church is a big, beautiful church. It sits beside the village common, looking down the valley toward Peterborough and Mount Monadnock. Behind it is a semicircular row of the best-preserved horse sheds in New England.

The first floor of the building is the Town Hall. Upstairs is the large auditorium that will hold an audience of four hundred people. Back in 1910 the average Sunday crowd was probably fifty or sixty. They sat in the rear pews of the church. I remember I once asked Father if it did not bother him to have the people sit so far back. He said, "No, that's human nature, and it gives me a chance to exercise my voice."

But the elder's family did not sit in a back pew. We sat in the fourth pew from the front, left-hand side of the middle aisle. Mildred and Edith used to argue the issue vehemently. Why should they have to sit way up front where all the women and girls in the rear could study the parson's family -- especially their hats and coats? It has long been a New England tradition that the minister's family should sit well up front. And that is where we sat, for Father was a believer in tradition. Mother sat on the inside, Nona next to her, then Mildred, then Edith beside me.

It did not bother me, so far as I can recall, to sit up front. Clothes were, and still are, according to comments, a minor concern with me.

This particular Sunday morning I could not seem to get comfortable with my thoughts. There were no fishing trips to plan; mail-order time was weeks away. I did not care to review mentally "The Unbelievable Adventures of a Lone Trapper in the Arctic Circle."

Father's preaching was not holding my attention. Not that Father was not a good preacher. He was powerful and dynamic. He often told good stories in his sermons and used illustrations from nature and farming that everyone liked because they understood what he was talking about. He exhorted the faithful to be more so and regularly gave the devil about all it deserved.

It was muggy, close, and uncomfortable in the church. I glanced over at Mother and saw that she was nodding off. She had been on the go since six o'clock, feeding her tribe, washing the milk pails, getting the four children, a man, and herself ready for church. The spirit of the Evil One entered me and I reached forward for a hymnbook. It did not disturb Mother. She was actually snoozing. I tore out a leaf of the Responsive Readings in the rear of the book. I tore the leaf in half, crumbled it slowly and carefully in my hand. Then I put it in my mouth and worked it into a solid round missile.

Father organized his sermons well, by firstlys, secondlys, and thirdlys. And when he came to the grand climax of a division of his sermon he had the habit of rising on his toes and throwing his muscular arms wide, as if to include the whole world.

By and by I had the spitball made to suit me. It was firm and round; it was large enough to handle efficiently. I took another look at Mother and shoved Edith over a bit. Then when Father was hitting on all fours, raised on my toes and arms wide-flung, I let go with a quick, snappy sidearm throw.

I am a bit ashamed to admit it, but I missed Father by at least four feet.

I have been told that even if New Hampshire men are not very smart they are persistent. I made a second spitball and bided my time while Father got steamed up to the climax of the next point. This time I aimed more carefully. The spitball whizzed by Father's ear, and just for the merest fraction of a second I thought he paused. Probably he thought it was an unusually large fly.

I was improving. I took special pains with the third one. I made it a little larger; I chewed it a little longer. I pushed Edith over a little farther. Then I waited. I was patient. I have been called a patient man -- as well as other adjectives. I knew Father had several points to cover and there was plenty of time. I waited while he checked off two or three climaxes. Then he came to another. Mother was still snoozing. Mildred and Nona were making horrible faces, trying to stop me. Edith, as usual, was co-operative.

Came the crucial moment. Father towered above us, his voice deep with emotion, his arms outspread. I let drive quick and hard.

The spitball went straight and true. Persistence and patience always pay off. The ball caught Father right in the middle of his chin.

It was one of those epochal moments in life. Silence was as thick as a double feather bed over that church.

A look of utter astonishment was in Father's eyes. His arms dropped slowly, very, very slowly to his sides. Slowly he bowed his head and looked down at the platform by his feet. Slowly he raised his head, and for some strange reason he looked straight at me.

Psychologists, those men and women who can use seven-syllable words without faltering, tell us that, in moments of great crisis, picayunish trivialities etch unforgettable gullies in our cerebral convolutions. It is thirty-seven years since that July day, and two minor points are still as clear as first November ice in my mind.

Eight or ten pews behind us, Eddie Kent sat with his father and mother. When Eddie grew excited he had a high, shrill, falsetto giggle. When that spitball conked Father on the chin, Eddie's giggle just sort of climbed upward toward the rafters. Then it was sliced off abruptly as his mother's elbow jabbed into his ribs. At the very instant the giggle was left dangling high in the air a young cockerel out behind Charlie Sheldon's barn let go with one of those croaking, raucous, quavering, long-drawn-out, juvenile cockerdoodledoos.

Silence again muffled the church. Father's eyes bored into mine, and I suppose the ravages of a criminal career were deeply lined in my face.

After one of those moments that seem an eternity Father said, "Excuse me," in a low, firm voice.

With portentous, unhurried dignity he walked across the pulpit platform. He methodically descended the four steps. I could tell from the set of his shoulders that he was in complete command of the situation. He started up the aisle. As he went by the pew he crooked a finger in my direction.

I got up and followed Father that long last mile. I remember the horrible clatter we made as we went over the big hot-air register. We went out into the entry. There Father sat down, took me across his knees, and performed a task that more parents today should perform on their offspring.

Then he opened the door to the auditorium, closed it carefully but emphatically, took me by the shoulder, marched me down the aisle, sat me down in the pew with a thud, climbed into the pulpit, and finished his sermon as if nothing had happened.

"That Darned Minister's Son" by Haydn S. Pearson.
c 1950 Doubleday & Co., New York

Little Morton was saying his goodnight prayers while his Dad and Mom stood by the bed. "Dear God," he intoned, "bless Mommy and Daddy who feed me and give me nice toys. And bless all those cows giving such good milk and, dear God, please bless all the camels that give us soup."

* * * * *

Grandma Thomas was giving her little grandson the dickens over his failure to go to church. "You will never get into heaven the way you are going today," she told him.

"Well, Granny, the reason I don't go is I got a problem. I can't for the life of me figure how I'm gonna get my shirt on over those wings I'll have."

"Never mind about shirts. The question in your case is how are you gonna get your hat on over those horns!"

* * * * *

The minister was talking to the Sunday School class about kindness to animals and cited the Biblical references to substantiate his case.

"Now let's suppose," he said, "that you saw a bad person cutting off the tail of a cat. What Biblical quotation would you use to tell him of the terrible wrong he was doing?"

"I would point out to him," one of the class said, "what God hath joined together, let no man put asunder."

* * * * *

One Santa Claus grabbed up a guitar and conked the other Santa Claus over the head with it, and that was when the fight started.

TOO MANY SANTA CLAUSES

The setting for this tale is in a country school not far from the town of Lenoir in Watauga County [North Carolina].

A couple of weeks before last Christmas, teachers and other members of the Parent-Teachers Association decided to put on a rip-snortin' Christmas program. Word leaked out about plans and preparations and all the children got tremendously interested.

One of the first things the kids wanted to know was whether Santa Claus was going to be present. They were informed that a letter had been sent to Santa at the North Pole but nobody could be exactly sure whether he would show up or not.

The children hoped and prayed that he would.

Three or four of the grown-ups got together and decided that Santa would have to be present by all means, otherwise there would be a lot of disappointment.

"Let's get Jimmy Walker to dress up," someone suggested.

They went to call on Mr. Walker, a middle-aged farmer who lived abut a mile from the school. He didn't much want to do it but they finally persuaded him to accept.

"Tell Mrs. Walker to make you a Santa Clause suit," they suggested. "All you have to do is stand around and let the children see you, and help distribute the presents."

Mr. Walker said okay.

Several other grown-ups, not knowing what the first group had done, called on Mr. Tom Hadley with the same proposition.

"We want you to act as Santa Claus at the Christmas celebration," they informed him. "Don't say anything about it, because we want this to be a big surprise to the children."

"Well, I don't know much about how to do it, but if the kids have got to have a Santa Claus, I reckon it's up to me to help out," he stated. "I'll get my wife to make me some kind of suit to wear at the celebration."

The event was to be held on the night of December 21. The children were still debating whether or not Santa Claus would put in his appearance. Teachers and parents continued to keep them in suspense. The adults knew that preparations had been made to have a Santa Claus present but they didn't know that a duplication had inadvertently been arranged.

When the program started at eight o'clock, the school auditorium was packed and jammed with children and grown-ups. The school orchestra rendered several selections. There was an appropriate Christmas talk by the preacher. And then --

In walked Mr. Walker, dressed in a perfectly nifty Santa Claus suit!

The children applauded joyously. Santa had come all the way from the North Pole to pay them a visit. They cheered him for several minutes, and Mr. Walker bowed and waved his hand at them.

And now, momentarily, we turn to Mr. Hadley.

It was close to Christmas. Mr. Hadley felt that the advent of the Yuletide season justified him in taking a drink. So he drank a toast to himself. Then he dressed up in the suit his wife had made for him. He surveyed himself proudly in the glass and decided it would be polite and considerate to drink a toast to Santa Claus, which he thereupon proceeded to do.

Just as he was leaving the house, he happened to think of Mrs. Santa Claus, 'way up there at the North Pole -- poor old lady -- so he drank a toast to her, too. And then, as a final thought, he also remembered the reindeer.

All of which meant that by the time he arrived at his destination he was in a highly festive mood.

He entered the back door of the auditorium and walked out on the platform.

The children gasped in amazement. They hadn't been sure whether one Santa Claus would show up or not, and here -- all of a sudden -- were two of them.

They yelled, stamped their feet and clapped their hands.

Mr. Hadley bowed in appreciation of the reception being accorded him. Then he happened to look over toward the side of the stage and saw Mr. Walker.

92

An interloper!

He walked somewhat unsteadily over toward Mr. Walker and said: "What are you doing here?"

"I'm Santa Claus," said Mr. Walker.

"Like hell you are!" said Mr. Hadley. "I'm Santa Claus."

"I was here first."

"Yes, and you're going to get out of here first."

The children sat with eyes and mouths wide open.

"I'm not," said Mr. Walker. "You've got no business here, and besides, you're drunk."

Mr. Hadley looked around him. Members of the school orchestra had left their instruments on the stage. A guitar was within easy reaching distance. He grabbed it, held it firmly in his right hand, took a long swing and crowned Mr. Walker with it.

The guitar burst into pieces. Mr. Walker staggered back from the blow. The children went wild. They didn't know what it was all about but they were having the time of their lives.

"You--you--you--" gulped Mr. Walker. And then he called Mr. Hadley something that little children aren't supposed to hear. But they heard and, naturally, were delighted. Mr. Walker reached over on a table, picked up a book and slung it at Mr. Hadley.

He socked him squarely in the face with it.

Then Mr. Hadley started cussing. The children discovered that he was even more fluent than the other Santa Claus. The latter started forward and landed a blow on Mr. Hadley's face. Mr. Hadley took a wild swing and missed.

"Sock him, Santa."

"Kill him, Santa Claus!"

"In the belly, Santa! Hit 'im in the belly!"

The entire auditorium was in an uproar. The two Santa Clauses were going at each other with everything they had. Four or five men sprang from their seats and went up on the platform. They succeeded in separating the combatants. They ushered them unceremoniously out of the building and told them to stay there and not come back in again.

Then the school principal said that in view of unforeseen circumstances, he himself would enact the part of Santa Claus. The kids didn't give a rap about the rest of the program. They had seen enough to last them a life-time, and they haven't quit talking yet about the dandy fight that Santa Claus and his brother put on for them.

Excerpts from "Just for the Fun of it." 1954 written by Carl Goerch, used with the permission of the Estate of Carl Goerch.

"DO YOU HAVE AN 800 NUMBER?"

* * * * *

One day, in Sunday School, the teacher told the class that if anyone needed to go to the bathroom, he or she should just raise their hand. A little boy asked, "Teacher, how's that going to help?"

* * * * *

Two six-year-old sisters knelt before their beds ready to say prayers. Ruthie was first, ending, "Amen. Good night, God. Now just stay tuned to Mabel."

* * * * *

One Sunday morning in church, little Elsa Schnable, who had accompanied her father to church, felt violently ill. "Daddy," she managed to whisper, "I'm sicker'n heck. I got to vomit!"

"Go to the bathroom," her father answered.

In a very few minutes, Elsa was back, saying, "Papa, I didn't have to go as far as the restroom. There's a tiny box by the door that says, 'For the sick.'"

* * * * *

Little girl said, "My Grandmother reads the Bible all day long...I think she's cramming for her finals!"

A little boy went to bed terribly upset over a request he had made to see the local ball team play. His father turned him down. That night he made the following prayer: "Please don't give my parents any more kids because they sure don't know how to treat the one they got!"

*****

The preacher's little boy asked him, "Papa, every Sunday morning when you come out to preach I notice that you bow your head and just sit there. What are you doing?"

*****

"Oh, Mamma," questioned the child, "Who's that?" He pointed to a passing nun.
"A Sister of Charity," was the answer.
"Which one," the boy asked. "Faith or Hope?"

*****

A little boy knelt beside his bed and said this prayer: "Dear God, if you can't make me a better boy who minds what his daddy and mama tell him, don't worry about it. I'm getting along just fine the way things are goin' now."

*****

A mother asked her little daughter, "Who said 'God's in His heaven -- all's right with the world'?" and the little girl's answer was, "Mrs. God."

*****

Sierra was almost twelve years old when she and her parents went to Chicago to visit her grandparents, Pastor and Mrs. John Hendrichs. All went well until Sierra became obsessed with knowing how old her grandmother was. She pestered her constantly until, finally, she came back into the room to say: "I know how old you are, Grandma. You're 73."
"That's right," replied Grandma. "How did you find out?"
"I looked at your driver's license. But tell me, Grandma, how come you got an F in sex?"

*****

Definition: A Sunday-school teacher is one whose job is to welcome a lot of live wires and make sure that they are well-grounded.

Returning from Sunday School, the little boy asked his mother: "Does God carry a comb, Mom?"

"What a question. What makes you ask that?"

"Well, in class this morning, the teacher said that God parted the Red Sea."

* * * * *

The three-year-old grandson looked out the window and saw lightning for the first time. "Look, Grandma!" he exclaimed. "God just took my picture!"

* * * * *

The Sunday School teacher was describing how Lot's wife looked back and was turned into a pillar of salt. Little Billy raised his hand and said, "My Mama looked back once when she was driving and *she* turned into a telephone pole."

* * * * *

Repentance as described by a small girl: "It's to be sorry enough to quit."

A minister asked a small boy, "Sonny, do you say prayers before meals?"

The boy replied, "Ain't necessary at our house, Pastor. My Ma is a darn good cook."

* * * * *

The Sunday School's subject was the prodigal son. "Everyone was having a great time," the teacher said, "except one, because to him the banquet meant bad times and bitterness and he hated the feast. Who can tell me who that one person was?"

One little boy raised his hand and said, "I know, teacher. It was the fatted calf."

* * * * *

"Son, I'll give you a quarter if you can tell me where God is," the atheist told a small boy.

The boy's polite reply was, "I'll give you a dollar if you can tell me where He isn't."

"IF GOD'S NOT IN, WILL HIS ANSWERING MACHINE GET THIS?"

* * * * *

Michael returned from Sunday School to ask his father, "Tell me, Dad...we had a story in Sunday School about the evil spirits that entered the swine. I wasn't sure what that meant. Could you explain it all to me?"

"Well, yes, I can do that. Just what, specifically, did you want to know?"

"Tell me...is that a description of how they made deviled ham?"

* * * * *

The Sunday School examination question read: What was Noah's wife's name?

Johnny Kirk wrote: Joan of Ark.

* * * * *

The sermon seemed endless to the little boy in church with his family. Finally, overcome with restlessness, the boy whispered, "Mom, if we give the money now, will he let us go?"

The Fifth Commandment is, let see now...Humor thy father and thy mother.

* * * * *

"Where have you been, Eleanor?"
"I've been to Sunday School, Daddy."
"What's that you have in your hand?"
"Oh, it's just an ad about heaven."

* * * * *

It has been said that the modern youngster's prayer ought not be: "Lead us not into temptation," but "tell us where it is and we'll find it."

* * * * *

Five-year-old Eddie Brighton was playing with the little girl next door. Her family had just moved in and this was the first play session of the two. They had been wading at the lake and had gotten quite damp. They decided to take off their clothes and enjoy the water without them. The lad looked the girl over and then remarked, "Gosh, Emma, I sure didn't know there was that much difference between Catholics and Protestants!"

* * * * *

An early pioneer story has it that there was a conference of country ministers assembled at the home of the president of their Association. They were all seated around the central stove trying to keep warm on this very cold day. The small son of the house came in from doing his chores and he was cold. Yet he couldn't find a place near the stove, so crowded was it with ministers. One preacher, seeing the boy shivering, asked, "Is it cold outside, boy?"
"You bet! Cold as hell!"
"But, Son, my Bible tells me that it's hot in hell, not cold."
"Oh, no, it's just like it is here. There's so darned many preachers that a fellow can't get close to the fire."

* * * * *

The minister visited his kindergarten class that was taught by a young lady named Murphy. While there, he witnessed the class reciting the Twenty-Third Psalm. But something seemed wrong with the recitation and he asked Miss Murphy if he could hear each child recite. She nodded. All went well, no errors, until one little boy ended his Psalm, saying, "Surely good Miss Murphy shall follow me all the days of my life."

All travelers have the patron saint named St. Francis of the sea sick.

$$* * * * *$$

When Mary was told she was to play the mother of Jesus, she sang the Magna Charta.

$$* * * * *$$

Back in World War II, two brothers, farm boys, met their death. They were brought back to the U.S.A. for burial. At the cemetery, a large crowd gathered to pay their respects and there was a military guard of honor and a squad of riflemen to fire the final salute for the two heroes.

It was a very said occasion and several women broke down and wept. At last the squad of riflemen fired the final salute and the Army bugler blew taps. This was just too much for the elderly aunt of the deceased and she fell over in a dead faint just as the riflemen fired the last salute.

There was a moment of dead silence broken by a little boy's voice that the entire crowd could hear as he screamed, "Damn, they shot Grandma!"

$$* * * * *$$

" MOM, I'M GOING UPSTAIRS TO SAY MY BEDTIME PRAYERS.
DOES GOD HAVE A FAX MACHINE? "

3
CONGREGATIONS

GASTRONOMICAL ENDEAVORS WON AND LOST

The main topic of this little story is gas. Not unleaded or ethanol or even regular -- just plain gas.

Where I was raised, you didn't mention anything about gas. And if the occasions should come to be noticed, you excused the problem and then slid out of the room with a red face.

When it comes to gas, there seems to be a double standard. When you're with boys, gas can create some highly competitive times. When you happen to be around a bunch of girls or some of them really radical church women, you have to be fully awake and on your toes.

One time Terry and I spent the night over at Larry's. It was a Saturday in the summer, the first day in quite a while that our folks had let us get together for more than two or three minutes at a time.

We ran and ripped all day, played world champion ropers on the milk pen calves, and managed not to get into any trouble. That evening, as we were helping Larry with his chores, the subject of gas came up. Bragging began and was followed by a series of challenges. It appeared we had just talked ourselves into a friendly gas war.

In our little area of the world, the main diet consisted of beef, beans, and vegetables. The beans, of course, had a little to do with our kind of competition. As we were finishing with the chores, we made up the rules for the contest. We could eat as much as we wanted of anything but the beans. We each had to eat three helpings of beans. That way each of us would have an equal shot at the title. So to speak.

Well, supper was great, plenty of everything, and the deviled eggs that Larry's mom fixed was probably the best I had ever eaten. Little did I know that after eating eight or nine along with three helpings of beans, I was fixing to acquire a championship title I would never lose.

When we finished eating, we went out to play some basketball, and after a while, Larry's dad hollered for us to come on in and get our baths and get to bed. He didn't want a bunch of dirty kids oversleeping and making everyone late for church.

Did he say church?

Good gravy...we had forgotten all about having to go to church, and here we were, fully loaded for the gas war to end all gas wars.

It was a terrible event. There we were, all three of us, in the same bed and with several dense clouds floating around the room. For some reason, I didn't get into the competition until daylight. It seems as though the beans and the eggs worked against each other until about breakfast time.

I excused myself from the table and slipped out the door. I could hear Larry and Terry laughing while Larry's mom chewed them out and explained that at least Curt had the manners to leave the room, and they shouldn't be laughing at someone's embarrassment.

As we pulled up to the church, we could see that just about everyone in the country was there, all the kids we went to school with and most of their parents. There was even that goofy red-headed girl who had a crush on me.

I don't know what made her like me, but I was stuck with her. She came over to us and said it was gonna be okay if all the kids in the fifth grade sat together because she had already asked her daddy, and he said so. Her daddy was the preacher.

She tried to grab my hand and I just snarled at her. Then she tried to step closer and I did it. I got back in the competition. Lucky for me it got laid off on Terry. I guess it was the way the wind was blowing.

She turned red, he turned red, and I headed for the church house. Larry was almost down on the ground laughing, and I was building pressure.

I began to wonder if I had made a mistake, entering the sweepstakes the night before church. I was trying to avoid any contact with other people, simply because I couldn't tell when the next round was going to start.

My mother called me over and said it was all right if I sat with the little red-headed girl, but there had better not be any talking or laughing. I assured her there would be no talking, but I thought to myself there was a very good possibility of some snickering.

The preacher got up and went to doing his thing. Larry and Terry was sitting behind me and that red-headed girl, and I was starting to suffer. That girl had crowded me 'til I was up against the end of the pew, and Larry and Terry was giggling about it.

I had crossed my legs and started to sweat. Somewhere between the third and fourth hymn, I started getting weak, and that little girl started getting closer. I had all I could do just to stay hooked, when the preacher said, "Let us pray."

Boy, if he only knew.

It was abut the time everyone had gotten down to some serious prayer that it happened. That little red-headed female poked me in the ribs. When I jumped from the poke, there was a slippage of gas. Sounded kind of like a two-by-twelve being ripped in half. The silent prayer came to a halt.

I jumped up, looked the little girl square in the eye, and hissed just loud enough for everyone to hear, "Sherry, couldn't you at least have excused yourself?!"

With that, I walked around and sat down next to Larry and Terry.

Them two traitors were laughing so hard, they were having minor gas problems theirselves, and I noticed from the corner of my eyes some other problems on the way. Our Dear Old Moms were on their feet.

The little red-headed girl stamped out of the church house, and we boys were sentenced to be separated for life -- again. But there was a bright spot. As we waited in the car for church to be over, Larry mentioned that I was now World Champeen Gas Passer.

From "A Snake in the Bathtub" by Curt Brummett. 1990 Reprinted with permission of August House, Inc.

✳ ✳ ✳ ✳ ✳

Faith -- we are told -- is that quality which enables you to eat blackberry jam at a church picnic without looking closely to see if the seeds moved.

✳ ✳ ✳ ✳ ✳

"HOW DO YOU LIKE MY NEW EVENING GOWN?"

Maybelle Hawkins was describing a wedding she'd recently attended. "And do you know that the groom and his intended...you all know Elizabeth Hawks, don't you? Been married at least six times. Well, as Elizabeth and her feller were walking up the aisle towards the preacher, all the lights went out in the church!"

"My goodness, Maybelle. What did they do?"

"Oh, they just went ahead because Elizabeth knew the way."

✳ ✳ ✳ ✳ ✳

The laziest man in Paducah, KY, joined the church and seemed to have gotten religion. All expected energy to come to the guy but soon changed their mind when they heard that he'd had someone type a bedtime prayer for him and that he had pasted it upon the ceiling above his bed. When he retired, he'd point to the prayer and fall asleep. Now that's *lazy*!

✳ ✳ ✳ ✳ ✳

When a man needs money he needs money and not a slap on the back, a headache tablet or a prayer.

✳ ✳ ✳ ✳ ✳

Eddie Joyce, married for several years, was troubled and went to see his pastor. "Pastor, I've got real problems at home with the woman you married me to, back in 1988."

"Sorry to hear that, Eddie," the Pastor said. "What seems to be the problem?"

"Money! The root of all evil, isn't it? All she wants is money. She keeps asking me for money! Money! Money!"

"Goodness sakes, Eddie...what does she do with the money you do give her?"

"How should I know, Pastor. I ain't never given her none."

✳ ✳ ✳ ✳ ✳

The gent who lives only for himself is supporting just about the meanest human being around.

✳ ✳ ✳ ✳ ✳

I did not attend his funeral; but I wrote a nice letter saying I approved of it.

Mark Twain

104

It's a funny old world -- a man's lucky if he can get out of it alive.
W.C. Fields

＊ ＊ ＊ ＊ ＊

They tell the story of the early days of the Women's Liberation Movement and the famous march on Washington. Two of the ladies in the march had grown too violent in their protests and were put in jail. The older of the two heard the other woman crying in her adjoining cell and moved to comfort her.

"Dear little girl," she comforted, "don't let this good work get you down. It'll all come out right. Just put all your trust, your confidence in God. *She* is sure to do right by you."

＊ ＊ ＊ ＊ ＊

Politicians have a constant need to be diplomatic. Witness this candidate for the Senate who traveled to a small town community to address the single church there. Unfortunately, he had forgotten to ask which denomination so that when it was time for his speech, he inquired in this way:

"My brethren, all. I must tell you that my great Grandfather was a Presbyterian (absolute silence); but my Grandmother was an Episcopalian (more silence); I must tell you that my other Grandfather was a Christian Scientist (deep silence); while my other Grandmother was Methodist (continued silence). But I must tell you that I had an aunt who was a Baptist through and through (loud cheers!) and I have always considered my aunt's path to be the right one!"

＊ ＊ ＊ ＊ ＊

I must say that our pastor's sermons are truly refreshing. The congregation feels so much better after it awakens.

＊ ＊ ＊ ＊ ＊

BURYING EXPENSES -- A big real estate operator's widow told the undertaker that she wanted him planted with all the trimmings, the best of everything. She got a bill for $12,000. She was outraged.

"But Madam," reminded the undertaker, "you said the best."

"Yes," she fumed, "for a few dollars more, I could have buried him in a Cadillac!"

Some people are so prejudiced they don't even listen to both sides of a cassette.

***** *

In the hills of Arkansas, a backwoods preacher was delivering his sermon on the wise and the stupid. "It ain't them thangs you don't know what gits ya into trouble, it's them thangs ya know fer sertain that...just ain't so."

***** *

Our leading soprano in the choir has an enormous repertoire. And her tight dresses sure do reveal every bit of it.

***** *

The Rabbi called on a member of his congregation for a pledge to the synagogue's fund to build an addition for a new library. "Sam, our congregation is growing larger every year and we really need this library. Could you pledge a hundred dollars?"

"No, Rabbi, I can't."

"Well, then, how about fifty?"

"I can't do it, Rabbi, I'm heavily in debt and I got to pay my creditors first."

"But Sam, you owe a great debt to God, too, and don't you think He deserves your input?"

"He sure does, Rabbi, But God isn't crowding me like my other creditors."

***** *

Prayer: A declaration of dependence.

***** *

The farmer had sent his hired hand along with the wagon and team of mules to get a load of feed at the grain elevator. But the man seemed never to return. He was gone an hour longer than needed and, when he finally drove up to the house, the farmer bawled him out. "So what excuse do you have for being late?" he demanded.

"Well, our preacher was walking along the road and I picked him up and after that them damned mules couldn't understand a word I said."

What did the insurance agent say to Adam and Eve?
"It's obvious that you aren't covered."

* * * * *

A traveling salesman stopped his car and entered a small town cafe for a cold drink to ease the sweltering heat of an insufferable Texas drought. "Holy smokes, it is h-o-t!" he exclaimed to the old man sitting at the counter next to him. "When was the last time you folks down here had any rain?"

"Well, do you remember in the Bible where it says that it rained 40 days and nights without stoppin'?"

"Sure do," the salesman replied. "That was Noah, wasn't it?"

"Somethin' like that," the old man said. "Well, back then, down here we only got half an inch!"

* * * * *

Bang's Law: Church sermons have an unsettling habit of relating to your questionable behavior of the previous week.

* * * * *

A black G.I., in World War II, was on sentry duty one night and he was prepared for any practical joke that might be played on him. Experience had taught him that much! Suddenly he heard footsteps and called out..."Halt. Who goes there?"

"Major Moses," a voice replied.

"Very well," the guard said, "advance and give the Ten Commandments!"

✳ ✳ ✳ ✳ ✳

Chauncey Depew, asked what kind of exercise he took, answered: "I get my exercise acting as a pallbearer to my friends who exercise."

Portland "Sunday Telegram"

✳ ✳ ✳ ✳ ✳

Company B of the 31st Infantry Regiment was assembled to hear a sermon on the Ten Commandments preached by the regimental chaplain. It was a long, distinguished sermon at the conclusion of which, Private Jones announced to his friend, "Well, at least I never made a graven image."

✳ ✳ ✳ ✳ ✳

The graveyards are full of people the world could not do without.

Elbert Hubbard

✳ ✳ ✳ ✳ ✳

A preacher from a downtown Chicago church was the guest preacher at a rural church near Middletown, Illinois. The congregation asked him to pray for rain and he did. In fact, he prayed so successfully that, before he had quite finished, it began to rain, then rained on and on with lightning and terrible thunder. Almost four inches of rain fell during the sermon. Everything was flooded. Outside, after services, one farmer turned to another and said, "This oughta be a lesson for all of us. In the future, there'll be no more city preachers invited here because they don't know a derned thing about prayin' for farmers."

✳ ✳ ✳ ✳ ✳

A lot of folks would do more prayin' if they could find a soft spot for their knees.

108

PUFF PUFF

SCHWADRON

EVOLUTION

✳ ✳ ✳ ✳ ✳

The most indolent, lazy, useless member of the congregation was attending church one Sunday and was called on to lead the congregation in prayer. "Please, Lord," he began, "use me! Please use me. But, if you please, only in an advisory capacity."

✳ ✳ ✳ ✳ ✳

It was President Clinton's home state of Arkansas where some families in the Ozark Mountains live very insular lives. The preacher drove to the isolated farm home of a parishioner and asked a young girl who came to the door if he could speak to her father.

"Ain't likely," she said. "He's in the penitentiary."

"Well, then, might I speak with your mother?"

"Ma ain't here neither. She is done gone to the hospital. She was seein' sarpents and the like."

"Sorry to hear that," the preacher murmured. "If you've got a brother, could I speak with him?"

"Well, Brother Jonas, he's off to college."

"How nice!" the preacher said, smiling. "And what is he

studying?"

"He ain't studying nothin' I knows of," said the girl. "The folks there are astudyin' him!"

＊＊＊＊＊

As an example of the myriad ways the Lord works, consider the following event:

Returning from Europe, Mrs. Edna Baker stood before the customs officer who asked if she had anything to declare.

"Nope. Don't think I do, Sir," she replied.

Rifling through her valise, the inspector found a bottle. "And this, Madam? What's in it?"

"Only some holy water, Sir," she said. "I've been to Lourdes."

The customs officer removed the cork and sniffed the contents.

"Why, lady, I'm shocked. The bottle contains whiskey!"

"Holy smokes and glory be the Lord above. Another miracle!"

＊＊＊＊＊

Vice
Is nice
But a little virtue
Won't hurt you.

Felicia Lamport, "Axions to Grind!"
Scrap Irony 1961

＊＊＊＊＊

Back in the 1850s, a traveling parson needed a horse so he went to a trader, selected, bought and paid for one. As he was about to mount, the trader restrained him, saying, "One thing, Parson, this horse doesn't respond to the usual 'giddap' and 'whoa'. He's just right for a preacher like you. To start, you say, 'Praise the Lord.' To get him to stop, you got to say, 'Amen!' Got that?"

The Parson nodded, mounted the horse, said, "Praise the Lord" and his new horse cantered off just as nice as you please. But he soon came to a deep chasm washed out of the road, a chasm at least a hundred feet deep with precipitous sides. The Parson had forgotten the "stop" word. "Whoa" didn't work! Then he remembered, just in time, and said "Amen!" The horse finally, in the nick of time, stopped. The Parson took out his handkerchief, mopped his face, looked toward heaven and murmured, "Praise the Lord!" And he was over the side and headed for the bottom before you could say, "Whoa!"

In the old days, when there were circuit riding preachers, one of them came by this tiny cabin set in the hills of Arkansas, and spoke to the woman who was standing on the porch. "Do you have any Baptists around here?" he asked.

"Nary a one as I know of," the woman replied. "But my mister has many kinds of cattle and you could see if one of them was minglin' with the herd."

"It is plain to me, Ma'am, that you are living in darkness."

"Not my fault. I been atryin' to git my old man to buy we'uns a kerosene lamp 'stead of candles, but he won't spend the money."

"Lady, do you know that Christ died for our sins?"

"Nope. Sure didn't. I ain't heard nothin' about nobody even bein' sick in these parts."

"I bid you good day, Madam, I'll see you again at the Pearly Gates."

"Not me, you won't. I was out talkin' to a feller at the front gate, t'other night, and my old man liked to have killed me."

It's not the cough that carries you off...it's the coffin they carry you off in.

My friend, Joe, hadn't been to a Sunday service in many months. Finally, I prevailed upon him to go and he sat through the entire service seeming to enjoy it. But on the way out, as we passed the minister standing in the doorway, greeting the parishioners, he pulled Joe aside and said softly, "Joe, I'm delighted to see you. I want to see you here regularly. I need you to join the army of the Lord."

"I'm there already, Pastor. I'm in the Lord's army."

"Then how come I haven't seen you in a year or more?" the minister asked.

"I'm in the Intelligence Branch, Pastor. Top secret. We gotta be unseen!"

✳ ✳ ✳ ✳ ✳

Said the old man to the preacher at the close of the service: "Fine sermon, everything you said applied to somebody or other I know."

✳ ✳ ✳ ✳ ✳

There is this man who is known as the most ignorant man in Burke County, North Carolina. Somebody once asked him if he knew what county he lived in, and he answered flat out, "Nope." Well, they then asked if he had ever heard of Jesus Christ. "No," he answered. Finally, they asked if he had ever heard of God. "I believe I have," he said. "Is his last name Damn?"

✳ ✳ ✳ ✳ ✳

Girl to mother: "I can't marry him, Mother, because he's an atheist and doesn't believe in hell," and the mother answered, "Marry him, dear, and between us we'll convince him."

✳ ✳ ✳ ✳ ✳

Mary Teasdale was the nemesis of her church and everybody disliked her. She refused to like anything that anyone else did and always insisted that she could have done it much better. She made a fuss about everything. This went on until her eightieth year, when she died. At the funeral, a terrible storm came up with overwhelming thunder and constant lightning. Suddenly, a teeth-chattering blast of thunder overwhelmed the congregation and one of the mourners announced, "Well, by golly, she *got* there!"

✳ ✳ ✳ ✳ ✳

The only thing that does not improve with use is your temper.

There was a good young lawyer who showed up at a revival meeting and was asked to deliver a prayer. Unprepared, he gave a prayer straight from his lawyer's heart: "Stir up much strife amongst the people, Lord," he prayed, "lest thy servant perish."

* * * * *

There was a man in Nash County who hadn't walked for years. He had his son push him in a wheelchair every time he went out of the house.

Near their house was a cemetery. One day two boys who had been fishing took their fish under the shade trees in the cemetery to divide them. They left the two biggest ones at the gate.

The son came long, pushing his father in the wheelchair. It was just twilight, and the voices issuing from the cemetery had a ghostly quality. "You take this one and I'll take that one."

The other voice protest. "But yours is bigger than mine." So it went.

The son heard, paused, whispered harshly, "The Lord and the devil are dividing the souls."

The father said, "Stop for a minute, I want to listen."

Just then the voice inside the cemetery said, "There's two at the gate. You can have one of them and I'll take the other."

The boy could stand no more. He fled, leaving the old paralytic sitting there. He ran home and dashed into the house crying, "Oh, Ma, I left Pa at the cemetery and the Lord and the devil are in there dividing our souls. They'll get Pa sure."

His mother answered, "Don't you worry none about Pa, son. He beat you here by a full minute, but somebody has got to go back after his chair. You know your Pa can't walk a step."

Reprinted from "Tar Heel Laughter," edited by Richard Walser.
©1974 by the University of North Carolina Press. Used by permission of the publisher.

* * * * *

WATER INTO WINE -- Not long ago, a law-enforcing friend told me he had just caught a bootlegger who had eluded him for months. That morning he had come on him with fruit jars covering the floor of his station wagon and asked him what he had in them. "Water," was the answer.

"Let me taste it," said the officer, and turning up a jar, started drinking and kept on drinking. When he put it down, he wiped his mouth and said, "It tastes like wine to me."

"Lord, Lord," the old bootlegger answered, "Jesus has done it again!"

So live that no matter what happens, it wouldn't have happened to a nicer person.

"Progress." Wells, NV

* * * * *

During World War II, an army chaplain was surprised when a G.I. came to him offering an envelope filled with a donation.

"Great!" exclaimed the chaplain. "We can sure use this to help fund the repairs needed on the chapel." He opened the envelope to see $20. "My, that's a lot of money, Private Jones, isn't it?"

"Yep! But to tell the truth, I won it."

"Wouldn't it be better, Private Jones, to give it back to the men from whom you won it?"

"They've gone overseas, Sir."

"OK, then, I'll accept it."

Twice more, the G.I. gave the chaplain donations and each time the chaplain accepted them only when the soldier explained that he couldn't give back the money to the donors. But when the G.I. showed up with $500, it was too much. "Now you look here, Private Jones, gambling is a bad habit, a sin. And your giving all your winnings to the church doesn't excuse it at all!"

"But I'm not giving it all, Sir. I'm giving only a tenth. Y'see after you'd finished that swell sermon about the Lord providing for folks who tithe, I tried it. And, I got to tell you, Chaplain, He sure does provide for us tithers."

* * * * *

*"PERHAPS IT'S MORE THAN JUST A COINCIDENCE
THAT WE'VE ALL NEVER BEEN AUDITED."*

If you want to know about the troubles the church is having, ask someone who hasn't been there for months.

* * * * *

Elmer Karas took his family on a visit to Washington and, while there, they visited the House of Representatives which was in session. One of Elmer's kids, Tommy, was interested in the opening prayer of the chaplain.

"Papa," he asked, "why do they have, the very first thing, the preacher pray for Congress?"

"He's not praying for Congress, son," Elmer replied. "He bows his head and then prays for the country."

* * * * *

It sure is strange how the little things can bug us! For instance, it's lots easier to sit on a mountain top than a tack!

* * * * *

Mark Twain told the story about his session in church one Sunday morning. It seems the preacher was very good and the sermon quite wonderful. About halfway through, Mark Twain decided to give $20 to the church. But the preacher went on and on until Twain thought to cut in half his contribution, to $10. On and on went the preacher until Twain thought that when the basket passed him, he'd give only $2.00. Finally, at long last, the sermon ended; when the basket came his way, Twain filched a dollar from it!

* * * * *

Sign on a church bulletin: After 2,000 years, we are still under the same management.

* * * * *

When Jackie Gleason was asked if he thought he'd make it to heaven, he said, "Under present rules, perhaps not. But I'm counting on two things: God having a sense of humor...and Him grading on the curve."

And then there was the church janitor who insisted on sweeping reforms.

* * * * *

"Do you take this woman for your wedded wife," the minister asked the nervous bridegroom, "for better or worse, for richer, for poorer, in sickness or..."

"Just a minute, Pastor!" interrupted the bride. "Stop now or you'll talk him right out of it."

* * * * *

Your sense of decency is the one thing you can't preserve in alcohol.

* * * * *

John Edgar was running for mayor of his town. He stopped by his church and asked his minister to support him.

"Before I say yes or no, John, you must tell me...do you indulge in liquor?"

"Before I answer that, Parson, let me ask you a question...Are you asking me or inviting me?"

* * * * *

Funeral: A coming-out party for a ghost. Also, the last bedtime story.

* * * * *

The announcement on the church bulletin board was telling! It read: This Sunday at the Mt. Pulaski Methodist Church, we will hold our annual strawberry feast. But, due to the present recession, applesauce will be served.

* * * * *

A hokey museum was started in Toone, Arkansas and one of the first visitors was Uncle Ed Aspin of Chicago. He was startled before an exhibit of a spike that was purported to be from the right hand of Jesus, nailing that hand to the cross.

Uncle Ed turned to another visitor standing beside him. "Heck that ain't so very old," he said. "Why my Uncle Dodder had a pencil he swore was used by Noah to check-off the animals as they came, two-by-two, on board the ark!"

116

Undertaker:	The boxer who always wins. Put another way, he's the guy who always -- in the end -- let's you down.

*****

Thirty years ago, they told this story about a wealthy white fellow who had a black for a person servant in his home. They would exchange information about the dreams each had the night before. But the boss seemed always to have the best dream.

One morning, the boss got out of bed and announced to his servant, "Y'know, last night I had the oddest dream."

"Yeah? Please, Boss, tell me about it."

"Well, last night I dreamed that I went to heaven and saw lots of garbage in the streets, many rotting houses, broken-down fences and simply filthy streets with nothing but poor, ragged black folks walking about."

"Well, well, Boss, let me tell you about my dream. Seems I went up to the paradise of the white folks and the streets were clean, paved with platinum and gold, with lots of milk and honey stashed around and the purtiest pearly gates you ever did see. And there wasn't a single white soul in the entire place."

*****

A sign above the door of a small-town church read: Come on in...you aren't too bad for that. Nor are you good enough to stay out!

*****

The church needed a new organ and the elders decided to raise the money to buy one. They hit on this scheme: To each parishioner who gave fifty dollars, they would dedicate a hymn to be sung, accompanied by the new instrument. One maiden lady rose to offer $100. The Pastor thanked her and asked which hymn she preferred.

The lady rose, pointed her finger and said, "I choose him or him or him!"

*****

Outside a Manhattan church, there was a sign that read: Designed and approved for general audiences.

Two generations ago, golfer Josh Sarasohn wrote this desperate plea to his God. It expresses the need of most golfers who resort to prayer in their game. We thought to offer it for consideration by all golf club swingers:

Golfer's Prayer

No man can count the vast amount
  Of ties and shirts and sox,
That I possess -- I only guess --
  (And hankies, by the box)
Cuff links and studs, and sundry duds,
  A bursting treasury --
It takes cube root to half compute
  My haberdashery!

I own cigars, in tins and jars,
  And "straw-tips" by the bale,
And pipes galore -- Bring me no more
  Near-meerschaums from a sale!
My humidor is flowing o'er
  With Turkish and perique --
No Christmas tree (alas!) for me
  Will bear the gift I seek...

Give me some token to invoke,
  Some charm or some device;
Some spell that's sure, some certain cure,
  I want to lose my slice!
A drive that will lift the old pill
  High, pretty, straight and clean,
Past hazard, rough -- I want the stuff
  That lands 'em on the green!

St. Nick, Old Dear -- hark, prithee, hear --
  One gift, (can it be done?)
Once while I live, give me, oh give:
  I WANT A HOLE IN ONE!
  "Steve! Is Mama Home" by Josh Sarasohn
  © 1933 Pennfield Press

* * * * *

Question: What do you get when you mix holy water and prune juice?
Answer: A religious movement.

A true story involves two old men discussing the hereafter and all events preceding it. One said, "If you come to my funeral, Tom, I'll go to yours."

* * * * *

Back in the 1950s, a story circulated about a black, man, a WWII veteran, who decided that he wanted to join the most exclusive church on New York's Fifth Avenue. The minister didn't want to hurt the man, so he told him to go home and think it over for a few weeks.

So the black man goes home but returns the next day to confront the minister, who asked, "I thought that I told you to go home and think about this for a few weeks. And here you are again, not twenty-four hours later. Why?"

"Well, I went home and prayed," the black man said, "and the Lord heard me and answered me."

"Really! And what did the Lord tell you?"

"He asked me what church I wanted to join and I told him it was yours, so he says, 'That church? Why, man, you can't get in there. I just am positive about that. Why, I have been trying to get in that church ever since it organized and I haven't made it yet!'"

* * * * *

Bulletin board notice: The ladies of the congregation have cast-off clothing of all kinds and can be seen in the church basement this Saturday afternoon.

* * * * *

Tom and Jack lost their good buddy, Pete. They went to the funeral home to pay their last respects, but before they got there, they had several drinks to dull their sorrow. They entered the funeral home and walked unsteadily to the casket, or what they thought was a casket, but it was a piano! They knelt before it, prayed, stood up and left the place. Walking home, Tom said to Jack: "That sure was a lovely casket, wasn't it?"

"It sure was," Jack replied. "And you know something...I never knew that our good buddy Pete had such a beautiful set of teeth."

* * * * *

At the McFarland Zone Center for mental patients, an old lady was a constant reader of the Bible. When asked why she did not try a more varied kind of reading, she said, "I can't. I'm cramming for my finals!"

Faith: Faith is believing what you know ain't so.

Mark Twain

"I THINK SHE'S GOING TO REGRET MARRYING A DOCTOR."

* * * * *

Old Elmer Johnson passed on and at the church service, someone remarked: "As I recall, old Elmer attended church only three times during his entire life...when he was *hatched*, when he was *matched*, and now, when *dispatched!*"

* * * * *

Man: A creature made at the end of the week when God was tired.

Mark Twain

* * * * *

One reason why the Ten Commandments are so succinct, direct, self-sufficient is that they were not devised by a committee.

Three young men and a fourth, an old man, were discussing the salvation of the world. One young guy said, "If we had no more profanity, this world would be lots better."

The second young fellow added, "And if we could quit drinking liquor, we'd sure as heck have a better world."

The third young guy announced that if the world could get rid of adultery and all other sinful things, the millennium would have arrived.

"The millennium, ha!" exploded the cantankerous old man, "sure, and then we'd have to put up with **that!**"

* * * * *

It was unseemly in the small town of Edinburg, Illinois, for a person to be buried without a good word spoken for him or her. But the deceased was so incorrigible that no one could be found to speak a decent, kind word. Finally, one man agreed to do the proper thing and the entire community came to hear what on earth (or heaven) he could say about this man!

The one-man delegate stood up. "Friends, about our deceased neighbor, let me say this. Sometimes he wasn't as bad as he was most all of the time."

* * * * *

Moral indignation: Jealousy with a halo.

H.G. Wells

* * * * *

The preacher was asked to give the family some advice on how to restrain and manage their six-year-old boy and his sister, two years older. "Pastor, they fight and fuss and feud all the time and we simply are at a loss for what to do. Can you help?"

"Your problem is not all that unusual, friend. The term for it is sibling rivalry."

"I'd think a better term would be sible war," said the father.

* * * * *

"By the time the meek inherit the earth," growled Old Man Gotrocks, "the taxes will be so high they can't keep it."

The new pastor of the Grace Lutheran Church was making his first sermon. He was terribly nervous, swallowed a lot and spoke in a muted voice. Finally, one of the members in back yelled: "Speak louder, Pastor, we can't hear you."

The preacher raised his voice but soon lapsed into a quiet monologue. Again, the voice yelled, "Louder, Pastor, speak louder. Can't hear you."

A voice from the front came back, "Quit complaining back there! Just shut up and thank God...or I'll change places with you."

✳ ✳ ✳ ✳ ✳

Thare iz sum pholks in this world who spend their whole lives a hunting after righteousness, an kant find enny time tew praktiss it.

Josh Billings

✳ ✳ ✳ ✳ ✳

Pastor John Hodges noticed a man stand, turn and begin to walk out of church during the most important part of his long, long sermon. "Excuse me, Sir!" Pastor Hodges called to the man. "Where are you going?"

"To get a haircut."

"Sir! You should have done that yesterday!"

"I didn't need it then."

✳ ✳ ✳ ✳ ✳

A big city paper reported: "Miss McIntyre's insipid singing caused the congregation to burst into applesauce."

✳ ✳ ✳ ✳ ✳

In 1929, *"Everybody's Weekly"* held this article: "The old-time woman who saved her wedding dress for her daughter now has a daughter who saves her own wedding dress for her next wedding!" (And we think multiple marriages are a contemporary problem!)

✳ ✳ ✳ ✳ ✳

Way back in 1929, the *"Wisconsin Octopus"* had this cynical saying about marriage: "A wedding is a funeral where you smell your own flowers."

The church chandelier was looking terribly shabby, rusting and in need of replacement. But a new one would cost over $2,500! A meeting was held to make a final decision on whether or not to buy one. An old man raised his hand and said, "We shore don't need no chandelier in thiseyer church. It costs too derned much money! Worst of all, there ain't nobody in thiseyer church what can play one."

* * * * *

Sometimes a minister can't win for losing. Example: "How do you like our new minister?" the question was asked by one parishioner of another.

"Don't much care for him," was the reply. "He preaches so derned long that I can't keep awake, and he hollers so blamed loud that I can't get to sleep."

* * * * *

A fellow appeared at church one Sunday morning and both of his ears were bright red. One of the deacons asked, "Fred! What did you do to yourself?"

"You wouldn't believe it! While I was ironin' a pair of pants last night so' to come to church this morning, the phone rang and, as you might guess, I picked up that dadblamed iron instead of the phone."

"Golly, that's sure sad, Fred. But what happened to the other ear?"

"The very same guy called back!"

* * * * *

It's Always Been Like That

Just the other day, Pastor Pedigrew, both his integrity and craftiness intact, finally completed his twenty-four-month Project Facelift.

Just over two years ago, the Cedar Gap Independent Full Gospel Non-Denominational Four Square Missionarian Church of the Apostolic Believers began contemplating a sanctuary renovation. As the ranking scholar and fearless shepherd of the small congregation, T. Edsel prepared the preliminary sketches.

Then Delmarine, his triple-chinned wife, went to work with the Ladies' Tuesday Bible Symposium on the proposed changes.

"Changes?" a bright-eyed lady chirped. "Whattaya mean changes! What's wrong with the way it's been since I joined back in '42?"

Delmarine tried to explain that the flaking paint above the pulpit gave the sanctuary a mildly leprous appearance, and while that was certainly Biblical, it did not bid one to come worship. "T. Edsel thought a nice muted blue-and-gray scheme would be comforting."

The announcement met with either stony squint-eyed staring or tight-lipped dissent. "Blue? What kind of blue? Are we talking sky, navy, azure, robin's-egg, electric, or what? I mean, I don't look good in every blue hue." The speaker fluffed her formerly gray hair. "Some colors clash."

"Well, I kinda like scarlet. Isn't that a religious color?"

"It was also the color on Hester's letter-jacket. Forget scarlet."

Blue alone ate up three Tuesday's symposia, not to mention the problems with ordering padded or unpadded seats.

"We're driftn', Brethren," a man in overalls said. "We're just gettin' too comfortable. There's somethin' in there about bein' at ease in Zion, ain't there, T. Edsel?"

But those were only surface ripples compared to the typhoon T. Edsel knew he would set off if he suggested rearranging the power sources at the front of the church. T. Edsel frowned at the auditorium situation and decided...the choir loft had to be moved.

Actually, "loft" was a tad presumptuous. The seven women and two men in the Adult Sanctuary Choir sat in folding chairs behind a two-by-four railing off to the north side of the auditorium. The pulpit stand, a hand-fashioned creation rescued from a defunct traveling drama group performing *Elmer Gantry*, stood directly in the center of the small stage area.

T. Edsel quickly realized that although the symbolism inherent in a centrally positioned pulpit perfectly mirrored his theology, it messed up his master renovation plan. That stand had to move off to the south side of the sanctuary, both to balance the choir's relocated seats and to open up the view for the new baptistery painting he still envisioned.

"Brethren," T. Edsel said, his voice low enough for a TV anchorman, "we've got to keep the Great Trinity of Faith plainly visible."

"Now, Pastor Pedigrew," Sister Oliphant, the chairwoman of the Sanctuary Committee, said slowly, "By 'trinity' you mean --"

"Preachin', singin', and baptizin' of course. The pulpit, the choir, and the baptistery, our three-sided keystone of Faith."

"Pastor, our pulpit has always been right there in the center, deviating neither to the left nor to the right." Sister Oliphant looked around, proud of her mishandling of scripture. "It's always been there in the middle, and it's gonna stay right there in the middle."

That was two years ago. Beginning that week, early every Monday morning, T. Edsel crept into the sanctuary, looked around warily for any stray Watchers or roving Holy Ones, then carefully nudged the pulpit stand one inch to the south. Then he fluffed up the telltale carpet and refocused the overhead floodlight.

Ninety weeks and ninety inches later, the migratory lumber arrived at the exact spot for balancing a choir loft. T. Edsel called a general meeting for that Sunday afternoon.

"I seem to remember, a couple a years ago, somebody suggested movin' the choir up on the pulpit area. For symbolic reasons, of course."

"Well, that'd be nice. That north wall has always looked sorta bare."

"Or, I just thought of another idea." T. Edsel played his trump. "We could leave the choir where it is, and move the pulpit stand over in the middle to balance the pulpit area."

Sister Oliphant, still chairwoman of the Sanctuary Committee, cleared her throat menacingly. "Sorry, we can't do that."

"What's the problem?"

"As long as I've been a member here, that pulpit's always been off to the south side, and it's gonna stay right there on the south side."

The nine-member choir is now up on the preacher's level, the cracked plaster looms symbolically behind the baptistery, and Pastor Pedigrew caroms his sermons in on his congregation from his new vantage point nearer the south wall.

That only proves that tradition is a wonderful thing and certainly more reliable than memory.

Reprinted with permission from "Life As It's Lived,"
by Jack Boyd, © 1989 Texas Tech University Press.

✳ ✳ ✳ ✳ ✳

Be careful how you live; you may be the only Bible some people will ever read.

✳ ✳ ✳ ✳ ✳

An elderly Quaker lady was driving her new car in Pittsburgh. At a cross street, she encountered a huge truck that was unable to stop until it had busted her fender, broken four windows and put a big dent in half the car. The lady was furious but managed to say, "When thee gets home to thy kennel this evening, Mister, I pray that thy mother bites thee."

✳ ✳ ✳ ✳ ✳

God may forgive your sins, but your nervous system won't.
Alfred Korzybski: "Healthways."

SCHOCHET

* * * * *

I know a humorist who, together with a good deal of rattle brain, had a grain or two of sense. He shocked the company by maintaining that the attributes of God were -- the power and risibility -- and that it was the duty of every pious man to keep up the comedy.

"Emerson's Journals"

* * * * *

God grant me patience...and I want it *now!*

* * * * *

A man walked into the office of the local newspaper and asked, "How much to publish a notice in the obituary column?"
"Two dollars an inch," was the reply.
"That's absurd! My brother was six feet, five inches tall!"

Wherever God erects a house of prayer,
The devil always builds a chapel there;
And 'twill be found, upon examination,
The latter has the largest congregation.
Daniel Defoe: "The True-born Englishman"

✳ ✳ ✳ ✳ ✳

Pete and Eddie loved to play baseball and belonged to an amateur team. When Pete heard that Eddie had been taken to the hospital with a terminal illness, he hurried to see him. There he found Eddie reconciled to his fate and at ease. They talked about baseball.

Eddie said, "I sure hope they play baseball in heaven."

Pete replied, "Well, I'm certain they do. But once you get there, please get in touch with me and tell me, will you?"

Eddie nodded, saying, "You bet!"

The next morning, Pete heard Eddie's voice as it awakened him from sleep. "Pete," Eddie said, "I have real good news and some bad, too. They do have wonderful games of baseball up here."

Pete asked, "And the bad news?"

Eddie: "You are playing second base next Wednesday."

✳ ✳ ✳ ✳ ✳

Do unto others the way he'd like to do unto you, an' do it fust.
Edward Noyes Westcott

✳ ✳ ✳ ✳ ✳

After the Congressman had delivered a speech at a political rally, a woman approached him and told him how much she had enjoyed his talk and that she would like to have a copy. The Congressman told her that his speech had not been prepared and had no printed text. "So you think you will ever publish the speech?" she asked.

"Perhaps posthumously," he said, and she replied, "Oh, good. I hope that'll be real soon."

✳ ✳ ✳ ✳ ✳

Conscience is that still, small voice
That quells a wicked thought
Then adds this sequence,
Besides, you might get caught.
"Supervision"

A woman called her friend and hysterically yelled this question: "Helen, did you see my name in the obituary column? Isn't that awful! How dare they!"

Her doubtful friend on the other end of the line asked tremblingly, "Tell me, Mary...where are you calling from?"

* * * * *

Some people go to church to see who didn't.

* * * * *

The American cowboy was...and is...a whiz at inventing and adapting words to fit his needs. In his revealing book of cowboy language, Ramon Adams included a few euphemisms for preachers and their world. Here are three:

Preacher: Fire escaper, Sin-buster, Sin-twister, Sky-Pilot.
Cemeteries: Bone orchard, Boneyard, Boot hill, Gampo Santo, Grave Patch, Still Lot.
Anxious Seat or Anxious Bench: At frontier revivals, a seat near the front reserved for those concerned about their spiritual welfare.

* * * * *

The devil iz sed tew be the "father ov lies." If this iz so, he haz got a numerous family, and sum very promising children amoungst them.

Josh Billings

* * * * *

A man was attending a strange church in Tennessee and saw that they had the nativity scene, but with firemen's coats and hats. This seemed strange and he asked why it was this way.

In East Tennessee dialect, the parishioner said, "Don't y'all recall whut the Bible say? It say, 'they come from a-far'!"

* * * * *

Churches: Soulariums.

Pik Thomajan: "Phoenix Flame"

* * * * *

The bars of the church are sometimes so low that any old hog with two or three suits of clothes and a bankroll can crawl through.

W.A. "Billy" Sunday

"NO, NO, HIGBY, IT'S DING BEFORE DONG
EXCEPT AFTER BONG."

＊ ＊ ＊ ＊ ＊

The minister gave his Sunday morning service, as usual, but this particular Sunday, it was considerably longer than normal. Later, at the door, shaking hands with parishioners as they moved out, one man said, "Your sermon, Pastor, was simply wonderful -- so invigorating and inspiring and refreshing."

The minister, of course, broke out in a big smile, only to hear the man say, "Why I felt like a new man when I woke up!"

＊ ＊ ＊ ＊ ＊

The middle-aged farm couple were without children and so they resorted to prayer in the hopes that she would become pregnant. And she did! At the end of the term, she delivered triplets. The wife said, "Dear, prayer really does work, doesn't it?"

Her husband replied, "Seems to, but I sure as heck didn't pray for a bumper crop!"

＊ ＊ ＊ ＊ ＊

Back in the hills of Arkansas, a traveling preacher stopped a resident and inquired, "Tell me, Sir, have you found Jesus?"

"Holy smokes, Preacher, I didn't have no idea He was lost."

There was a great meeting in San Francisco for one of the nation's leading evangelists. Thousands came to hear him. Halfway through his exhortation, he said, "There has never been a perfect man. If anyone with us at this assembly knows of a perfect man, let him stand!" None stood. The evangelist continued, "And there is no such thing as the perfect woman, anyone who has known such may now stand and testify."

One middle-aged lady stood.

"Amazing!" said the evangelist. "Have you truly known a prefect, faultless woman?"

"Not personally, Mister Preacher, but I've learned a great deal about her. She was my husband's first wife."

* * * * *

A New Englander enjoyed making his own additions to the Beatitudes and his favorite one bears repeating: "Blessed is the man who having nothing to say, abstains from giving wordy evidence of the fact."

* * * * *

A young preacher, now at his first congregation, said, "I will take for my text the words 'and they fed five men with five thousand loaves of bread and two thousand fishes.'"

Hearing the misquotation, an old parishioner said, "Heck, Pastor, I could do that myself."

The new preacher said nothing but the following Sunday, he talked on the same subject and this time got it right: "And they fed five thousand men on five loaves of bread and two fishes."

He looked at the old man and said, "And you think you could do that, too, my friend?"

"Yep. I sure could," was the reply.

"And just how would you do it?" the young preacher asked.

"With all those leftovers from last Sunday," the old man said.

* * * * *

Bigots, enthusiasts, and clothes pins, all hav the same sized heads on them.

Josh Billings

* * * * *

We have a young minister who is sure to go far...and the sooner the better!

130

"How did you enjoy my sermon, Mr. White?" the new young clergyman of the Tennessee Hill Country Church, asked.

"Let me tell ya this about it, Mistuh Preacher. I don't hardly git to hear those sermons of yours. Y'see, I'm an old man and I got to sit way back close to the stove to keep warm. And there in front of me sits ol' Missy Jenkins and widow Jergens, and old lady Strepper and her kids, all asettin' in front of me with their mouths wide, wide open, takin' in ever derned thing you say, Parson. Well, by the time what's left gets back to me, it's pretty pore stuff, Pahson, mighty pore stuff."

❋ ❋ ❋ ❋ ❋

" NOW THIS IS A CITY I LIKE...WHERE CLEANLINESS IS DEFINITELY NEXT TO GODLINESS!"

❋ ❋ ❋ ❋ ❋

A widow from Penbickatee,
    Married ten times and persnickety,
She led with a halter,
    Poor Mick to the altar,
They sang "Him" Number 'leven for poor Micky.

Cowboy saying: Hot words lead to a cold slab.

* * * * *

The minister of a large congregation was invited to a small town to marry a young couple. He did just that, and the ceremony was much appreciated by bride, groom and family.

When the service was over, the groom told him, "I very much appreciated your coming out here, Pastor, and to show my 'preciation, ah, since I ain't got no money, ah-m gonna give you my favorite coon dawg thet I was aiming to sell for twenty bucks. But because you done so good for me, ah-m gonna let you have him for ten!"

* * * * *

"I'll give till it hurts," said the parishioner, "but you ought to know I'm terribly sensitive to pain."

* * * * *

The country church was badly in need of repair, so Brother Thomas, the minister, called a special meeting to raise funds.

At the assembly, Brother Thomas announced the need and stated that everyone knew of that need and that they would now ask for contributions.

After a brief pause, Brother Eakins, the richest man in the congregation, volunteered he would give ten dollars. Just as he sat down, a hunk of plaster fell from the ceiling onto Brother Eakins's head. He jumped up, looking terribly startled and corrected himself: "I meant to say fifty dollars."

The congregation could only sit there, silent and stunned. Then a lone voice cried out: "Oh Lord, hit him again!"

* * * * *

A stockbroker was asked why he never joined a church. "Too commercial," he replied. "Too derned commercial. Why most every one of them has a 'plus' sign on it."

* * * * *

Three skore years and ten iz man's furlo, and it iz enuff -- if a man kant suffer all the mizery he wants in that time, he must be numb.

Josh Billings

The Pierson family included Mama, Papa and eight kids, a fine family but not much account at attendance at the Baptist Church. The elders got together and raised funds to buy clothing for the entire family, thus canceling their stated reason for not attending church.

The clothing was elegant, the very best quality and the entire congregation waited expectantly for them to appear the following Sunday. But they did not attend. After services, the angry ladies who had supervised the clothing purchases stormed over to the Pierson home and demanded an explanation.

"Well, ladies, we did get all dressed up to go to your church, but we looked so darned good in all that fine clothing that we went to the Episcopal Church instead!"

* * * * *

O'Reilly had an emergency call to come help his friend, Tim Flannigan, who was injured in an automobile accident. Eddie got in his car and drove to the spot where Tim lay in a ditch, groaning and moaning. It was a terrible night with heavy rain, lightning and thunder.

"I ain't gonna make it, Eddie. Call a Rabbi will you? Quick!"

"A Rabbi? Are you crazy, Tim! You need a Priest, not a Rabbi."

"Do as I say, Eddie. I wouldn't ask a Priest to come out here on a night like this!"

* * * * *

The sage of Fancy Prairie used to say: "Folks who talk and gossip and think by the yard, ought to be moved by the foot."

* * * * *

Among other things to pray for when going to church is a place to park.

* * * * *

If all the people in church were laid end to end, they would be...more comfortable.

* * * * *

Hilda Spooner was wonderfully impressed by the sermon of a missionary guest speaker. She was ecstatic in telling a friend about him.

"He was the most realistic, exact preacher I ever heard," Hilda told her friend. "Why do you know, he talked about hell just as if he was born and raised there."

The Headfast Computer Company sales executive finished a hectic week and decided to have a drink before going home. He stopped in the bar and asked for a pick-me-up, saying, "I'm worn out! I need it."

"Brandy? Bourbon? Scotch? Highball? What'll it be?"

"I need something different, for a change."

"Well, I have this thing we do for Father Tompkins. It's called a Parish Priest special."

"That'll do," the man said. "Fix it up for me."

The sales manager took a long draught, then another and still another. He ended up drinking three of the Parish Priest specials before he left the place.

The next morning, Sunday, he jumped out of bed, fixed breakfast for the family, put all of them in the car and took them to Mass. When all was finished and they'd left the church, that's when the trouble started. He turned to his wife and said, "Susie! What in heck were we doing there? We're not Roman Catholics...we're Baptists."

"It always happens like this after an earthquake."

A collection is a church function in which most members take but a passing interest.

***** *****

A Rabbi preached a sermon to a small group of Jews in the small town of Ashland, Illinois. But among the congregation was a very learned, wealthy and sophisticated visitor from Chicago. The Rabbi was immensely flattered by the presence of such a distinguished person, both a thinker and a philosopher...and, as said before, very wealthy.

The next day, the Rabbi saw the visitor from Chicago and asked how he had liked the sermon.

"I can tell you this, Rabbi...after hearing your unusual sermon, I couldn't sleep a wink last night."

"Isn't that flattering," said the Rabbi. "I had no idea my talk made such an impression on you."

"Well, it wasn't exactly that," the rich man replied, "but whenever I sleep during the day, I can't sleep at night."

***** *****

A Quaker lady, never married, was asked why. She replied: "It takes a mighty good husband to be better than none."

***** *****

Some stories have the veritable ring of truth about them, and this one fills that bill. It seems that when services were over, an effusive member of the congregation came striding forward and said, "Oh, that was just a wonderful sermon! So true and to the point. And, everything you said applied to somebody I know."

***** *****

"Oh Lord," the pretty, unmarried girl prayed, "I'm not asking for anything at all for myself. But for my mother...would you please bring her a son-in-law."

***** *****

Heard in the elevator of an office building: "The only time I believe, truly believe in reincarnation is five o'clock of an afternoon when all the really dead people come back to life."

135

Old Herman Brown was the biggest, most consistent liar in town and everybody knew it. Well, a revival was in process near where he lived and his drinking buddies prevailed upon him to go, hoping that something might happen to break him of his constant, hateful lying. The members got him to join up and took him to the river to be baptized. And it was cold! Bitter cold. Every candidate came out of the baptismal water shivering and teeth chattering. When they put old Herman under, he came out the same way, shivering, teeth chattering, sputtering and blowing. "Are you cold, Brother?" the preacher asked. "No, I'm doing dandy," the perennial liar said.

The deacon remarked, "We better douse him under one more time, Reverend Jones, he ain't quit lyin' yet."

* * * * *

Sojourner Vanity had eyes fixed on heaven, her mind set on Emancipation and her feet most firmly planted on the ground.

A friend tried to make her abandon her constant use of tobacco, saying, "In the Bible, it says, Sojourner, that there ain't no unkind thing gonna git into heaven."

"That's sho nuff what they say?"

"An' tobacco is filthy," her friend went on, "defiles yo' breath, stains yo' teeth, dirties yore dress. However do yo' expect to git into heaven with tobacco on yo' breath?"

"Mah goodness, Honey," Sojourner smiled, "now you quit worryin' 'bout little ol' me. 'Cause when ah die, I 'spects to leave mah breath behind me."

* * * * *

The average man's idea of a good sermon is one that goes over his head and hits a neighbor.

* * * * *

A fellow was in Montgomery, Alabama on a business trip and, as it happened, was marooned there over a Sunday. That morning, he was taking a walk when he met a black man and asked, "Excuse me. What denomination is that church across the street?"

"Baptist, Sir."

"Great! I'm a Baptist. I'll just go visit it."

"Hey, wait! That church ain't for you."

"Why not? What do you mean? I'm Baptist...it's Baptist!"

"Because it's African Baptist. The one fer y'all is four blocks ahead, then first turn to your left for one block. That's it."

"But this one is Baptist. Why not here?"

"Well, at that Baptist Church four blocks ahead and one over, dey figures and believes dat Pharoah's daughter discovered Moses in de bulrushes. And at this one heah, across de street, dey believes 'Dat what *she* say!'"

* * * * *

Have you heard how Caspar Brown describes his minister's pulpit style? "In his sermons, he dives down the deepest, stays down the longest and comes up the driest of any preacher we have ever had."

* * * * *

The Lord gets some people into trouble because that is the only time they ever think of Him.

* * * * *

A minister met a church member on the street and he said, "I've been pleased to see you in church these last several Sundays." The man replied, "Well, Pastor, it's simply that I'd rather listen to your sermons than hers."

* * * * *

Grunt: The "in" way of saying Amen.

Reverend Charles was exhorting his congregation on the everyday meaning of Christian virtues, and the congregation was responding both spiritually and verbally.

"Brethren, we must not only talk about Christian virtues, but we must practice them every day!"

Four elderly ladies in the front row, regular churchgoers, responded, "Amen!"

"And we must stop that constant gossiping!"

"Amen!" said the ladies in unison.

"And we must cease our constant back-biting."

"Amen, brother! Amen!"

"And dirty, sinful songs! We must stop them!"

"Amen! Amen! Amen!"

"And this regular -- or even now and then -- nipping at medicinal whiskey...it must stop!"

"Oh! Oh!" moaned the ladies, "now he's quit preachin' an' gone to meddlin'."

✳ ✳ ✳ ✳ ✳

Church is kind of like a filling station...you get filled up on Sunday, but by Saturday, you've run dry and have got to go back for a refill!

✳ ✳ ✳ ✳ ✳

On the outskirts of a small Indiana town was pitched a huge revival tent. Just as the road turned into the tent, there was a sign about the gospel assembly: "IF YOU'RE WEARY OF SIN AND SINNING, COME ON IN." Underneath the sign, someone had written: "IF NOT...CALL 544-2094."

✳ ✳ ✳ ✳ ✳

Sadie Lowenlee was an elderly spinster of ninety when she passed on. When her will was read, the lawyer found a clause reading: I don't want to have the word "Miss" put on my tombstone because I haven't missed as much as some folks may think I have.

✳ ✳ ✳ ✳ ✳

Money isn't everything...but it sure is far ahead of whatever is in second place.

Abraham Lincoln was besieged by preachers to make new regulations about the selection of military chaplains since they were then selected by the regiments. He told the story of a little boy who was playing with some mud outside his home. He had a building, fence, dog, cat and other items all made out of mud. A passerby asked him what he was doing. "Oh, I'm amaking a church with all the stuff that goes in and out of them."

"But I don't see the minister," the passerby said.

"Well, Mister, I just don't have enough mud to make one of them!"

In the church questionnaire, the old lady filled it all out but at the address, when it came to "zip," she put "normal for my age."

* * * * *

* * * * *

Although you can't take it with you, you should know that it can sure brighten up the port of embarkation.

Cy Pearce

The common sense of the American pioneer is illustrated in the story about a horrendous drought in West Texas. Cattle were dying by the thousands. There was no moisture to germinate grain and the creeks and ponds and wells were going dry. A call to pray for rain was issued and the preacher read about God's benevolence and the power of prayer. "Now let us pray," the preacher said, ending the session.

One old rancher stood and said, "I done lived heah all mah life and I 'ppreciate what y'all are doin'. But I want to tell ya, jest in case...thar ain't a bit a use in prayin' for rain so long as thiseyer wind is in the west."

* * * * *

Out in Tombstone, Arizona, a cowboy wandered into town on a Sunday morning. He saw people going into a church and decided to join them, taking a seat in the rear. After the sermon, the preacher called upon all those who were Christians to stand. Nobody stood.

"What!" blared the preacher, "not a single friend of Jesus in this entire congregation?"

The cowboy then stood. The preacher was delighted to find at least one Christian in town.

"Stranger," said the cowboy to the preacher. "I don't know who this feller, Jesus, is, and I ain't never heard of him before. But I'm gonna stand up for any gent who hasn't any more friends than him!"

* * * * *

Isn't it amazing how a dollar appears to be so big in church. But when you take it to the store? My! How small it looks!

* * * * *

Eddie Alfred was the stingiest member of the church. And so when the annual church supper was scheduled, tickets printed and solicitation begun, Paul Barker was assigned to sell Eddie a set of tickets. As was expected, Eddie said, "Terribly sorry, Paul, but I simply won't be able to attend. But, rest assured, my spirit will be with you."

"Great!" said Paul. "I got $5, $8 and $10 tickets. And just where would you like your spirit to sit?"

* * * * *

Isn't it great that charity can be deducted from income tax? But it's a cryin' shame that it must also be deducted from income.

An elderly woman was mailing the old Family Bible to her grandson in a distant city. The postal clerk asked: "Does this package contain anything breakable, Madam?"

The old lady responded: "Only the Ten Commandments."

* * * * *

Then there was the saint who taught her dog to heal.

* * * * *

The story is told about Supreme Court Justice Hugo Black whom propriety demanded attend the funeral of a man he genuinely disliked. A colleague came in late for services, sat next to Justice Black and asked, "How far has the service gone?" Judge Black whispered back, "They just started the defense!"

* * * * *

Too frequently, an anonymous gift is a donation by someone who hopes everyone will find out without his telling them.

Herbert V. Prochnow

* * * * *

Two youngsters, one fifteen-years-old and the other, sixteen-years-old, were determined to marry in spite of their parents' disapproval. During the ceremony, the preacher asked the lad to repeat after him: "With all my worldly goods, I thee endow," and the groom's mother turned to her husband and whispered, "There goes his paper route!"

* * * * *

After the first week of service by the new minister, a church member was asked how he had enjoyed the sermon. "For the first time in my life," he answered, "I envied my feet...they were asleep!"

* * * * *

Everyone knows how proud of their state are all Texans. And it was about just such a proud fellow that the following story is concerned. It seems that he was born in Dallas and had lived there all his life. Now he wanted to join a church so he went to a Methodist minister that he knew and asked to join. The preacher thought he ought to find out first, just how much the man knew of the Bible. "Tell me, Sir...where was Jesus born?" "San Antonio," was the reply. The preacher told the man to study his Bible some more before joining the church.

Now the man went to see if the Baptists would accept him. This minister, too, needed to know something of the man's knowledge and asked the same question as had the Methodist. The old fellow thought a bit and then said, "Lufkin." "I think you need to study your Bible more, Sir, then come back and we'll talk about joining our church."

In desperation, because he knew his days were numbered, the anxious fellow went to the minister of the Presbyterian Church and asked to be admitted. "We'd welcome you," the minister said, but before he went further, the old man interrupted him, "Tell me, Pastor, tell me where Jesus was born."

"In Palestine, Sir," was the reply.

"Well, whataya know," grinned the happy man. "I was just positive it was in one of our Texas towns."

✳ ✳ ✳ ✳ ✳

"CAREFUL, DEAR, SOMEONE FROM THE CONGREGATION MIGHT HEAR YOU."

✳ ✳ ✳ ✳ ✳

Have you noticed how seldom one four-letter word is heard these days? The word? Cash!

142

Here is another one of those inimitable Carl Goerch stories, set in North Carolina:

THE MISSING SUIT

When your suit gets mixed up with somebody else's at a cleaning and pressing establishment, it usually isn't very difficult to get the matter straightened out.

W. R. Grant, of Troy, NC, didn't find it quite so easy to do this, however.

He sent his suit to the cleaner. It came back in two days, but instead of being a 44 stout -- which is his regular size -- it turned out to be a perfect 36.

Naturally, Mr. Grant was upset. He rushed around to the cleaner's and demanded his suit.

The cleaner made an investigation and then announced very apologetically that it was impossible to return the suit.

"Why?" inquired Mr. Grant.

"Because we sent it to another man," he was informed.

"But why can't you send for it and let me have it?"

"Because they buried him in it early this afternoon," the cleaner explained.

Excerpts from "Just for the Fun of It." 1954.
written by Carl Goerch, used with the permission
of the Estate of Carl Goerch

＊ ＊ ＊ ＊ ＊

Anyone can borrow trouble. It's the only thing for which you don't need a nickel of collateral.

＊ ＊ ＊ ＊ ＊

There was a terrible hail storm in Central Illinois and the corn crop was almost entirely destroyed. The minister met one of his congregation, a farmer, and asked, "Did you save any of your corn crop?"

"Not a single bushel," replied the farmer.

"Was it insured!"

"No, Sir! Not a penny."

"I'm sure sorry," replied the minister. "That's a shame."

"Thank you, Sir," said the farmer. "If anybody but the Lord had done it, I sure woulda been madder'n heck!"

＊ ＊ ＊ ＊ ＊

When I was young I thought that money was the most important thing in life; now that I am old, I know it is.

Oscar Wilde

143

Mrs. Burke stood in the living room, her arms loaded with four coats, ready to clothe the children and go to church. As her husband came into the room, she handed him the coats for the kids and said: "Here! You put these on 'em. I'll go out to the car and this time, *I'll* honk the horn!"

＊ ＊ ＊ ＊ ＊

"THEY'LL NEVER GET IT OFF THE GROUND."

＊ ＊ ＊ ＊ ＊

Tightwad: A congregant with an impediment in his reach.

＊ ＊ ＊ ＊ ＊

Cowboy saying: Few things are tougher to put up with than a good example.

＊ ＊ ＊ ＊ ＊

Much of a man's religion is in his wife's name.

The members of the Grace Lutheran Church, located in the country near Emden, Illinois, were debating whether to put up a fence around the cemetery located just back of the church. The preacher was very much for the fence. "It'll beautify the entire place," he said, "and dignify it, too. Let's do it."

One of the most penurious, conservative members of the church raised his hand and, when called upon, said, "I don't see no need fer sech a thing. Them as is outside the cemetery sure as heck don't want to get in and them as is inside sure as heck cain't get out, so why in the all-fired dickens do we need a fence?"

✻ ✻ ✻ ✻ ✻

Deacon Hornblower heard that the apple crop was likely to be a water-haul that year, because of threatened invasions by pests. To the other apple growers assembled, he said solemnly, as he started to kneel down:

"Let us pray."

But Ike Hardboyle took his hat and started out of the room saying: "Let us spray."

Moral -- Faith without works is dead.

✻ ✻ ✻ ✻ ✻

An American truism: Absence makes the heart grow fonder. If that is so, a heckuva lot of people sure love their church.

✻ ✻ ✻ ✻ ✻

There was once a congregation that was continually asked for money, so often, in fact, that they asked the pastor to speak of them not as his flock but as his fleeced.

✻ ✻ ✻ ✻ ✻

Abraham Lincoln was debating whom to hire as Indian Commissioner. He called in Ben Wade and Senator Daniel Voorhees for assistance in selecting the right man.

"Gentlemen," said President Lincoln, "I want an honest, decent, caring, moral Christian man, a man frugal and self-sacrificing!"

"Mr. President, I feel certain you won't find him," said Voorhees.

"And why not?"

"Because he was crucified more than eighteen hundred years ago," said the Senator.

A BIRD IN THE HAND

Uncle Bob Jordan was the out-prayingest Christian on the Green plantation. He had long been known for his prayers, but now he was praying more than he had ever prayed. He was seventy-two years old and, as he could no longer work much, his master had promised him his freedom for twenty dollars. So Uncle Bob would go down into the woods near the big house every night about seven o'clock and get down on his knees and pray, asking God to please send him twenty dollars for his freedom.

He had been praying for about a month, when the master passed near the tree where Uncle Bob was praying one night and overheard the prayer. The master decided the next night he would have some fun out of Uncle Bob. So just before dark he went down to the prayer tree and climbed up in it.

At dark Uncle Bob came under the tree, got down on his knees, and started praying as usual, "Oh, Lawd, sen' me twenty dollars to buy my freedom."

"All right, Uncle Bob," came the master's voice from overhead, "look down at the foot of the tree and you will find a ten-dollar bill."

Sure enough, Uncle Bob looked and found a ten-dollar bill.

"Come back tomorrow night," said the voice, "and you will find a five-dollar bill."

"Sho, sho, Lawd," said Uncle Bob, taking the ten-dollar bill and sticking it in his pocket. "Thank you, thank you."

The next night the master beat Uncle Bob to the tree again and hid in its branches. At dark Uncle Bob came and prayed his accustomed prayer: "Oh, Lawd, please sen' me ten mo' dollers to buy my freedom."

"Uncle Bob," responded the voice from overhead, "look at the foot of the tree and you will find another five-dollar bill. Take the ten-dollar bill I gave you last night, and the five-dollar bill I gave you tonight, and bring them back tomorrow night. Put them underneath the tree so that I can get them, and the next night I will bring you a twenty-dollar bill."

"No, sah, no sah, dat's aw right, Lawd," answered Uncle Bob. "I sho thanks you for de fifteen, but I'll get de udder five some place else."

From "Juneteenth," by J. Mason Brewer, in "Tone the Bell Easy," Publications of the Texas Folk-Lore Society, Number X, 1932.

＊ ＊ ＊ ＊ ＊

One thing a child learns at his mother's knee is...look out for the ashes!

146

A woman goes into the post office and asks for five dollars worth of stamps.

"What denomination?" the clerk asked.

"Religion and government aren't supposed to mix, young man," she replied. "But if you insist on knowing, I'm a Baptist."

＊＊＊＊＊

A politician had been invited to a church in a city in his constituency. He was seated and, after a while, he began to fidget. He leaned over to the elderly gentleman beside him and asked in a whisper, "How long has he been preaching?"

"Nigh onto thirty or more years," the old man replied. "I ain't exactly sure."

"Well, I'll stay then," said the politician. "He must be nearly done."

＊＊＊＊＊

By the time some folks learn how to be decent, they are too dadblamed old to do anything else.

＊＊＊＊＊

They tell the story in South Carolina about this old black lady who was terror-stricken during a terrible earthquake. She tried to run but the quaking earth was too much for her so she fell on her knees and, as people hurried to help her, she prayed: "Oh deah Lawd Gawd, dis is sholy Jedgment Day, so come on down hyah Lawd and he'p us through all dis trial an' tri'lation. But jes be sho and come you'self, Deah Gawd, and doan sen' yo' Son, 'cause this ain't no time fo' chillun!"

From "Cryin' in de Wilderness," Alfred Holmes von Kolnitz, Charleston, S.C., Walker Evans and Cogswell Company.

＊＊＊＊＊

The reports of my death are greatly exaggerated.
Mark Twain -- in a cable from Europe to the Associated Press.

＊＊＊＊＊

In his book *"Carolina Chats,"* Carl Goerch told this delightful tale of a "misplaced" funeral.

The Squire was taken seriously ill and Dr. Josh Tayloe -- now dead -- was summoned. After examining the sick man, Dr. Tayloe immediately ordered that he be removed to the hospital in Washington for a vitally necessary operation.

One of the neighbors loaned his automobile for the purpose and the Squire was carried to the hospital. Dr. Tayloe notified Lewis's wife and children that his case was a serious one and that it was doubtful whether he would recover.

At the hospital, however, the operation proved a success. Within a very short time the Squire was convalescing nicely. He was so rejoiced over his recovery that he determined to do something by way of celebrating, so he asked one of the nurses to summon an organ dealer to the hospital. There used to be two or three of them in Washington.

When the dealer arrived, Squire Lewis instructed him to send an organ to his home immediately. His instructions were carried out. The organ was securely boxed and was sent to South Creek in charge of a drayman, who didn't know what was inside the box and didn't care.

In the meantime, the Squire's family had been greatly worried about his condition. He had told one of the nurses to write his wife and tell her that he was getting along all right, but the letter evidently had miscarried, or else the nurse forgot to write. At any rate, members of the family were in total ignorance as to the outcome of the operation. They hoped for the best, but they feared the worst.

And then, one bright, cool morning, one of the children, playing out in the yard, observed the Negro drayman stop at the farm-gate, get down, open it and drive up to the house. The child ran into the house and told its mother that somebody was coming. Mrs. Lewis went out on the front porch. She took one look at the box on the dray and then threw up her hands in despair. Her wail of anguish brought the other children to the front door.

"It's your pappy!" she cried. "He's daid and he's inside that box. He must have passed out when they were operating on him, and they've sent his body home from the hospital!"

It might be mentioned in passing that Squire Lewis, although only 5 feet 7 inches in height, weighed over 200 pounds. The shape of the box, therefore, did not surprise the family.

The neighbors were notified of the death, and on Tuesday morning the funeral services were held. Many flowers were placed upon the "casket." The choir from the Methodist Church rendered several appropriate selections. The minister dwelt lovingly upon the fine traits of the deceased. It was a swell funeral from every point of view.

And then, on another bright and cool morning -- Thursday, to be exact -- one of the children, who was sitting on the front steps, observed a man approaching the house. The child gave one look at him and dashed inside.

"Pappy's come home!" she cried. "He's coming right now!" Mrs. Lewis ran to the door. Her husband greeted her with a cheery wave of his hand and a bright smile. She fainted and fell full length on the front porch. The children scattered in all directions. It took some time to bring Mrs. Lewis to, but when she finally regained consciousness and was able to look at her "dead" husband, she told him of the funeral services which had been held Tuesday morning.

"And just think!" she cried. "We must have buried the wrong corpse. It must have been intended for some other home, and the drayman made a mistake."

Suddenly a great light dawned upon Squire Lewis.

"Mistake!" he shrieked. "Mistake -- hell! That was our new organ you buried. Gimme a shovel!"

Finding the implement out in the backyard and calling upon one of the older boys to help him, he went out to the family burial ground, found the newly-filled grave and started to work. In a few minutes the box was unearthed. Squire Lewis knocked off the lid and the organ was found inside, intact. He and the boys carried it to the house and set it up in the front parlor. Mrs. Lewis struck a few notes; it played fine.

The organ is still there, and so is Squire Lewis, although he is getting along in years. However, he never gets tired of telling how his family held funeral services over him, buried him in grand style and are now playing on him in the parlor.

Excerpts from "Carolina Chats." 1994. Written by Carl Goerch, used with permission of the Estate of Carl Goerch

✳ ✳ ✳ ✳ ✳

Charlie Owens went home during summer vacation from college only to find the town a mess. Houses were torn up, trees uprooted, and wreckage was everywhere. Luckily, his parents' home had suffered only minor damage and the family hadn't been hurt.

"What happened?" he asked his father.

"A cyclone hit us. It wrecked the town."

"Is everyone else OK?"

"All except Uncle Zeke. His house was lifted off the ground and ended up the other side of town right on the steps of the Methodist Church."

"How terrible!"

"Not so bad. Uncle Zeke said he'd been plannin' some on goin' to church anyway."

"COME IN, PASTOR, I'VE
BEEN EXPECTING YOU."

✳ ✳ ✳ ✳ ✳

WAYLAND SPRUILL

"Cousin Wayland" is a resident of Bertie County, down in the eastern part of the state. He's a big farmer and also has a number of other business interests in that section.

He is puckish in appearance. Rather stout; and whenever he laughs, which is almost constantly, he shakes all over. Smokes a pipe must of the time.

Cousin Wayland has been in the North Carolina Legislature a number of times and is always one of the most popular members at each session. He has a slow, drawling style of speech. When he gets up to make a talk on some legislative matter, he folds his hands across his stomach, cocks his head to one side, closes his eyes and proceeds to go to it. He can be both serious and funny. Whenever he gets to talking about the State Hospital, in which he is keenly interested, he can bring tears to your eyes. On the other hand, when he gets off on the rippling waters of the Cashire River, or the somber depths of the pellucid Roanoke, it's a regular riot.

Possessed with a keen sense of humor, he loves practical jokes. Like the one he played on the Rev. B. Townsend, for instance.

Mr. Townsend was a well-known preacher in eastern Carolina.

His home was in Duplin County. The people at Republican Church, Bertie County, asked him to come and hold a revival meeting for them.

Mr. Townsend wrote back that he'd be glad to come, and the following Sunday he arrived and was extended a most cordial welcome.

Among those at the meeting was a Mr. George L. Harrison, a farmer who lived about three miles from Republican. He was a deeply religious man and keenly interested in the progress of the revival. At every service he sat in the front row, and when the singing started, Mr. Harrison would participate in lusty fashion.

The first time the Rev. Mr. Townsend heard Mr. Harrison's voice, he looked at him in a somewhat startled manner. And there was ample justification for his being startled, because Mr. Harrison had one of the most ungodly voices you've ever heard. Not only that, but he had no sense of time, and at the end of the song, he was liable to be two laps behind or three laps ahead -- it didn't make any difference to him at all.

After the third service, Mr. Townsend sadly decided that something ought to be done about the matter. And so, knowing that Mr. Spruill was a man of prominence and importance in the neighborhood, he went to see him about it.

"Brother Spruill," he said.

"Yes, Brother Townsend," said Cousin Wayland.

"I want to talk to you about Brother Harrison. I hate to say this, but his singing is -- well, it's rather terrible."

"I agree with you, Brother Townsend."

"I was wondering if you wouldn't talk to Brother Harrison about the matter and get him to sing in more subdued tones. I'm sure the congregation would appreciate it immensely."

"I'll be glad to do it, Brother Townsend."

"Thank you, Brother Spruill."

So Wayland stopped Mr. Harrison as the latter was leaving for home after the service was over, and he said to him: "Brother Harrison, the preacher was talking to me a little while ago about your singing. He said you were one of the best singers he has ever heard."

"Did he really, Brother Spruill?"

"Yes, Brother Harrison. But he said there was one thing wrong with it."

"What was that, Brother Spruill?"

"He said that with a voice like yours, you ought to sing louder: sort of lead the rest of the congregation so that they, too, would sing more enthusiastically."

"You just wait until tomorrow night!" exclaimed Mr. Harrison happily.

The next night, when Claude Evans, the song-leader, announced the first selection, Mr. Harrison took a deep breath and cut loose. He let 'em have it with the full power of his lungs. The very rafters of the church trembled, and Brother Townsend shuddered.

At the conclusion of the service, the preacher sought out Wayland a second time.

"Good heavens, Brother Spruill!" he exclaimed. "He was worse tonight than he's ever been before."

"Yes -- too bad, Brother Townsend."

"We must stop it. Ah -- I have an idea!"

"What is it, Brother Townsend?"

"We'll sing some song tomorrow night that he doesn't know. Now you've been going to church here for a long time and you know the songs with which Brother Harrison is acquainted. Can't you suggest some song that will be strange to him and that he won't be able to sing?"

Wayland went into a deep study. Presently he said: "Yes, Brother Townsend, I believe I can. I've just been going over in my mind some of the songs which we sing regularly. There's one familiar hymn which we've never sung, so far as I can recall. It's 'I Love to Tell the Story.' Try that out tomorrow night, Brother Townsend, and I believe it'll put an end to your worries."

"Thank you, Brother Spruill."

"Not at all, Brother Townsend."

The next night Claude Evans announced Hymn No. 342.

Brother Harrison turned the pages of his book and his face beamed as he recognized the song. Among all the others, this was his special favorite. He could hardly wait until Mr. Evans started off. After that, Mr. Evans and the rest of the congregation might just as well have been out in the woods, 'coon hunting: there was nothing heard in the church except Mr. Harrison's awesome and terrifying performance.

"I'm afraid," said Mr. Townsend, after the services, "I'm afraid it's a hopeless proposition, Brother Spruill."

"Looks that way, Brother Townsend."

"But I want to assure you of my sincere appreciation for what you tried to do."

"Not at all, Brother Townsend," said Wayland. "I'm always glad to be of service in any way I can. It's been a pleasure."

Excerpts from "Carolina Chats. 1994" written by Carl Goerch, used with the permission of the Estate of Carl Goerch.

✳ ✳ ✳ ✳ ✳

Sarah Fulton once sang in the choir but for several sessions, she had been in the congregation, not in the choir. When asked why she no longer sang, she explained, "One Sunday when I was home sick with a cold, several folks asked if the organ had been repaired!"

By the time the average father gives away the bride, he hain't got nothin' else to give.

Abe Martin

* * * * *

Shortly after his marriage, a backwoodsman was asked how he liked married life. He replied that if things didn't change, he was going to leave his wife for good. "But you can't do that, Son," the Parson said. "Remember...you took her for better or worse!"

"I know that, Suh," the hillbilly said. "But she's a hyall of a lot wuss than I took her for!"

* * * * *

Heard in the pool hall: "I'm an atheist...thank God."

* * * * *

It is unusual to find three generations of a family all living under one roof. But in this one family, that situation was real. Grandpa was Robert. The father was Robert II and the nine-year-old son was Robert III.

One day, the mother answered the phone and heard a voice say, "I'd like to speak with Robert, please."

The mother responded, "Do you want the Father, the Son or the Holy Terror?"

* * * * *

I have alwus noticed one thing, when a man gits in a tite spot, he don't never call on hiz friend the Devil tew help him out.

Josh Billings

* * * * *

In his later years, a friend discovered W. C. Fields reading a Bible. This seemed amazing, given the irreverent attitude of the man, and the friend asked, "Have you finally come to religion, Mr. Fields?"

"No, no," Fields assured him. "I'm just looking for loop-holes."

* * * * *

If you don't go to your friends' funerals, they won't come to yours.

153

The minister joined all the bereaved relatives of the departed soul to hear the will of the deceased. Of course he, like the relatives, hoped that a large sum would be left to the church.

The attorney asked the pastor to read the will and this is how it read and only this: "Being of sound mind, I spent it all."

✳ ✳ ✳ ✳ ✳

And then there was the religious moth who lived in a church closet. He gave up woolens for lint.

✳ ✳ ✳ ✳ ✳

For an entire month, Mrs. Jones wept bitter tears over the loss of her husband, buried with full honors. Then the insurance agent called at her home and presented her with a check for $100,000. She took the check, brushed a tear from her eye and said, "Sir, I sure miss my husband something terrible. Why, I'd give half this, all $50,000 of it, just to have him back!"

✳ ✳ ✳ ✳ ✳

We're all cremated equal.

Goodman Ace, 1977

✳ ✳ ✳ ✳ ✳

I never see our preacher's eyes,
　　He hides his orbs divine,
Cause when he prays, he shuts his own,
　　But when he preaches, mine.

✳ ✳ ✳ ✳ ✳

A prayer for politicians:　　"Teach us, O Lord, to utter words that are tender and gentle, for tomorrow we may have to eat them."

✳ ✳ ✳ ✳ ✳

It was the final, championship game between Notre Dame and Southern Methodist University. Shortly after the game began, Notre Dame scored a touchdown and a spectator threw his hat in the air, yelling a wild "Hurrah!" and pounded his neighbor on the back. A bit later, when Southern Methodist scored, he was just as ecstatic and active. The neighbor asked, "Sir, just which team are you for?"

"I don't give a damn who wins. I just love to watch football."

"Oh," the neighbor sneered, "an atheist, eh?"

Cowboy saying: Love your enemies, but keep your gun oiled.

＊ ＊ ＊ ＊ ＊

The directors of the Fearsome Valley Baptist Church accused the sexton of doing less and less work at his job as grave-digger. Further, they claimed that the graves were getting shallower and shallower, saying, "Each grave that you dig, Sexton, is shallower than the one preceding it. Now why? What's behind this? And what do you have to say about it?"

The sexton took off his hat, scratched his head, then looked up and said, "Well-l-l, y'aint seen anybody climb out of them yet, have ya!"

＊ ＊ ＊ ＊ ＊

Not only is it more blessed to give than to receive...but it's also tax deductible!

＊ ＊ ＊ ＊ ＊

The neighborhood church had installed a new set of electronic chimes and they were intended to spread the sound of sacred music all through the neighborhood. Following the first Sunday of use, members were assigned areas to call on residents and get the reaction of the folks living near the church.

One member knocked at the door of a nearby house and an elderly lady came to the door. "Good day, Madam, I'm from the church and we want to know..."

"What are you saying, Mister?"

"I said, I'm from the church and we want..."

"What are you trying to say?"

In a loud voice, the caller said, "I'm...from...the...CHURCH, and..."

"You'll have to speak louder, Sir. Those damned chimes are making too damned much noise!"

＊ ＊ ＊ ＊ ＊

Some folks are late to church service because they have to change a tire; yet others are late because they have to change a dollar.

＊ ＊ ＊ ＊ ＊

The laziest man in the congregation was asked by his pastor what passage in the Bible he most preferred. He responded: "That one about the feller who loafs and fishes."

"Giv the devil hiz due," reads wel enuff in a proverb, but mi friend what will bekum ov you and me if this arrangement iz carried out?

Josh Billings

* * * * *

Two congregants had just come from church and the sermon on Sodom and Gomorrah from the Book of Genesis. "You know, George, I always thought that Sodom and Gomorrah were man and wife."

His friend replied: "I can believe you because I thought the Epistles were the wives of the Apostles."

* * * * *

"WE THANK THEE, O LORD, FOR THE BIG BEAT COFFEEHOUSE FIVE"

* * * * *

An acquaintance of an enormously rich -- oil rich -- Texan's funeral, watched the rich guy being carried off in his Cadillac, in which he was literally to be buried! He remarked: "Man, that's what I call living!"

When the town miser passed away, a very few kind-hearted souls gathered for his funeral. As they were about to close the casket, the preacher said: "We are about to send this man's soul to heaven. It would be good to have someone get up and say a nice word about him." But silence greeted the request. "Please, my friends," the minister begged, "just a few kind words." After a pause, a voice floated up from the rear pew, "For sure, his brother was worse."

* * * * *

Just about az cerimonys creep into one end ov a church, piety backs out at the other.

Josh Billings

* * * * *

An old hillbilly was brought into court for a minor offense. The Judge asked, "Your name is Joshua, is it not?" "Yes, Suh, Judge," the old man replied.

"And are you the Joshua who stopped the sunshine?"

"No, Suh," said the hillbilly, "I'm the Joshua who made the moonshine...and the sheriff stopped that!"

* * * * *

Bulletin Blooper: This being Easter Sunday, we will ask Mrs. White to come forward and lay an egg on the altar.

Bruce Pilcher, Chaplain

* * * * *

A backwoodsman was elected the financial secretary of the tiny church in his area and was asked to come forward and give a report of the financial condition of the church.

"Give us the status quo of things, Mr. Financial Secretary," the head deacon said.

"Deacon, some of us folks out back don't know what status quo means."

"The status quo means...means...well, it's the Latin for 'the mess we'uns is in.'"

* * * * *

Operating a funeral home is a serious "undertaking."

* * * * *

During a political debate, a heckler kept bad-mouthing the candidates. Not only the candidates but the audience became irritated at the smart aleck! At last, the nasty guy yelled, "I wouldn't vote for you if you were St. Peter!"

"Man, you couldn't!" shot back the candidate. "If I were St. Peter, you wouldn't be in my district!"

* * * * *

I know I'm OK because God doesn't make junk!

* * * * *

Bulletin Blooper: Tuesday evening there will be an ice cream social. All ladies giving milk, please come early.

Bruce Pilcher, Chaplain

A revival was under way in a small Baptist church and the preacher, at the epitome of his exhortation, asked his listeners to rise and indicate that they were ready to be saved. All stood except for one man.

"Hey, Brother," the preacher shouted, "are you asittin' there atelling us that you don't want your sins washed away, leavin' you pure as the drivin' snow?"

"I done had 'em washed away," the seated man replied.

"Just where you done had that done?"

"Over to the Methodist Church."

"You ain't been washed...you been dry-cleaned!"

＊ ＊ ＊ ＊ ＊

Too many well-meaning people wait for the hearse to bring them to church.

＊ ＊ ＊ ＊ ＊

A farmer had four sons, only one of whom left the farm and went to the city where he became enormously rich. But the city son was always too busy to visit the farm and told his brothers that he'd take care of all funeral expenses of the father when he passed away. Eventually, this happened, the father was given a fine funeral and the bill was sent to the city brother. He paid it once but kept getting a monthly bill for $32.50. He soon got tired of paying it, and asked why the charge was coming every month.

"Well, you told us that you'd pay the burial expenses when Dad died. Well, we rented him a tuxedo."

＊ ＊ ＊ ＊ ＊

A man was asked why he refused to fly an airplane. The man said, "because it's against my religion. I'm a very devout coward."

＊ ＊ ＊ ＊ ＊

A $20 bill and a $1 bill were in a bag of old, tattered money that was being returned to the U.S. mint to be destroyed. The two bills discussed their lives.

"What a ball I've had," said the $20 bill. "Great stores, fancy restaurants, night clubs. Wow! What a life it's been. How about you?"

The $1 bill responded, "All I ever did was go to church."

Conscience, we are told, is the still small voice which tells us that somebody is looking.

$$* \quad * \quad * \quad * \quad *$$

The minister was preaching his sermon on the mortality of man, saying, "Everyone in this town, everyone here will die!" The congregation was hushed except for one laughing parishioner who cackled loudly to the embarrassment of everyone else. "Why do you laugh when you know that everyone in this town, including you, will die and soon?" said the minister.

"Well, Parson, y'see...I ain't from this town."

$$* \quad * \quad * \quad * \quad *$$

The Reverend Charles Mitchell, a former Chicago minister, was introduced to an audience as Dr. Mitchell, soon after he had received his formal Ph.D. Since he was a modest man, he told the audience, "I think most of us misunderstand the meaning of advanced degrees," he said, "the real meaning of M.D. is 'moderately dumb'; and D.D. means 'decidedly dumb'; and Ph.D. means...'phenomenally dumb!' That's ME!"

$$* \quad * \quad * \quad * \quad *$$

If all the philanthropists in the world were laid end to end, most of us would agree that it'd be a good thing!

4
JEWISH HUMOR

Most of the stories herein are from the Christian faiths, Protestant and Catholic. Naturally, that is so because most churches and congregations are Christian. In all fairness and interest, we decided to add a chapter of Jewish and synagogue humor. It is purely delightful, typically American and loads of fun. See if you don't agree.

✳ ✳ ✳ ✳ ✳

A Tennessee hillbilly was on his first trip to New York. He was looking the city over and had walked his way to the east side where he stood in front of a synagogue. Not having anything better to do, he walked inside, listened and looked at the services for a while. Then he asked one of the congregants, "Tell me, Suh. What kinda show does y'all put on heah? Is it worth my while to watch?"

"Well, it just might be worth your while...and it is a good show. But then it should be, because we've been running now, let's see, for four thousand years."

✳ ✳ ✳ ✳ ✳

If you could put all the world's troubles on a hook on the walk, everyone would pray for his own.

✳ ✳ ✳ ✳ ✳

Could this be the answer to the unanswerable question that Job posed, in that famous, tearful Book?

It seems that Nathan Cohen was pious, always was and would be. One day, he came to Sabbath services and moaned, "Dear God, today I have troubles as I have had every day of my life. Nothing but poverty, misery, illness and want have I know. Yet, I have always and daily prayed to you. Never have I forgotten you or blamed you. Always, have I praised and blessed you.

"Why is that you always burden me with pain while that no-good Levy has nothing but good luck with wealth and happiness? He never prays to you, never enters a synagogue, yet always he comes out on top with health, wealth, happiness...everything you do not give me. Why? Why? Why?"

Suddenly, a voice sounded, a deep, powerful, commanding voice, saying: "Because Levy doesn't constantly bug me, that's why!"

Anger and rage will make you age.

* * * * *

Rabbi Shlomo Riskin, now in Israel, says that a person's essence can be recognized by three things: "His cup...what happens when he drinks. His pocket...how he spends his money. His anger...what he says when provoked."

* * * * *

"Thou hast chosen us from among the nations but just why, dear God, didn't you choose another bunch!"

* * * * *

Curse: May you back into a pitchfork and grab a hot oven for support.

* * * * *

"WHERE HAVE YOU BEEN, JONAH? YOU SMELL LIKE FISH!"

A noted Los Angeles Rabbi opened his sermon with these words: "As you know, I have always welcomed the poor to our synagogue, at all times and, my dear congregants, I want to tell you that, according to our income last month, they have arrived!"

* * * * *

Having money is a fine thing, but...using your power over money is far better.

* * * * *

David Epstein was without sin. All his life, he had thought of and practiced virtue. Never, yes, never in his entire life of sixty years, had he done grievous things. Always, he had lived virtuously, justly, loved mercy and walked humbly with God. But when the angel at the Pearly Gates let him in and consulted his record, he paused, saying: "I don't know quite what to do about you, David. You are such an exemplary figure, without blemish or sin, that I fear there will be jealousy, fighting, violence against you on the part of those here. But I have an idea. I'll give you six more hours on earth where you must commit a sin. Then you can get in."

So back to earth went Epstein where he sat thinking about how to sin. Suddenly, he thought of a widow who had cast covetous eyes at him whenever they met. He went to her door, knocked and she met him with delight. "Can I enter?" he asked.

"You sure can, honey. Come right on in." She locked the door behind her, led him to the bedroom and the fun began. When he felt that his six hours were up, Epstein got out of bed, excused himself from the exhausted lady and started out the door.

"One moment, David," she called softly. "I can't begin to tell you what a wonderfully good and holy thing you have done for me this day."

* * * * *

To do good is noble; to advise others to do good is also noble...and much less trouble.

Mark Twain

* * * * *

If you don't want people to ride you, don't act like an ass.

* * * * *

You can go a long way with lies, but the problem is that you can't return.

"Rabbi, I need your help," said the worried father. "My boy is ready for Bar Mitzvah and all he ever thinks or talks about is baseball."

"Not to worry," said the Rabbi, "your son is merely doing what we Jews have been doing for thousands of years. Did you know there are several references to baseball in the Bible?"

"That can't be. What do you mean? Give me some examples," said the boy's father.

"All right. Consider that Eve stole first and Adam stole second. Do you begin to see what I mean? And then there was Gideon who rattled the pitchers; and Goliath was struck out by David. And do you recall that the prodigal son made a home run? Oh yes, your son is following the tradition. In short, with so much anguish in the world, you should worry about those terrible troubles, not your son."

✳ ✳ ✳ ✳ ✳

Ann Landers, in her wonderful column, told that she had received the following notice from Father Theodore Hesburgh, President of the University of Notre Dame. It had been written by Sam Levinson and was titled: *"An Answer to an Anti-Semite."*

"It's a free world. You don't have to like Jews, but if you don't I suggest that you boycott certain Jewish products like insulin, discovered by Dr. Minkoski; the vaccine for hepatitis, discovered by Baruch Blumberg; streptomycin, discovered by Dr. Selman Abraham Waxman; the polio pill by Dr. Albert Sabin; and the polio vaccine by Dr. Jonas Salk.

"Good! Boycott! But humanitarianism requires that my people offer all these gifts to all the people of the world. Fanaticism requires that all bigots accept diabetes, hepatitis, convulsions, syphilis, infectious diseases and infantile paralysis.

"You want to be mad? Be mad! But I'm telling you, you ain't going to feel so good."

✳ ✳ ✳ ✳ ✳

If it cost no money to be charitable and good deeds caused no aggravation, you'd have a world of righteous people around you.

✳ ✳ ✳ ✳ ✳

The Sabbath School teacher was testing her pupils on the subject of Proverbs. "Tell me, class, what you know about the proverb, 'Cleanliness is next to'...what?"

"Impossible!" said a pupil.

Advice is something that we give by the bushel but take by the peck.

✻ ✻ ✻ ✻ ✻

The subject at the Hebrew Day School was the story of Moses.

"Please tell me, class," concluded the teacher, "just what you would have done if you, like Pharaoh's daughter, found a baby in the bulrushes?"

Little Rebecca's hand shot up. "I know what I'd do, for sure," she said, "I'd change him."

✻ ✻ ✻ ✻ ✻

A pagan says he won't believe in God until the month has three first days.

✻ ✻ ✻ ✻ ✻

The enthusiastic lady pushed herself through the crowd after services and shook the hand of the renowned Rabbi, D. Stephen S. Wise. "Doctor," she said animatedly, "after hearing you talk so often and so well about Palestine, I made it my business to see the country for myself. I just got back from Palestine and I tell you, it is a wonderful place. I really liked -- a lot-- Lake Tiberias and the Sea of Galilee. They are simply wonderful."

"Really?" queried Dr. Wise with a mischievous smile. "But the Sea of Galilee and Lake Tiberias are synonymous."

"Yes, I know," said the lady confusedly. "But it seemed that the Sea of Galilee is just a wee bit more synonymous than Lake Tiberias."

✻ ✻ ✻ ✻ ✻

In the introduction of a Jewish sermon, use this: "You should so live that when the roll is called up yonder, you won't have to cram for your final exams."

✻ ✻ ✻ ✻ ✻

It was a very hot summer day and the building was not air-conditioned. But the Rabbi spoke on and on -- rather did he drone on and on -- until the congregation, one by one, had left and the synagogue was empty. The janitor walked down the aisle and handed the Rabbi the keys to the building, saying, "Here's the key, Rabbi. When you are done, please lock the front door after you."

165

Rabbi Isaac Mayer Wise (1818-1900) was walking slowly down the street one day, shortly after his 81st birthday. He met a former student, Rabbi Yosef Alman, who said, "Good morning, Rabbi, and how do you feel today?"

"The Rabbi is quite well, thank you," said the aging Rabbi. "But this house is growing dilapidated. It is tottering on its foundations. Time, season and weather have almost destroyed it. And its roof is terribly worn...almost worn out. Its walls are damaged and it trembles in every wind. The old tenement is almost uninhabitable, and I think that Rabbi Wise will soon have to move out of it. But he, himself, is quite well, thank you."

* * * * *

While you live, the entire world isn't big enough; after death, the grave is.

* * * * *

If you fail Jacob, you help Esau.

* * * * *

Manny Goldberg had lived a long, fruitful life but now, 83 years old, he lay on his deathbed surrounded by sons and daughters who were discussing (they thought unknown to him) funeral arrangements.

"Shall we get him a metal or a wood casket?"

"Wood'll do. Metal is too expensive."

"Well, what about flowers?"

"A wreath will do. Flowers cost a lot."

"Shall we go to Abrams or Levy Funeral Directors?"

"Take Abrams. Levy is terribly expensive."

Just then, the old man opened his eyes and said, "Children, forget about the hearse. I'll just walk to the cemetery."

* * * * *

Isn't it amazing how bearable are other people's troubles?

* * * * *

Rabbi Litvak received an invitation to speak at the American Legion Post in Kewanee. It read, "We invite you to be our main speaker at the forthcoming Independence Day celebration. The Mayor will speak, then we will have recitation of the Gettysburg Address by our Post Commander, then comes your talk, after which the firing squad takes over."

The angel of death never looks at the calendar.

＊ ＊ ＊ ＊ ＊

A wealthy industrialist was having financial difficulties and went to the synagogue to find comfort. As he bowed to pray, he heard the supplicant next to him say, "Oh help me, Divine One. I need five hundred dollars to save me from bankruptcy." The industrialist took out his wallet and gave the man the money he needed. The man was overwhelmed, took the money and ran from the synagogue.

The industrialist began, once again, to pray for help, saying, "And now, God, may I have your undivided attention!" And, evidently, God heard him.

＊ ＊ ＊ ＊ ＊

Pray that you will never suffer all that you can endure.

＊ ＊ ＊ ＊ ＊

In earlier days, when American hotels in some few areas would not rent rooms to Jews, a Mrs. Cohen, finding herself stranded in an exclusive resort town, went to the nearest hotel and up to the desk.

"I vould like please, von room for this effening."

The clerk sized her up and said, "Sorry, but all rooms are rented."

"So vy the sign says, 'rooms available'?"

The desk clerk shrugged, then said, "We don't rent rooms to Jews. And if you'll just try at a hotel on the other side of town..."

Mrs. Cohen hummphed and hawed, then said, "Jewish? Who says I'm Jewish? It happens that I'm a convoitable."

"What? You're a what?"

"A convoitable. Way back from, I been hearing the Fulton Schine and he's made me a convoitable, a Kedillac."

"Ah hah! I understand. You are now a Cadillac convertible."

"That's it!"

"Well, I'm a Catholic myself," said the clerk, "and if you don't mind, I'll test you with the catechism. How was Jesus born?"

"By a himmeculit contraption from out of heaven. The Mama's name was Mary and Papa was Yussel."

"Now, please, tell me where Jesus was born."

"He vas geborn in a menager, he vas."

"And why was he born in a manger?"

"Because some joik like you vouldn't give to a Jewish lady a room for the night."

"WELL, WHAT DID YOU EXPECT? THIS IS THE RED SEA."

* * * * *

God protect us from our friends. Our enemies, we can handle by ourselves.

* * * * *

Do you want to know what really happened in the Garden of Eden? Well, here's the way it was.

"Hey, baby," Eve said to Adam as she handed him a fresh dish of delicious dates. "Are you really and truly and always and forever my man?"

"You can bet on it," said Adam. "Who else?"

* * * * *

There's one measurement that makes us all equal: six feet deep!

* * * * *

Those coming to the fund-raising meeting in a Chicago synagogue were greeted by this sign on the bulletin board: "You Can't Take It With You. But You **Can** Send It On Ahead."

The Rabbi was handed a package of fish by one of his congregants. "Rabbi, I want you to have these," said the congregant. "But I must tell you that I caught them on the Sabbath."

"Never mind, my son," said the Rabbi. "We both, the Lord and I, know that the fish were not to blame."

* * * * *

Never leave your mouth open for old man Satan to enter.

* * * * *

A husband and wife were involved in such a bitter quarrel that they decided to visit the Rabbi about it. It seems that their recent first-born son was the cause of it all. The mother wanted to name him after her father, "a superb scholar of the Torah!" she said. And the husband replied that, "the boy must be named after his grandfather, one of the most learned men of all time."

"Why not compromise?" asked the Rabbi. "Just give the child the name of both grandfathers."

"That's not possible," said the wife. "It is absolutely out of the question. Both of the boy's grandfathers were named Moses."

* * * * *

"WAIT!"

Most of us are unaware that the art of press-agent harks back to biblical days and the Book of Exodus. Moses's brother, Aaron, was also his press agent. When the Israelites were camped on the banks of the Red Sea, with the Egyptians hot on their tail, Aaron proposed that Moses build a bridge to cross over the sea and escape the tyrant Egyptians.

"No time for that," Moses shouted. "I figure on getting the sea to part and let just our folks cross, then closing the water on the Egyptians trying to follow us. What do you think of that notion?"

Aaron, ever the press agent, said, "You get that job done, Mosie, old boy, and I'll guarantee you at least two full pages in the Bible."

＊ ＊ ＊ ＊ ＊

A curse: Let all his teeth fall out except one and that one should have a toothache!

＊ ＊ ＊ ＊ ＊

An Israeli farmer was seeing his son off on an El Al plane, bound for the United States.

The father said to his boy, "May you live to one hundred and forty, the age of Moses."

"Daddy! The quote is, 'May you live to one hundred and twenty'...*not* forty!"

"I know that, my son. But in Israel, inflation is awful, affects everything."

＊ ＊ ＊ ＊ ＊

There are many folks who claim they have no faith in God or heaven, yet they'll invest their last dollar in a lottery or a crap game.

＊ ＊ ＊ ＊ ＊

Gertie, a shady lady of considerable sexual talent, died and went to meet that great Broker in the Sky. But when she came to the Pearlies, she was halted by St. Peter, who said, "I see by your record that you married four times, and that's bad enough. But I also see that you married a banker, then an actor, then a preacher and finally, an undertaker. Explain, if you can, your ridiculous choice of husbands and remember, your explanation will determine whether you get in heaven or not."

"Thanks, St. Pete," said Gertie. "The reasons why I married in these categories are that I had one for the money, two for the show, three to get ready and four to go."

To raise children, you need Solomon's wealth and wisdom and Samson's strength.

*****

There was a special meeting of the Joliet, Illinois, Kiwanis Club and the two guest speakers were Rabbi Edwin Gottschalk and Father Thomas Huxley. Unfortunately, the main course included ham. The Rabbi, of course, ordered a chef salad without ham.

The priest smiled at all this, speared a juicy piece of ham on his fork and turned to the Rabbi. "Isn't this beautiful, Rabbi? I do think you should get over that ancient superstition about ham and have a piece with me."

The Rabbi solemnly replied: "I'll make a deal with you, Father Huxley...I'll eat my first piece of ham at your wedding. OK?"

*****

Two hogs on their way to the slaughter house: "I wish everybody was Jewish!"

*****

The bellhop at a New York hotel was complaining to his buddy: "I sure don't much enjoy working for this hotel when they have a rabbinical convention. Wow! Those guys are somethin'. Those Rabbis bring ten-dollar bills and the Ten Commandments and they sure as heck don't break either one of them."

*****

The worst wheel always squeaks the loudest.

*****

An Orthodox Israeli was looking over a display of paintings and then he turned to the artist himself. "It is disgraceful that you paint portraits when the Torah clearly states, 'Thou shalt not make a likeness of anything in the heavens above or the earth beneath."

The painter replied: "That's exactly what everyone who sees my portraits says!

*****

The Rabbi was served toast by his wife. He took a look at the toast, then picked up a piece and said to his wife, "My dear, we no longer practice the rite of burnt offerings."

171

A priest, a Protestant minister and a Rabbi were old friends and enjoyed a three-handed game of cards every Monday night. Unfortunately, the tiny, blue-law town in which they lived, forbade such games and they were raided and brought before the Justice of the Peace. The priest was first to be called up.

"Were you gambling, Father?"

The priest looked toward heaven and whispered to himself, "Forgive me, oh Lord," then turned to the Judge and said, "No, Your Honor, I was not gambling."

"And how about you?" The Judge asked the Protestant minister, who looked heavenward and begged forgiveness, then said aloud, "No, Your Honor, I was not gambling."

The Judge turned to the Rabbi. "And you, Sir, were you gambling?"

The Rabbi looked the Judge squarely in the eye and replied, "With whom, Sir?"

* * * * *

An oath and an egg are all too soon broken!

* * * * *

A man is visiting the President in the Oval Office and he sees the several phones there and asks what each one is for. The President says, "Now this red one goes directly to the Premier in Moscow. The white one connects me directly with God."

"Really! Wow! How much does it cost to call God?"

"Two thousand dollars a minute!"

The guy is impressed, leaves and finds that he must visit the Prime Minister of Israel. And he does. There, too, he sees several phones on the Prime Minister's desk and asks, "What are they for?" The Prime Minister says, "The black one is to your President in the U.S.A. The blue one is to the Prime Minister of Russia. And the white phone goes directly to God."

"How much does it cost to call directly to God?" the visitor asked.

"Fifty cents a minute, is all," the Prime Minister replied.

"Fifty cents a minute! But it costs our President two thousand bucks a minute to call God. How come it's so cheap here?"

"Here, you see," said the Prime Minister, "it's a local call."

* * * * *

When you climb a ladder be sure you count the rungs.

*"DAVID, WHERE HAVE YOU BEEN WITH THAT SLINGSHOT?
MRS. GOLIATH HAS CALLED THREE TIMES!"*

* * * * *

An Israeli bird-breeder has managed to create a remarkable mutation with parrots. He has developed a breed of parrots that lays only six-pointed eggs, resembling the Star of David. Unfortunately, in doing this remarkable feat, the parrot has lost all power of speech, except to say, "**Ouch!**"

* * * * *

One of the easiest things is to be charitable out of another's pocket.

* * * * *

Sol Rubin moved to Florida and was happy there with the exception that he did not see his son, George. He called him in New York, and invited him to come down, and that he did. But he was gone every day to the race track and, finally, Sol got fed up and said, "Here you are, come to be with me in Florida, and all you do is go to the racetrack and I never see you. Now, I'm going to the synagogue tomorrow. Will you join me?"

"You bet I will, Dad."

They went to the synagogue together and on the way home, George said, "I enjoyed being with you, Dad. Were you pleased at how well I remembered the Hebrew you taught me?"

"You did just fine, my boy, but the word is 'Hallelujah' not 'Hialeah!'"

The Rabbis say: "Everyone in life gets some ice...the rich in the

The Rabbis say: "Everyone in life gets some ice...the rich in the summer and the poor in the winter."

* * * * *

Rabbi Elkanan was playing golf and was told by his caddy that he had about 150 yards to go to finish the last of eighteen holes. Further, the caddy told him to select a number four iron.

"No!" the Rabbi argued, "I think this calls for a number three iron." He selected his club, addressed the ball, hit it and was at least fifty yards short of the green and...in the rough.

"Shucks!" exclaimed the Rabbi, "I guess that God didn't hear me."

"I'm sure he did," the caddy said. "But He knows, just as I know, that prayer is not enough. You...have...got...to...keep...your...head...down!"

* * * * *

If you have honey, you must expect flies [good and bad go together].

* * * * *

Rabbi Eliezer Datz was in the habit of wearing both belt and suspenders to hold up his pants. A congregant asked him if, because of this double precaution, he lacked faith. The Rabbi thought for a moment, then said, "No, my faith is intact. In fact, I'm following valid Torah (Bible) advice as advised in Ecclesiastes IV: 9-10, which states: 'Two are better than one; because they have a good regard for their labor. For if they fall, the one will lift up his fellow; but woe to him who is alone when he falleth; for he hath not another to help him up.'"

* * * * *

If we only thanked God for the good He gives us, we would have no time for the bad.

* * * * *

One doesn't often hear of it, but there is a case of a Rabbi who was given to excess when drinking alcohol. A friend gave him a case of first-rate peach brandy but told the Rabbi he expected him to announce the gift from the pulpit. And the Rabbi did, in this way:

"My friends, I want to thank my dear friend, Herbert Levy, for his generous gift of fruit and the spirit in which it was given."

Every jackass loves to hear himself bray.

✳ ✳ ✳ ✳ ✳

"Rabbi," gushed the admiring woman at the close of Friday night's service, "I have to tell you that the only reason I come on Friday is to hear your superb sermons. I think you should print them in a book."

"Oh, I don't think I should," the Rabbi said modestly. "I don't think my sermons are that good. But, who knows, perhaps they'll be published posthumously."

"Oh, let us hope so," the woman gushed. "And I hope that'll be real soon."

✳ ✳ ✳ ✳ ✳

All locks will open with a golden key!

✳ ✳ ✳ ✳ ✳

The reform synagogue in Springfield, Illinois had hired a new, young Rabbi, only recently graduated from the Hebrew Union College. The congregation liked him except for this one problem...his sermons were too long.

One Friday night, at services, in the middle of his usual long, extended sermons, the congregation was startled to hear the Rabbi say: "It doesn't bother me much when now and then some of you look at your watches. But it bothers the dickens out of me when I see you put your watches up to your ears to see if the things are still running!"

✳ ✳ ✳ ✳ ✳

If it's appearances you chase, you'll find mud on your face.

✳ ✳ ✳ ✳ ✳

The Rabbi had never learned to keep a sermon short, trenchant and meaningful. Trenchant and meaningful? Yes. But not short. One of his sermons went on interminably until the congregation grew so restless that the good Rabbi seized a gavel and smashed it on the flat surface of the *bimah*! So hard did he hit, that the gavel broke and the head of it sailed out to strike the forehead of a man sitting in the first row! The poor guy sank back, glassy-eyed and moaning. But in a moment, he sat up, saying, "Hit me again. I can still hear him."

175

When you feel good you have lots of worries. But when you are sick, you have only one.

* * * * *

Recently, there was an article in the newspaper, really an advertisement, of a New York railroad company seeking 200 sleepers for their cross-country line. A certain Rabbi in Chicago offered his entire congregation.

* * * * *

A certain cantor in New York City was unemployed and yet was growing rich at it. How? He learned the wedding March backwards and sang it at divorces.

* * * * *

A rabbinical student was discussing his future with his hometown Rabbi.

"I sure hope I can make it," the lad said, "I do so want to be a Rabbi. Aside from study, can you tell me what other all-important qualification I need?"

"Consider the matter of imagination," the older man said. "You will just have to imagine that somebody is really and truly paying attention to what you say."

* * * * *

The baby was born at the right time, but the wedding itself was a bit late.

* * * * *

The Rabbi prayed fervently all that morning, with only one brief interruption did he pray. Finished, he looked up to see a member of the congregation approaching him.

"Rabbi, I sure hope you prayed for something specific," the congregant said to him with a touch of sarcasm.

"I did," the Rabbi responded. "I prayed that the rich should give generously to the poor."

"And do you reckon God heard your prayers?"

"Yes, I do think so...at least half of it. The half where the poor have agreed to accept!"

* * * * *

Always remember...there are no pockets in shrouds.

"TEN **MORE** COMMANDMENTS?"

✻ ✻ ✻ ✻ ✻

An Orthodox Jew's wife had been having a terrible time giving birth and seemed nowhere near delivery. The Rabbi suggest that it was time for prayer and that the customary ten Jews be gathered to recite Psalms as the favored way to help the mother deliver.

The ten men needed for the prayers were gathered and the recital of appropriate Psalms began. Soon the midwife appeared before the father and announced the arrival of a boy. Congratulations followed. In a few minutes, she was back to announce another baby. Again, congratulations were ardent. But soon, the midwife came out to announce a third baby and the father stood, turned to the ten men and said, "That does it! We ain't gonna sing another Psalm because I think we already overdid it!"

✻ ✻ ✻ ✻ ✻

A thief has a good heart...he takes pity on the possessions of others.

On their way to school, two youngsters were discussing the differences of their faiths.

"Why I bet you don't know what makes the difference between a Methodist, a Baptist and a Jew," the one boy taunted his Jewish friend.

"The heck I don't," the Jewish boy said. "A Baptist gets shoved clean under the water, but a Methodist only gets sprinkled."

"And the Jew? What happens to him?"

"A Jew, well, y'see a Jew...a Jew gets dry-cleaned!"

* * * * *

Adam was a mighty lucky man...he hadn't a mother-in-law.

* * * * *

A rabbinical student felt bad about an event in his class and he told his roommate about it. "Well, I asked if it'd be okay if I smoked while praying. The teacher turned me down emphatically!"

"You went at it wrong," his roommate said. "Use your head! I reversed the question and asked if it'd be okay to pray while smoking and got an OK!"

* * * * *

If God will it, even a broom can shoot.

* * * * *

Three rabbis were engaged in an argument as to the relative merit of their respective forms of Judaism.

"It's quite clear," said the Reform rabbi, "that the wisest way to approach Jewish theology is as if we were umpires at a ball game. Now take me, a Reform Rabbi, I call 'em the way I see 'em."

"In my case," said the Conservative Rabbi, "I call 'em just the way I see 'em."

"Enough of this nonsense," said the Orthodox Rabbi, "it doesn't make a bit of difference how you guys call it, it's nothing until I say what it is!"

* * * * *

Time is the best healer.

178

An old Jew was ill and went to a Catholic hospital for treatment. There he was told that he'd need surgery and was asked to whom the bill should be sent.

"I'm not married," the old man said, "and I have no children. My only relative is my sister and she is an old maid and converted to Catholicism and she's a nun!"

"Hold on there!" said the hospital nun. "What makes you think nuns are old maids? We are brides of Christ!"

"Well, whatdyaknow!" said the old man, grinning. "Since that's the case, just send the bill to my brother-in-law!"

✳ ✳ ✳ ✳ ✳

Mark Twain said he preferred: "Heaven for the climate, Hell for the company!"

✳ ✳ ✳ ✳ ✳

Sol Cohen had spent his entire life in Chicago, enjoying every minute in the windy city. Then Sol died and awakened in the hereafter, a wonderful place with hurrying crowds, tall buildings and the feel of a metropolis.

"Y'know," Sol said to a fellow he had pulled to one side. "This is just like good old Chicago and I feel right at home! I'd have bet a million bucks heaven wouldn't be like this!"

"Mister," said the stranger he had talked to, "whatever gave you the idea that this is heaven?"

✳ ✳ ✳ ✳ ✳

"He that sitteth in heaven, laugheth" -- Why not? It's easy for Him!

✳ ✳ ✳ ✳ ✳

Manny Levy died at the wonderful age of 94. He arrived at the Pearly Gates and was admitted by an angel who said, "We're having you stay at the Angelic Hotel tonight. Please sign the register."

The old boy signed.

"We'll need information about you first. How old were you when you died?"

"Ninety-four!"

"Really! I'll bet you saw a lot of changes in your time."

"Yep! Sure did. And I was against every dadblamed one of 'em!"

If one person says you have the ears of an ass, hit him on the nose. If two say so, best that you buy a saddle.

✳ ✳ ✳ ✳ ✳

Seymour Seigel was on a tour with a group from Memphis and they were now in Beverly Hills examining a new, very modern synagogue. The guide was explaining the architecture, quite modern, that combined the dome of the White House with a second dome resembling the Taj Mahal. A huge Roman ampitheatre was present along with something resembling the Vatican and a section that looked like one of those sterile New York tall buildings.

"I have a relative that goes to that synagogue," one of the tourists said proudly. "Isn't it elegant...beautiful...just stunning!"

"Well, to tell you the truth," replied one of the tourists, "if I was a member, I wouldn't know whether to pray in it, at it, or for it!"

✳ ✳ ✳ ✳ ✳

It is never too late to marry or to die.

✳ ✳ ✳ ✳ ✳

A Rabbi and an agnostic were discussing whether there truly was a God...a soul.

"You surely know," the agnostic said, "that Spinoza, the great philosopher, wrote that man stands on a level with the animals and is of the same nature."

"Yes, I know the statement," the Rabbi replied. "But do, if you please, tell me why it is that the animals have never produced a Spinoza?"

✳ ✳ ✳ ✳ ✳

When two on a pillow are fixed, another should not mix betwixt.

✳ ✳ ✳ ✳ ✳

Another fellow, an atheist since his youth, became not only interested but devout in his late years. At the age of seventy-five, he decided to come back to the faith of his fathers.

One evening, he attended services at Temple Israel, the first time he'd been in a temple since his Bar Mitzvah days at the age of thirteen. He heard the Rabbi announce that the next week's sermon would address the question of the great and terrible biblical flood that destroyed all life in the world.

The old man approached the Rabbi after services and said that he was sorry not to be able to attend services next week, that he'd be out of town, "But don't worry, Rabbi, put me down for $20 to aid the flood victims."

It's not that life's so good with money, it's that it's worse without it.

✱ ✱ ✱ ✱ ✱

Ira Loeb was now eighty years old. Although he was a declared atheist and constant jeerer at all forms of religion, he decided to attend synagogue on the Day of Atonement. And he prayed so hard he could hardly maintain his kippah atop his head.

"I thought you were an unbeliever," his Rabbi said later, "and here you are praying. Wonderful. What brought this on?"

"I'm still an atheist," the old man said. "But at my age, just suppose I'm wrong?"

✱ ✱ ✱ ✱ ✱

God, please send us the remedy because the affliction, well, we can manage that on our own.

✱ ✱ ✱ ✱ ✱

The Rabbi paid a visit to one of his congregants. It was a unique day, combining both the Sabbath and the important holiday, Rosh Hashana. To his surprise and disgust, he found the man playing cards with four other Jews.

"It's Sabbath! It's Rosh Hashana!" thundered the Rabbi. "How dare you play cards on a holy day like this. Atheists, that's what you are...rotten atheists!"

One of the players looked up: "Rabbi," he said, "let me assure you that in this high-stake game, there are no atheists!"

✱ ✱ ✱ ✱ ✱

From too many swigs one becomes a pig.

✱ ✱ ✱ ✱ ✱

A group of rabbinical students was caught red-handed, on the Sabbath, playing...pinochle.

The Rabbi pounded on the table. He was furious. "What have you got to say for yourselves, dumkopfs?" he shouted.

"I just forgot, Rabbi, forgot that it's the Sabbath," said one student.

"All right, yet," replied the Rabbi. "I can understand that. Just don't let it happen again."

"I hate to admit it, Rabbi," said a second student. "But I forgot that gambling is not permitted on the Sabbath."

"All right, I'll forgive you. Just never do it again. And you, young man?" the Rabbi asked of the third young man.

"Well, Rabbi," replied the third fellow. "I just forgot to pull down the shades."

"WHAT ABOUT MY NAME?"

* * * * *

Sure, life's a dance! But the heck of it is...learning the steps.

* * * * *

A religious Jew left his little village in Russia and went to America. Several years later, having done well, made money and completely assimilated to American ways, he returned to his village in Russia to see his parents.

His ninety-year-old mother almost didn't recognize him, he'd changed so much!

"You look so strange in those clothes," she murmured.

"That's the way we dress in America" he said.

"But why aren't you wearing a beard like all good Jewish men?"

"Well, Mama, all men shave in America."

"And your eating? You do keep a kosher kitchen, don't you?"

"Mama, it's darn near impossible to follow our dietary laws."

The old woman shook her head, wiped a tear from her eyes, then looked up and asked, "You're still circumcised?"

Both a miser and the fatted calf are useful...after death.

* * * * *

Grandmother Sarah went to the beach with her young grandson whom she watched as he paddled around not too far out. But suddenly, a huge wave came far up on the shore and in its backward flow, carried her grandson out to sea. Grandmother Sarah wailed to God to save her boy and it worked! Another wave washed the boy back to shore. Grandmother dried him, looked him over, saw what was missing, looked heavenward and shrieked, "So where's his hat?"

* * * * *

For thirty years, the Rabbi and the synagogue president were deadly enemies, truly hating one another. Finally, the Rabbi left the synagogue for a new congregation. The next morning, for the first time in thirty years, the president didn't attend morning prayer service. The congregation, fearful that something had happened to him, sent a delegation to his home. The group found the president eating a hearty breakfast and asked him why he hadn't attended prayers that morning.

"When that jerk of a Rabbi left, my prayers were answered," he said, simply.

* * * * *

A mohel (a Jewish circumsizer) entered his yacht in a world-wide competition. He had an appropriate name for his boat: *The Yankee Clipper*!

* * * * *

The Bar Mitzvah lad, expecting a rich present from his wealthy uncle, was terrible disappointed to discover that the package contained a mere prayer book. After that, the family had nothing to do with the uncle and only bothered to attend the reading of his will in the hope that they'd been left something. The lawyer read: "As for my dear nephew, I knew he'd be disappointed with the Bar Mitzvah present I gave him -- otherwise he would have opened it and found and cashed the $1,000 cheque I put inside."

* * * * *

Old Jake Gingiss was an honorable man -- it says so on his gravestone.

The new Rabbi was requested to put more pizzazz, more fire, lots of fire in his sermons. After he'd delivered a few of his new, fiery sermons, the congregation asked him to put his sermons in the fire!

* * * * *

If you insist on litigation, you can be sure of tribulation

* * * * *

Abe Levy was finally persuaded to go to a seance because his friends said that the seance guy could make a connection between him and his long-dead grandfather.

Sure enough, the thing worked and a voice said, "My dear grandson, I'm happy that you are here. Are there any questions you'd like to ask me?"

Abe nodded. "Yes, there is. Tell me, Grandpa, where did you learn to speak English?"

* * * * *

Overheard in the synagogue: "You must be a friend of the groom?"

"I should say not! I'm the bride's mother!"

* * * * *

"And now, Mr. Cohen, what is your problem?" asked the psychiatrist.

"People. They are the problem. They don't listen to me, they just laugh and walk away from me."

"What do you say to them, Mr. Cohen? Please start at the beginning."

"O.K. In the beginning...I created the heavens and the earth. And the earth was without form and void..."

* * * * *

Hell ain't so bad as the getting there.

* * * * *

Asked why he had suddenly begun to attend synagogue, Moe Levy said, "I can hear again! I got this new hearing aid and it made all the difference. It's great...cost $2,000!"

"$2,000! Wow! That's unbelievable," his friend, Sam, remarked. "It sure must be a dandy. What kind is it?"

"Two P.M.," Moe said.

Liquor is an unreliable helper. Send it to the stomach and it goes right up to the head.

* * * * *

The American had visited the Wailing Wall in Jerusalem every morning for a week. He spent an hour there, in prayer. Finally, he quit going and, when asked why, said, "It's no use. It's like talking to a wall."

* * * * *

It's better to be honorable than pious.

* * * * *

"IF YOU SHOULD LOSE THE TABLETS, DON'T WORRY. EVERYTHING IS HERE ON COMPUTER TAPE AT CENTRAL DATA STORAGE."

* * * * *

A Rabbi was trapped by a lion while on a tour in darkest Africa. Not only was he cornered by the lion that looked terribly ferocious, but the lion started to pray.

"A miracle," said the Rabbi. "That lion should pray...I'm saved by a miracle."

"Be quiet," said the lion. "I'm saying the blessing before meals."

185

Life may be no more than a dream...but I don't want to wake up!

＊ ＊ ＊ ＊ ＊

Rabbi: "Mr. President, I met old man Goldberg on the street this morning."
President: "That lazy, stingy, no-good bum. He never comes to Temple and yet interferes with everything we do."
Rabbi: "He told me he wants to make a large donation."
President: "As I was saying, he's a man of firm principles, a sterling character. How much is he giving?"

＊ ＊ ＊ ＊ ＊

The deafest of all are those who won't hear.

＊ ＊ ＊ ＊ ＊

It is said that heaven and hell are separated by a brick wall of great depth and height. But one day, the wall was discovered to have been badly damaged by hellish vandals. God noticed this and, in great anger, sent for the Devil, saying, "Your people have damaged the wall!"

"What can I do about that?" smirked the Devil.

"You can repair it or I'll sue."

"Haw! Haw!" laughed the Devil. "I ain't agonna repair it and you can't sue me."

"I sure can," screamed God.

"Oh, yeah? Just where are you gonna get any lawyers?"

＊ ＊ ＊ ＊ ＊

"Can you hear me at the back of the synagogue?" asked the Rabbi.

"Yes. We sure can. But we can move."

＊ ＊ ＊ ＊ ＊

My wife divorced me for religious reasons. She worshipped money and I didn't have any.

＊ ＊ ＊ ＊ ＊

When predictions are for fair weather, everybody has an umbrella to lend.

A congregation had moved to a new location in Minneapolis. It is customary to dignify the move by having a band play proper selections of music when the sacred objects are moved to a new synagogue.

They engaged a non-Jewish band and asked that they play religious music during the march. That's why the bearded Rabbis, clad in their rabbinic clothing, marched to the tune of: "Onward Christian Soldiers."

✳ ✳ ✳ ✳ ✳

A Rabbi was the only professional religious person on the large airliner that was struggling against a terrible storm. The pilot instructed all to fasten their safety belts and prepare for dangerous weather. An elderly lady turned to the Rabbi and said, "Do something religious for us, please, Rabbi."

The Rabbi thought for a moment, then said, "All right. I'll take up a collection!"

✳ ✳ ✳ ✳ ✳

Virtuous precepts are fine, but endorsed by example, they are much more negotiable.

✳ ✳ ✳ ✳ ✳

A New York Rabbi was at an advanced age and very sick. A physician was called and the Rabbi was thoroughly examined. After the examination, the doctor asked, "How old are you, Rabbi?"

"Ninety-five," said the Rabbi.

"I'm really sorry, Rabbi, but I can't make you younger."

"I don't want to be made younger, Doctor, I want you to make me older!"

✳ ✳ ✳ ✳ ✳

There is one thing sure about Noah...he certainly didn't miss the boat.

✳ ✳ ✳ ✳ ✳

It was the day of the funeral of a very rich Jew, and one of the mourners was beating his breast and crying louder than all others. The Rabbi, very concerned, tapped him on the shoulder.

"Take it easy, my friend. It is sad, but you must take it easy. You are one of the relatives of the deceased?"

"No! No! That's the trouble. I ain't."

You can tell which of our members believes in God by the way they drive!

✳ ✳ ✳ ✳ ✳

Herman Cohen owned a remarkable parrot, one that could pray in Hebrew. He decided to take the bird to the synagogue and make some money from it. So, following services, he called together fifteen friends and said, "Fellows, this parrot of mine can actually pray!"

All his friends scoffed at the notion, so Herman said, "OK guys, I'll bet you a hundred bucks he can. Who'll take it?"

All the assembled men nodded and agreed to the bet.

Odds of twenty to one were agreed to and the money lay on the table.

"OK, parrot o'mine, start praying!" But there came forth not a word! "Go on, Pray!" yelled Herman, but it did no good. He paid his loss.

When Herman got home, he thought about strangling the parrot and raised his hands to begin, when the parrot said, "Hold on, man. Wait and see what odds you're gonna get **next** week!"

✳ ✳ ✳ ✳ ✳

"HOW MANY DAYS AND NIGHTS ARE LEFT?"

"A prostitute," said the Rabbi, "is a girl who hates poverty worse than immorality."

* * * * *

A well-known Rabbi was known everywhere as a "wit." He called himself "The Chief Rabbi of America." He was asked by one of his fellow Rabbis, just who it was who had given him this unbelievable title. "The sign painter," said the Rabbi.

* * * * *

If a man is going to make a business of serving God, he ought to see to it when he sells a bill of goods as well as when he prays.

* * * * *

A congregant called on the Rabbi and complained about the bad way things were going in the synagogue under his administration.
"If I had four more like you, I'd be in a position to do the best ever job for our synagogue," the Rabbi replied.
"How can you say that! I'm your worst critic, Rabbi!"
"That's an easy one to answer," said the Rabbi. "I have 90 just as critical of me as you are. But if I only had five, I'd feel a lot better."

* * * * *

Favored by God are those who have nothing to say, and who can't be persuaded to say it.

* * * * *

One of the best refusals in terms of charity occurred in an Iowa City congregation. A rich member of the temple was approached by a very young man and asked for a contribution for the Lord. The rich member said, "How old are you, young man?"
"I'm 18," said the lad.
"In that case, since I expect to see the Lord before you, because I'm 65, I'll personally hand the contribution to Him."

* * * * *

"You can be sure," said the Rabbi, "that happiness consists in having lots to do and to then keep doing it."

In Chicago, a Jew had as his closest friend, a Catholic. Both had sons who planned on going to professional schools. The Jewish lad would go to law school and the Catholic boy was to prepare for the priesthood.

"What's the position when your lad becomes a Priest?" asked the Jew.

"Why, in a few years, he may get appointed Bishop," said his friend.

"And after that, what?"

"Maybe he'll get to be Archbishop, then a Cardinal and, if all goes well with him, he might get to be Pope."

"Is that all?" asked the Jew.

"What did you expect him to become?" asked the Catholic, "the Lord?"

"Well, one of our boys made it," said the Jew.

* * * * *

Someone has suggested that the world today is in such a sorry state that if Moses were to come down from the Mount today, he'd probably take different kinds of tablets...aspirin!

* * * * *

Sol Goldman was a very wealthy man, but not known for his charity. And now, he was very ill in the hospital, attended by his Rabbi, who hoped that his will would include a decent contribution to the synagogue.

"Rabbi," said Sol, "I know I've not been a very charitable member, but I have been thinking of putting in my will a sum of $25,000 for the use of the synagogue."

"Wonderful," said the Rabbi. "How good of you."

"But I am worried about one thing, Rabbi. Heaven! Do you think I'll make it there?"

The Rabbi, knowing Sol very well and not wishing to say anything that might jeopardize the gift, was at a loss as to how to reply. He dearly wanted that money. Yet, he must be honest. Here was his solution. "So, let us put it this way. When your time comes, consider yourself on standby!"

* * * * *

Curse: May the heartburn after one of your meals be strong enough to heat the Metropolitan Opera House.

" I DON'T KNOW WHERE IT CAME FROM, BUT I DON'T LIKE IT. "

5
HEAVEN AND HELL

What is the oldest sin on earth? Stealing apples!

＊＊＊＊＊

The minister was asked why he didn't talk about hell more often, and why he didn't describe the torments and pain that would be suffered by those members of the congregation who went down there. "Is it too hard to do?" he was asked.

"Nope. It ain't hard at all. It's just that when I gets going good at describing hell, well, the congregation makes so derned much noise fanning themselves that I have to let 'em out on recess every five minutes or so."

＊＊＊＊＊

He: Is the accordion mentioned in the Bible?
She: Yes, the Gospel *according* to St. Mark.

＊＊＊＊＊

Picture the earth as only a mass of dirt and fire since it was blown to bits during the final, thermonuclear war. Above the black, flashing ruins, towers the figure of God. He surveys the destruction below him, shakes His head mournfully and says, "Well, there's six days work wasted...shot...gone to hell."

＊＊＊＊＊

"My boy," asked the boss, "do you believe in life after death?"
"Yes, sir."
"Then that makes everything fine," the employer continued softly. "About an hour after you left to attend your grandfather's funeral, he came in to see you."

＊＊＊＊＊

The traveling evangelist was preaching to the people assembled in a huge tent. Everyone loved his preaching until he got to the part where he asked that all those wishing to go to heaven would stand. The entire tentful of people stood...except for one dour-looking old man. "Sir," the preacher asked the old fellow, "don't you want to go to heaven?"

"I sure do, Parson, but I sure as hell don't want to go on no excursion."

The old anvil laughs at many hammers.

*****

A poor man died and went to heaven, knocked at the Pearly Gates. St. Peter asked, "Who's there?" The guy announced himself and St. Peter asked if he's riding or walking. "I'm walking," he says. Whereupon St. Pete tells him he can't let anyone in who isn't riding.

The guy goes off down the road and meets a well-dressed fellow, quite rich, who announces that he's going to heaven. "You can't get there awalkin'," the poor man warns him. "I'll carry you up there and that way we'll both get in." So the rich guy straddles the poor guy's back and off they go to the Pearlies.

St. Peter responds to the rich guy's knock and asks if he's walking or riding. "I'm riding," the rich guy replies.

"Fine," St. Peter says, "hitch your horse outside and then you come on in!"

*****

When choosing between two evils, I like to take the one I've never tried before.

Mae West

*****

When Benny and Sam died, each went in the opposite direction, Benny to heaven. When he had a moment, Benny went to the phone and called his buddy, Sam. "How's it goin', Sam?" he asked. "How's life in hell?"

"Not bad, Benny, not bad at all. We gets up around four of a morning, puts on red clothes and our horns, then shovel more coals on the fire and eat burnt toast and roasted ice cream for breakfast. How about you up there?"

"It's mighty tough, Sam. We get up at four, take in the stars, roll up the moon, put out the sun and then we hustle those clouds along every which way. Man, it's tough up here. We don't hardly get any rest atall."

"That's too bad, Benny," Sam replied. "But I thought heaven would be easy, restful, delightful. How come?"

Benny replied, sighing, "I hate to say this, Sam, but we're mighty short-handed up here."

*****

It used to be that when the son began to sow wild oats, Pop began to use the threshing machine.

Just after the turn of the century, a balloon began to have trouble while flying over Union Springs, Alabama. The pilot managed to land the ailing air ship in a cotton field and, as he was clambering out of the basket, an aged black man came running up to him, saying: "Howdy, Massa Jesus. And how's your Pa this mornin'?"

✳ ✳ ✳ ✳ ✳

Curse: May your corns grow higher than the Empire State Building.

✳ ✳ ✳ ✳ ✳

Johnny Jones was a wonderful guy but given to irregular and prolonged drinking bouts. But his good deeds outweighed his bad ones so that when he died, he managed to make it into heaven. There he looked everywhere to find one of his drinking buddies, but none were to be found. After some thought, he hied himself to the guardian angel and managed to get a weekend pass to Hell.

Sure enough, down there, he found his old buddies and he truly had a ball...limitless booze, plenty of willing girls, air-conditioning everywhere so that he was reluctant to return to heaven. But he did.

The next weekend, he wrangled another pass and rejoined his old friends only to have an even better time than his first trip down below.

"Enough is enough!" he told the guardian angel. "I want to move down to Hell permanently where all the action is."

"It's OK by us," the angel replied, "but remember, once you leave here, there's no coming back. Ever! Y'understand?"

"Ya dern tootin'," Johnny Jones replied gleefully. "Who in hell would ever want to come back here?"

Well, when Johnny returned this time, he found things altered more than somewhat. It was hot as blazes, fire everywhere, devils at every step and jabbing with three-pronged tools they used to move him about constantly. Finally, after a week of this, he staggered to the head honcho at the gate and asked, "How come things are so changed? It used to be fun down here. Now it's plain hell."

"Heh! Heh! Heh!" sneered the honcho. "The last two times you were here, old buddy, you came as a *tourist!*"

✳ ✳ ✳ ✳ ✳

The old adage that "marriages are made in heaven" doesn't tell it all...because thunder and lightning are made there, too.

"I'M ORIGINALLY FROM AUSTRALIA. HOW ABOUT YOU?"

* * * * *

Elmer Tonkins was the greatest fund-raiser that was ever known in the huge state of Indiana. That ol' boy could get a contribution out of a bankrupt miser. His entire life was spent in the holy work of raising funds for worthy causes.

But, as to all men, death came to Elmer Tonkins and he appeared at the Pearly Gates and requested permission to enter. The guardian angel looked over his record and said, "Sorry, Elmer, but I find that you've been assigned a place in Hell."

"What!" Elmer screamed. "Why I've spent my entire life helping others, raising funds for worthy causes. This is a rampant injustice that you do me."

"Nevertheless," said the angel, "you must go to the devil."

When Elmer got down there, the Devil nodded, saying, "We've been expecting you. Come on in."

Scarcely a month passed before the guardian of the Pearly Gates got a call from the Devil. "Say, Father Angel," the Devil began, "I want you to get this fellow Tonkins out of here. I can't use him."

"Really?" the angel was surprised. "How come? He's perfect for your kind of facilities, or so my records show."

"Can't use him. He's already raised almost enough funds from the residents down here to air condition the place."

Curse: May you be famous for your hospitality to God's
          creatures...such as rates, bedbugs, ants, worms and
          maggots.

＊ ＊ ＊ ＊ ＊

Three ladies appeared before the Pearly Gates to be greeted by
the guardian angel who asked them to be seated and to wait a bit
since he had important business that must be attended to. Then
the angel disappeared.

The angel was gone a long time but eventually arrived back,
whereupon he called in one of the ladies and asked if she had
been upset over his absence. "Not a bit, dear Angel," she replied.
"I'm just delighted to be here and to be considered for entrance."

The angel thanked her, then said, "There is just one question for
you -- as a kind of final exam -- in what country is the Vatican
located?"

"Italy, your honor. Rome, Italy."

"Excellent. Please take your place in heaven."

The angel called in a second woman and asked the same
question. "I hope you haven't minded waiting. I had some
compelling business."

"Not at all, your angelic majesty, not at all. I've been praying for
this moment, praying every day and in church on Sundays for this
very moment. I was pleased to wait."

"But I must know one thing before you enter," the angel said. "In
what country is London?"

"In England, your angelic presence. In England."

"Fine and dandy, Ma'am. Please enter heaven."

The angel then called for the third woman to enter. "I do hope my
delay in admitting you was not resented, Ma'am. Was it?"

"You're damned right it was. On earth, I could understand waiting
in line...at the polling booth, at concerts, at the movies...
everywhere one must wait. But here? In heaven? To wait as I did,
is simply disgraceful!"

"Well, OK, if that's the way you feel! But I must ask one question
before allowing you to enter heaven. What is the capital of
Barundi?"

＊ ＊ ＊ ＊ ＊

God gave women a delicious sense of humor...so they could
better understand the jokes they married.

"ARE YOU SURE THIS REALLY IS HEAVEN?"

✳ ✳ ✳ ✳ ✳

Eric Thompson had spent the sixty years of his life making bum decisions! For example, if he shot craps, he lost. If he played the horses, he'd pick the loser. If he bought a new car, it never ran properly and if he dialed a phone number, most of the time, it was wrong.

Well, he had to make a business trip to an isolated city served by only one airline. That pleased him because he had no decision to make.

He took the plane, but in mid-flight, both engines caught fire and he knew they'd soon explode and destroy them all. He broke down and wept, then prayed, "Dear God, in all my life I never made the right choice. I have borne these ordeals without complaint. But now when I had no choice but to take this one plane, I still am besieged with trouble. Why?"

Suddenly he was transported from the plane to be suspended, all alone, miles above earth where a voice spoke to him. The voice pierced the clouds. "Eric! Eric Thompson! Have you in truth called upon Me to save you?"

"I have. I most certainly have, dear One. I prayed to be saved by you, St. Francis."

"Well, that's interesting. But tell me, before I open the gate...did you pray to Saint Francis of Assisi or Saint Francis Xavier? Which did you choose?"

Cowboy saying: Don't repent. Just stop sinning.

✳ ✳ ✳ ✳ ✳

I saw a cartoon in a church newsletter which showed two angels sitting on a cloud. One is asking the other: "Tell me the truth, Robert. Do you believe in the heretofore?"

✳ ✳ ✳ ✳ ✳

A HENPECKED HUSBAND AT THE GOLDEN GATE
St. Peter stood guard at the Golden Gate,
    With a solemn mind and an air sedate,
When up to the top of the golden stair
    A man and a woman, ascended there,
Applied for admission. They came and stood
    Before St. Peter so great and good,
In hope the City of Peace to win,
    To ask St. Peter to let them in.

The woman was tall and lank and think,
    With a shaggy beard on her chin,
The man was short and thick and stout;
    His stomach was built so it rounded out;
His face was pleasant and all the while,
    He wore a kindly and gentle smile;
The choirs in the distance the echoes awoke,
    And the man kept still while the woman spoke.

"I've talked and talked to Him loud and long,
    For my lungs are good and my voice is strong,

So St. Peter, you'll plainly see
    The gate of heaven is open to me.
But my old man, I regret to say,
    Hasn't walked straight in the narrow way.

He smokes and swears, and grave faults he's got,
    And I don't know whether he'll pass or not."

So St. Peter sat and stroked his staff,
    But in spite of his office he had to laugh,
Then said with a fiery gleam in his eye:
    "Who's tending this gate your or I?"
And then he arose to his stature tall
    And pressed a button on the wall,
And said to the imp who answered the bell
    "Escort this lady around to (The Bad Place)."

Slowly the man turned by habit bent,
    To follow where ever the woman went.
St. Peter standing on duty there,
    Observed the top of his head was bare.
"Halt," he said, "Give him a harp,
    He's been too long with a tongue too sharp.
A jeweled harp with golden strings
    Good Sir, pass in where the angels sing.

Gabriel give him a seat alone,
    One with a cushion up near the throne;
Call up the angels to play their best,
    Let him enjoy the music and rest."
            "Nothin' Ain't No Good," E.P Holmes. 1955
            Reprinted with permission of John Wesley Clay.

"Do you remember old Deacon Jones? He is still living. Do you remember his son Abe? He was a good-for-nothing sort of fellow. Abe gave the old man a great deal of trouble. The deacon got terrible mad at Abe one day and told him to leave the house and never come back. He said, 'Go down there and never come back.' Abe went away. They never heard anything more from him until one night last winter. The deacon had invited all the preachers in the surrounding country to the house. It was a bitter cold night. All the preachers were sitting around the stove, when they heard a knock at the door. The deacon got up and went to the door and there stood poor Abe, cold and shivering. The deacon said, 'Where have you been?' He said, 'Where you told me, down there.' 'How did you find things down there?' 'Just like they are here at home, so many preachers there I couldn't get to the fire.'"

"On A Slow Train Through Arkansaw"
Thomas W. Jackson. 1903.

* * * * *

"IT USED to BE CALLED 'REINCARNATION', BUT TODAY SOUL 'RECYCLING' SOUNDS MORE TRENDY."

When his time had come, old Paul found himself in heaven where St. Peter bade him welcome and took him on a tour of the place. They came to a long, long hallway filled with boxes on shelves and each box held a clock...millions of them.

Old Paul asked, "What in heck do you use all these clocks for?"

"Each clock lets us know when a person sins," was the reply. "Each time the hands move, it tells us that a person has sinned."

So Pete started looking around. He found his friend Jim's clock ticking away real gentle-like. Then he tackled Eddie's and it wasn't moving at all. Then he looked for his worst friend, old Dirty Sam. He couldn't find it anywhere, so he asked, "Tell me, how come Dirty Sam's clock isn't here?"

St. Peter said, "Well, it's been a little hot in our restroom up here and we moved his clock in there because it makes a very good fan."

＊ ＊ ＊ ＊ ＊

Church Notice: Learn all about hell. Come early and hear the choir practice.

＊ ＊ ＊ ＊ ＊

A mountain climber falls off the edge of a precipitous cliff but, luckily, grabs a protruding root and hangs on, halfway to the bottom of the cliff. He casts his eyes heavenward and cries, "Is anyone up there?" A voice floats down to him, saying, "Yes, my son. Let go of that root you hold and I will bring thee up here."

There was a long pause and then the man cried, "Anyone else up there?"

＊ ＊ ＊ ＊ ＊

Heaven: A place you can reach if you turn **right** and then go straight forward.

＊ ＊ ＊ ＊ ＊

A Bishop and a Congressman arrived at the Pearly Gates at the same time. Both gained admission and were presented with a car. The Bishop was given a Ford pick-up while the Congressmen got a luxurious Cadillac. "This seems unfair," said the Bishop. "I get a Ford pick-up, but this Congressman gets a Cadillac. Why do you treat me this way?"

"We've got hundreds, thousands of Bishops up here," said St. Peter, "but this guy is one of three Congressman in the place."

Heaven iz ever kind tew us, she puts our humps on our backs so that we kant see them.

Josh Billings

* * * * *

Minister to his wife: "I made seven people truly happy today, my dear." His wife replied, "That's mighty good to hear, John. What did you do for them?"

"I married three couples."

"But that's only six...you said seven."

"Dear, I don't give my services away for nothing, you know."

* * * * *

He: "Is the flea mentioned in the Bible?"
She: "Yes, the wicked flea when no man pursueth."

* * * * *

This guy died and went to Hell. The Devil gave him three choices on how he could spend eternity. He opened up a big door and there were people standing on their heads on spikes and nails. The newcomer said, "Let's go on and see what the next one is like."

They went on to another door, the Devil opened it, and there were people standing on their heads and the heads were all resting on red-hot coals. "Let's go on, Mr. Devil," the newcomer said. And they went to another door, opened it and there were people standing up to their waists in manure. "This one looks best of all. I'll take it." So the Devil has him remove all his clothes and get ready for it. Then another Devil comes by and says, "All right, everybody. Coffee break is over, so get back on your heads again!"

* * * * *

Prayer -- a little message to God, sent at night...to get the cheaper rate.

* * * * *

Brother Smith, a member of a hillbilly church, was impossible to get along with. He was always arguing, disagreeing and nothing seemed to please him. Well, one night at prayer meeting, a member told the congregation that he wished Brother Smith was in Hell.

The minister said, "Please, Sir, I'm shocked at such a wish."

"Well," the member replied, "I figure that if that old cuss was in Hell, he'd have the place busted up in three or four months."

"I'M AFRAID THERE IS NO 'UP,' SIR. THERE'S ONLY 'DOWN!'"

* * * * *

Man waz kreated a little lower than the angels, and he haz been a gittin' a little lower ever since.

Josh Billings

* * * * *

A well-to-do farmer was on his deathbed. He told his wife to take his billfold up on the roof of the farmhouse and hide it under a shingle so that he could grab it on his way to heaven.

After his death, the wife climbed up on the roof and looked under the shingle and, sure enough, the billfold was still there. "Just as I thought," the wife said to herself, "he never made it!"

* * * * *

An ex-sailor from the U.S. Navy died and stood before the Pearly Gates. He was invited in, then handed a golden harp by the guardian angel.

"Dadblameit," growled the sailor, "just one more derned thing to keep polished."

The preacher was a great exhorter, full of enthusiasms and obsessed with hell-fire and damnation. He finished his Sunday sermon by shouting to his flock: "All those who want to go to heaven, raise their hands!"

Only one old man in the back row did not raise his hand,.

The preacher repeated his demand and still the old fellow sat still.

"You in the back row, with your hand down, don't you want to go to heaven?"

"What's the big rush," the old fellow said quietly. "I like it just fine here where I am."

"Sir! Remember this! All will go eventually!"

"Maybe so, Mister Preacher, but I tell you...right now, I ain't goin' no place!"

* * * * *

A clergyman passed on up to the Pearly Gates and was told they were out of rooms at the moment. The minister raised heck and finally was told that if he could find Adam and Eve, recently disappeared, he could be given entrance to heaven.

"I'll be back real soon," said the minister.

Sure enough, in just a couple of hours, the minister was back with Adam and Eve in tow. "How did you find them?" asked St. Peter.

"Easy. I looked for a couple without navels."

* * * * *

It iz a statistikal fakt that the wuicked work harder tew reach Hell, than the righteous do tew git to heaven.

Josh Billings

* * * * *

An infantryman lost his courage during a terrible fight and started to run to the rear. "Hey, soldier, come back here!" the sergeant roared after him. "What if you do get killed, man, then heaven'll be your home."

"Maybe so, Sarg," the fleeing soldier yelled back. "But right now I ain't homesick!"

* * * * *

Eternal: God's epitaph.

They tell the story of the time Mark Twain was in London at the invitation of a literary group that was giving a banquet in Mark's honor. The Bacon-Shakespeare controversy came up and one of the members asked Twain for his opinion.

"I really haven't thought much about it," said Twain.

"Come on now, Mr. Twain, surely you have a theory on the subject!"

"I figure on waiting until I get to heaven and then to ask Shakespeare just who did write his plays."

"Mr. Twain," said one of the urbane members, "I don't think you'll find Shakespeare in heaven."

"Then you ask him," said Twain.

* * * * *

Thar iz plenty ov pholks in this world whoz hart bleeds for the poor, but whoz pocket-books never do.

Josh Billings

* * * * *

The head of the Ku Klux Klan died and found himself at the door to Paradise. He knocked for admission.

"Who dat knockin' at de do'?" called St. Peter from inside the gate.

The Klan head paled. "Never mind," he muttered as he turned to leave. "Forget it!"

* * * * *

There's a time to speak and a time to be quiet. A perfect example appears in the case of three Christians who appeared at the Pearly Gates just after God had determined that there were too many folks in heaven and admittance regulations had to be made more rigorous.

When the first Christian appeared before St. Peter, the angel asked, "What is the meaning of Easter?"

The woman hemmed and hawed, finally saying, "It's...it's a holiday when eggs are colored and ..."

St. Peter sent the lady to hell.

The next entrant walked up and asked to be admitted. St. Peter asked the same question: "What is the meaning of Easter?"

The fellow said, "Well, there's a rabbit and he hops here and there..."

"Go to hell!" exclaimed St. Peter.

The next applicant, an old man, walked up and was asked the same question. But he responded, "That's when Jesus was crucified and he arose from the dead and came out..."

"Hallelujah!" exclaimed St. Peter. "A wise and worthy angel."

"...of the cave and saw his shadow," the old man continued, "it indicated there'd be six more months of winter."

Curse: May all your teeth grow hysterically angry so they
           can chew off your head.

＊ ＊ ＊ ＊ ＊

It iz a grate deal eazier tew be a philsopher after a man haz had
hiz dinner, than it iz when he don't kno whare he iz a going tew git
it.

Josh Billings

＊ ＊ ＊ ＊ ＊

Supreme Court Justice Tom Clark told a story about a most
virtuous lady who died and was totally dismayed to discover that
she was consigned to hell. She phoned St. Peter and was told that
the assignment was only temporary, that heaven was so
overcrowded at the moment that she'd just have to wait till things
cleared up.
A couple of weeks later, she again phoned St. Peter to tell him
that they were teaching her to drink and smoke. St. Peter
cautioned patience and will power and that she'd soon be
accommodated in heaven.
Two weeks later, the paragon of virtue made a last, final call:
"Howdy, Pete. **Forget it!**"

＊ ＊ ＊ ＊ ＊

SCHWADRM

"SINCE THE ATT SHAKEUP, TELEPHONE SERVICE IS REALLY SCREWED UP.
EVERY TIME I CALL 'DIAL-A-CURSE', I GET 'DIAL-A-PRAYER.'"

One ov the hardest things for enny man to do, iz tew fall down on the ice when it iz wet, and then git up and praze the Lord.

Josh Billings

✳ ✳ ✳ ✳ ✳

In 1964, the Burlington Liars Club awarded first prize in the club competition for tall tales to Philip Strandvold, for this one.

There was a lady back home who was always late for everything. One day, she died. No, she wasn't late for her own funeral but when she arrived at the Pearly Gates, St. Peter had to put in for his first overtime.

✳ ✳ ✳ ✳ ✳

A man who'd spent his life as a pickpocket died and got down on his knees before St. Peter, begging for admission through the Pearly Gates. St. Peter listened to his plea for entry, then said, "Sorry, old man, but this is not the place for you. Downstairs you go. Meanwhile, give me back my watch."

✳ ✳ ✳ ✳ ✳

I find it iz a grate deal eazier for mi philosophy to ackount for original sin, than for an attack ov the jumping tooth ake.

Josh Billings

✳ ✳ ✳ ✳ ✳

A pint of example is worth a barrel of sermons.

✳ ✳ ✳ ✳ ✳

A physician dies and appears before the Pearly Gates. The angel asks, "Who are you?" And the guy says, "Peter Evans, a cardiac specialist."

"What can I do for you?"

"I want in."

"And what have you done that makes you think you belong up here?"

"One time I saw a bum on the street in my hometown and gave him a dime."

"Anything else?"

"Sure. Lots. One time I was going into the hospital and a little boy stopped me and asked if he could have some money to get something to eat. So I gave him a nickel."

"Anything else?"

"Nope."

Turning to Gabriel, the angel asks, "What should we do with this gent, Gab?"

"Give him his 15¢ back and tell him to go to hell!"

Someone has aptly remarked that in the Garden of Eden, it wasn't the apple in the tree that caused all the fuss, it was the "pair" on the ground!

✳ ✳ ✳ ✳ ✳

Wisdom can't be bought at the shopping center.

✳ ✳ ✳ ✳ ✳

Adam was feeling bad in the Garden of Eden. God noticed this and said he'd furnish a partner, a lovely, wise, kind and intelligent wife for him. "She'll truly take care of you in all ways," God promised.

"Hey, that's swell. I hope it's soon. But tell me, Lord, just how much is it going to cost me?"

"Not so much...only an arm and a leg and you've two of both."

"Yeah, I know. But I need 'em both. Say, Lord, how about settling for a rib?"

✳ ✳ ✳ ✳ ✳

Why did Noah take two of a kind of each breed of animal aboard? Because he wouldn't swallow that story about the stork.

✳ ✳ ✳ ✳ ✳

Each week the lad would return from Sunday School with an illustrated card depicting the Ten Commandments. The first week showed people in church. A view of Cain slaying Abel illustrated the lesson against murder.

"I was kind of uneasy about that seventh week," the lad's father said. "And it was with relief that Johnny came home with the card illustrating that adultery commandment. The card for that week showed a dairyman leering hideously as he poured a huge pail of water into a container of milk!"

✳ ✳ ✳ ✳ ✳

I read the Book of Job last night, and I don't think God comes well out of it.

Virginia Wolff

✳ ✳ ✳ ✳ ✳

Did you know that Noah was the first of all financial investors? Yep! The *"Pun American Newsletter"* states that "he floated his stock while everyone else was being liquidated!"

A farmer along the Mississippi was put out of business by the terrible floods of 1993. The floods were all he could talk about after that. Eventually, he died and went to heaven and St. Peter asked if there was anything they could do to make life in heaven good for him.

"Well, if it's not too much trouble, I'd like to talk to the folks up here abut the awful floods of 1993."

"We can arrange that," St. Peter told him. "And we will."

The next evening, a large crowd had gathered to hear the newcomer talk about the floods that had ruined him. Just as he was abut to speak, St. Peter told him: "Now you watch yourself, son. Noah is in the audience."

✳ ✳ ✳ ✳ ✳

If I ever reach heaven, I expect to find three wonders there: first, to meet some I had not thought to see there; second, to miss some I had expected to see there; and third, the greatest wonder of all, to find myself there.

John Newton

✳ ✳ ✳ ✳ ✳

"YOU'RE HERE, MR. HENNYPACKER, BECAUSE TOO MUCH OF THE GOOD LIFE CAN BE A BAD THING."

One of the oldest stories in the Jewish tradition has to do with God seeking people to whom he could give the Commandments. He first went to the Russians, who looked it over, then handed it back, saying, "That part about 'Though shalt not steal' is impossible!"

Then God took the offer to the French and asked them to accept it.

"What!" they yelled. "You're telling us that we shouldn't commit adultery? That's ridiculous!" They handed it back to the Lord.

Finally, they brought it to Moses who asked, "How much do you want for it, God?" Who replied, "Not one shekel. It's free."

"OK, then," said Moses, "Give me ten!"

$$* * * * *$$

IRISH STEW

To fulfill the blarney requirement for his winning nomination as honorary grand marshal of today's St. Patrick's Day parade, Pat Grady told this one.

Saying he had recently returned from a trip to New York City, Grady claimed he left this note on his windshield:

"I realize my car is too close to a fire hydrant, but I have circled the block ten times, and if I don't park here I'll be late for work and lose my job. Forgive us our trespasses."

When he returned to his car, he found a parking ticket under the windshield wiper and this note from the Irish cop on the beat:

"I have circled the block for ten years, and if I don't give you a ticket, I'll lose my job. Lead us not into temptation."

©1994 "The State Journal-Register," Springfield, Illinois

$$* * * * *$$

Man says, "So so."
Heaven says, "No, no."

Chinese aphorism

$$* * * * *$$

EVE

Apropos de Rien
It is not fair to visit all
The blame on Eve for Adam's fall
The most Eve did was to display
Contributory negligee.

Oliver Herford

211

METHUSELAH

Methuselah ate what he found on his plate,
    And never, as people do now,
Did he note the amount of the calory count;
    He ate it because it was chow.
He wasn't disturbed as at dinner he sat,
    Devouring a roast or a pie,
To think it was lacking in granular fat
    Or a couple of vitamins shy.
He cheerfully chewed each species of food,
    Unmindful of troubles or fears
Lest his health might be hurt
    By some fancy desert;
And he lived over nine hundred years.

Author unknown

✶ ✶ ✶ ✶ ✶

The Navy Chaplain preached a sermon on the Ten Commandments. After he had finished, an Ensign, who had listened raptly said, "There's still hope for me. I haven't ever made a graven image."

✶ ✶ ✶ ✶ ✶

"SMOKING OR NON-SMOKING?"

212

Did you know that when Noah was admitting life to the Ark, three camels tried to get aboard?

"All right, you three," said Noah, "one of you must stay ashore."

First camel: "Not me, Boss, 'cause I'm the camel so many people swallow while straining at a gnat."

Second camel: "I got to come in 'cause I'm the camel whose back was broken by a straw."

Third camel: "You better let me aboard because I'm the camel that passes through the eye of a needle sooner than a rich man enters the Kingdom of Heaven."

What to do? Of course, Noah let all three aboard!

✳ ✳ ✳ ✳ ✳

When Eve upon the first of man
    The apple passed with specious cant,
Oh, what a thousand pities then
    That Adam was not adam...ant!
                 Thomas Hood, 1799-1845

✳ ✳ ✳ ✳ ✳

Adam Haddem...or, the agelessness of the flea.

✳ ✳ ✳ ✳ ✳

A pilot was coming into LaGuardia Field in New York City, but he was having trouble. He wired, "I'm coming in now, but I'm out of gas and falling. Don't think I can make it. What shall I do? This is urgent!"

The tower replied: "Repeat after me: Our Father who art in heaven...."

✳ ✳ ✳ ✳ ✳

Isn't it a curious phenomenon that when it comes to the biblical principal of tithing, it seems that some people stop at nothing!

✳ ✳ ✳ ✳ ✳

There was a dear lady of Eden,
Who on applies was quite fond of feedin',
    She gave one to Adam
    Who said, "Thank you, Madam."
And then they both skedaddled from Eden.

Did you ever wonder how many fig leaves Eve tried on before she made up her mind and said, "I'll take this one."

* * * * *

Leslie Gibson of Dunedin, Florida, is certain that the three most constipated men mentioned in the Bible were:
Cain, because he wasn't Abel.
David, because neither heaven nor hell could move him.
Solomon, because he sat on the throne, trying like
everything, for forty years.

* * * * *

Then there was the floundering, debt-ridden business woman who turned to her Bible for solace. Luckily, she turned to Chapter 11.

* * * * *

The reason why God created woman last was that He didn't want anyone telling Him how he should create man.

* * * * *

6
EARLY AMERICAN

The eastern, as well as the frontier-western, preacher of the 19th century was "full of beans" and as vigorous in delivery as hot pepper. Abraham Lincoln once said that when he listened to a sermon, he wanted to see the preacher go at it as if "he were fighting bees!"

Another and equally colorful description of the frontier preacher at work was given by A. E. Rector in his advice to all young, aspiring clergymen: "Begin slow, go slow. When most oppressed, be self-possessed. Rise high, catch fire. Wax warm, close out in a storm."

A truly effective preacher was described thus: "He drank water, spit and pawed and with all his awkwardness he was cheered, huzzahed as if a thunderstorm of eloquence was flowing like a burning river of fire."

The enthusiasms of the preacher, his vigorous movements, loud voice and demanding tone often overrode the announced subject of the sermon. Fiery, thunderous delivery gave the expected sound and the subject matter was overwhelmed by volume! A church member described a preacher's recent sermon in this way:

"He preached nigh onto two hours."

"What did he talk about?"

"He never did say," was the reply.

Acting, movement, sound, dramatics, rather than serious and logical subject matter, was the motive behind the frontier sermon. Entertainment and enthusiasm were the two most important qualities. And that says much about both preacher and congregation. But then, Americans have always accorded a high place to inspired entertainment.

＊ ＊ ＊ ＊ ＊

An anecdote that goes back just before this century began, has it that a Presbyterian home missionary was traveling through West Texas and came to a sod shack occupied by a woman.

"Are there any Presbyterians in this area?" he asked the woman.

"Now, I jist don't know 'bout that," answered the woman. "Got all kinds of varmints in these parts, but I ain't paid much attention to 'em. If'n my husband was heah, he'd know fer sho. He keeps his hides on the south wall of ouah cabin and if you'd care to walk around theah, you could see if'n theah was any Presbyterian hides ahangin' theah."

"My friend," the missionary said, "I think you are a soul in the dark."

"Ah knows it. I been aftuh mah husband to saw me a winder, but he ain't done it."

"You don't understand. Do you have any religious convictions at all?"

"Naw. And my old man ain't got none either. They done tried him fer hog stealin' oncet, but they never convicted him nohow."

✳ ✳ ✳ ✳ ✳

The big debate between William Jennings Bryan and Clarence Darrow was underway. Both were erudite men. Bryan held out for the literal interpretation of the Bible, Darrow took a somewhat broader view to say the least.

During a recess, a reporter asked Mr. Darrow, "Sir, how does it feel to be debating with a distinguished Bible scholar?"

"I wouldn't know," snapped Darrow. "Ask Bryan."

✳ ✳ ✳ ✳ ✳

PASSOVER

On one occasion, a Hebrew fellow-citizen presented a member of the Sazerac Lying Club with a cake of unleavened, or Passover bread. This being exhibited at the next meeting of the Club, led to a discussion on the origin and uses of the Jewish holiday of Passover. Uncle John asserted that the holiday was kept by the Jews in commemoration of the deliverance of Moses from the bulrushes, and his being "passed over" to Pharaoh's daughter; but the "Theological Member" told him to "shut up" talking of something he knew nothing about; and if the President would maintain order and enforce the rules, he would tell them what Passover bread was for. Mr. Fibley said he would, and the "Theological Member" turned himself loose in a narrative, of which the follow is the substance, as nearly as I am able to reproduce it from memory.

"When the Pharaoh was Khedive of Egypt he was building government buildings by contract, and the Israelites were working for him making brick by the day. Like all government contractors, he neither furnished a good article nor treated his employees with justice.

"The Israelites struck for higher wages and eight hours a day, and organized a trade union and elected a man named Moses as President. Moses was in the clothing business; and because he didn't know anything about labor the Israelites thought he would make a good presiding officer of a labor organization.

"When the Israelites struck, old Pharaoh hired a new set of hands, and they (the Israelites) concluded to go on a prospecting

216

trip into Canaan District, where there was represented to be a big milk and honey ledge. Owing to the snow blockade on the Suez Canal the market was bare of yeast powders, and the mill that made the self-rising flour had shut down; and as the Israelites were afraid the claims would all be located if they didn't get there quick, they started off with a few sacks of flour and mixed their bread in the flour sack and baked it on a hot rock.

"After they had crossed the creek Pharaoh missed some picks and shovels, and thinking the Israelites had stolen them, he swore out a search-warrant and sent a sheriff's posse after them. The sheriff's party missed the ford and were drowned, and to this day the Israelites eat unleavened bread in commemoration of the event."

Sazerac Lying Club. 1888

✳ ✳ ✳ ✳ ✳

Weavin' Way: State of excitement. "Oncst upon a time a powerful young preacher come...and held a meeting over at Bark Log...and when he got into one of his *weavin' ways*, he could fairly make your blood run cold."

✳ ✳ ✳ ✳ ✳

Flat-Boat Preacher: Bill Arp explained that a flat-boat preacher was of a rough and tumble lot who peddled and preached up and down rivers...and tied up for the double purpose of preaching and selling whiskey!

✳ ✳ ✳ ✳ ✳

"I could have forgiven him fer sleepin' through mah sermon," said the Southern preacher, "but I shore hated it when he began to saw gourds [to snore]."

✳ ✳ ✳ ✳ ✳

Pastor Elmer Richards said that when a man is offered a drink, he ought to turn it down by saying, "I wouldn't take a drink even if you offered me a clear deed to a ten-acre lot in heaven."

✳ ✳ ✳ ✳ ✳

Response to a stupid action: "I guess you didn't have a seat in the Amen corner when they passed around brains."

It was a great revival meeting in the deep, rural South. The tent was filled for this night's service and the subject was eternal damnation. The preacher urged those seated to abjure sin, to fear the wrath sure to come from it. "On that last day, my friends, on that last day before the final reckoning and the end of things, there's gonna be cryin' and sobbin' and weepin' and wailin' an' gnashin' of teeth!"

An elderly gentleman stood up and shouted, "But, Pastor, I ain't got no teeth."

"Don't worry, mah friend. Teeth will be provided."

* * * * *

Catching the Lord

It happened that, in an early day, a Methodist circuit rider came to a crossroads in the state of Wisconsin where stood a typical country lad--barefooted, pants rolled up, one suspender, and shirt bosom open. The preacher was mounted on about the poorest horse that had ever been seen in these parts. Addressing the boy, he said, "My son, which one of these two roads will take me to Stoughton?"

The boy paid no attention to the question. He had never seen a respectable man mounted on so sorry a steed. The minister repeated the question, and the boy, looking up, queried, "Who are you?"

Back came the answer, "I am a follower of the Lord."

"Well," said the boy, "it won't make any difference which road you take. You'll never catch him with that hoss."

* * * * *

When a man gits to going down hill, it duz seem az tho everything had been greased for the ockashun.

Josh Billings

* * * * *

REV. MR. HALLELUJAH'S HOSS. (1886)

There are a good many difficult things to ride, I find, beside the bicycle and the bucking Mexican plug. Those who have tried to mount and successfully ride a wheelbarrow in the darkness of the still night will agree with me.

You come on a wheelbarrow suddenly when it is in a brown study, and you undertake to straddle it, so to speak, and all at once you find the wheelbarrow on top. I may say, I think, safely, that the wheelbarrow is, as a rule, phlegmatic and cool; but when a total stranger startles it, it spreads desolation and destruction on

218

every hand.

This is also true of the perambulator, or baby-carriage. I undertook to evade a child's phaeton, three years ago last spring, as it stood in the entrance to a hall on Main Street. The child was not injured, because it was not in the carriage at the time; but I was not so fortunate. I pulled pieces of perambulator out of myself for two weeks with the hand that was not disabled.

How a sedentary man could fall through a child's carriage in such a manner as to stab himself with the awning and knock every spoke out of three wheels, is still a mystery to me, but I did it. I can show you the doctor's bill now.

The other day, however, I discovered a new style of riding animal. The Rev. Mr. Hallelujah was at the depot when I arrived, and was evidently waiting for the same Chicago train that I was in search of. Rev. Mr. Hallelujah had put his valise down near an ordinary baggage-truck which leaned up against the wall of the station building.

He strolled along the platform a few moments, communing with himself and agitating his mind over the subject of Divine Retribution, and then he went up and leaned against the truck. Finally, he somehow got his arms under the handles of the truck as it stood up between his back and the wall. He still continued to think the plan of Divine Retribution, and you could have seen his lips move if you had been there.

Pretty soon some young ladies came along, rosy in winter air, beautiful beyond compare, frosty crystals in their hair; smiled they on the preacher there.

He returned the smile and bowed low. As he did so, as near as I can figure it out, he stepped back on the iron edge of the truck that the baggage man generally jabs under the rim of an iron-bound sample trunk when he goes to load it. Anyhow Mr. Hallelujah's feet flew toward next spring. The truck started across the platform with him and spilled over the edge on the track ten feet below. So rapid was the movement that the eye with difficulty followed his evolutions. His valise was carried onward by the same wild avalanche, and "busted" open before it struck the track below.

I was surprised to see some of the articles that shot forth into the broad light of day. Among the rest there was a bran fired new set of ready-made teeth, to be used in case of accident. Up to that moment, I didn't know that Mr. Hallelujah used the common tooth of commerce. These teeth slipped out of the valise with a Sabbath smile and vulcanized rubber gums.

In striking the iron track below, the every-day set which the Rev. Mr. Hallelujah had in use became loosened, and smiled across the road-bed and right of way at the bran fired new array of incisors, cuspids, bi-cuspids and molars that flew out of the valise. Mr. Hallelujah got up and tried to look merry, but he could not smile without his teeth. The back seams of his Newmarket coat were more successful, however.

Mr. Hallelujah's wardrobe and a small boy were the only objects that dared to smile.

From "Remarks" by Bill Nye. 1886.

✳ ✳ ✳ ✳ ✳

Almost enny phool kan prove that the bible ain't true, it takes a wize man to beleave it.

Josh Billings

✳ ✳ ✳ ✳ ✳

REVERSE PUBLICITY

Amos Skinner, the leading deacon of his church, was chuckling in high glee when he ran into another deacon on the village green.

"Got it at last, by heck," he cackled to his friend.

"What you cal'late you got, Amos?" asked the other.

"Just a little dee-vice, Ezry, but it's a-going to make me rich. Every meetin' house in the hull country'll want one."

"Haow you figger that out, Amos?" persisted Ezra.

"Well, it's a patent contribution box. Coins fall through slots of different sizes. Dollars, half dollars and quarters on velvet; nickels and pennies drop on a Chinese bell!"

The following piece is perhaps the most famous, most read piece of literary humor from the mid-nineteenth century. It is included in all collections of humor from that period.

GEORGE W. HARRIS
Parson John Bullen's Lizards
[1867]

AIT ($8) DULLARS REW-ARD
"TENSHUN BELEVERS AND KONSTABLES!
KETCH 'IM! KETCH 'IM!"

This kash wil be pade in korn, ur uther projuce, tu be kolected at ur about nex camp-meetin, ur thatatter, by eny wun what ketches him, fur the karkus ove a sartin wun SUT LOVINGOOD, dead or alive, ur ailin, an' safely giv over tu the purtectin care ove Parson John Bullin, ur lef well tied, at Squire Mackjunkins, fur the raisin ove the devil pussonely, an' permiskusly discumfurtin the wimen very powerful, an' skeerin ove folks generly a heap, an' bustin up a promisin, big warm meetin, and' a makin the wickid larf, an' wus, an' wus, insultin ove the passun orful."

Test, JEHU WETHERO
Sined by me,

JOHN BULLEN, the passun.

I found written copies of the above highly intelligible and vindictive proclamation, stuck up on every blacksmith shop, doggery, and store door, in the Frog Mountain Rane. Its blood-thirsty spirit, its style, and above all, its chirography, interested me to the extent of taking one down from a tree for preservation.

In a few days I found Sut in a good crowd in front of Capoehart's Doggery, and as he seemed to be about in good tune, I read it to him.

"Yasm, George, that ar dockymint am in dead yearnist sartin. Them hard shells over thar dus want me the wus kine, powerful bad. *But*, I spect ait dullers won't fetch me, nither wud ait hundred, bekase that's nun ove 'em fas' enuf tu ketch me, nither is thar hosses by the livin jingo! Say, George, much talk 'bout this fuss up whar you're been?" For the sake of a joke I said yes, a great deal.

"Jis es I'spected, durn 'em all git drunk, an' skeer thar fool sefs ni ontu deth, an' then lay hit ontu me, a poor innersent youf, an' es soun' a belever es they is. Lit, lite, ole feller an' let that roan ove yourn blow a litil, an' I'll 'splain this cussed misfortnit affar: hit hes ruinated by karacter es a pius pusson in the s'ciety roun' yeye,m an' is a spreadin faster nur meazils. When ever yu hear eny on 'em a spreadin hit, gin hit the dam lie squar, will yu? I haint dun nuffin tu one ove 'em. Hits true, I did sorter frustrate a few lizards a littil, but they haint members, es I knows on.

"You see, las' year I went tu the big meetin at Rattlesnake Springs, an' wer a sittin in a nice shady place convarsin wif a frien' ove mine, intu the huckil berry thickit, jis' duin nuffin tu nobody an' makin no fuss, when I hed been knocked inter by a four year old hickory-stick, hilt in the paw ov ole Passun Buillin, durn his alligater hide; an' he were stndin an striddil ove me, a foamin at the mouf, a-chompin his teeth -- gesterin wif the hickory club -- an' a-preachin tu me so you cud a-hearn him a mile, about a sartin sin gineraly, an' my wickedness pussonely; an' mensunin the name ove my frien' loud enuf tu be hearn tu the meetin' ouse. My poor inntersent frien' were jun gone and' I wer glad ove hit, fur I tho't he ment tu kill me rite what I lay, an' I didn't want her tu see me die."

"Who was she, the friend you speak of Sut?" Sut opened his eyes wide.

"Hu the devil, an durnashun tole *yu* that hit wer a she?"

"Why, you did Sut" -- --

"I *didn't*, durn ef I did. Ole Bullin dun hit, an' I'll hev tu kill him yet, the cussed, infernel ole talebarer!" -- --

"Well, well, Sut who was she?"

"Nun ove y-u-r-e b-i-s-n-i-s-s, durn yure littil ankshus picter! I *sees yu* lickin ove yure lips. I *will* tell you one thing, George; that night, a neighbor gal got a all fired, overhandid stroppin frum her man, wif a stirrup leather, an' ole Passun Bullin, hed et supper thar, an' what's wus nur all, that poor, innersent, skeer'd gal hed dun her levil bes' a cookin hit fur 'im. She begged him, a trimblin, an' a-cryin not tu tell on her. He et her cookin, he promised her he'd keep dark -- and' then went strait an' tole her man. Warnt that rale low down, wolf mean? The durnd infunel, hiperkritical, pot-bellied, scaley-hided, whisky-wastin, stinkin ole groun'-hog. He'd a heap better a stole sum *man's* hoss; I'd a tho't more ove 'im. But I paid him plum up fur hit, an' I means tu keep a payin him, ontil one ur tuther, ove our toes pints up tu the roots ove the grass."

"Well, yere's the way I lifted that note ove han'. At the nex big meetin at Rattilsnaik -- las' week hit wer -- I wer on han' es solemn es a ole hat kivver on collection day. I hed my face draw'd out intu the shape an' perporshun ove a tayler's sleeve-board, pint down. I hed put on the convicted sinner so pufeckly that an' ole obsarvin she pillar ove the church sed tu a ole he piller, es I walked up to my bainch:

"'Law sakes alive, ef that ain't that *orful* sinner, Sut Lovingood, pearced plum thru; hu's nex?'

"Yu see, by golly, George, I *hed* tu promis the ole tub ove soap-greas tu cum an' hev myself converted, jis' tu keep him frum killin me. An' es I know'd hit wudn't interfare wif the relashun I bore tu the still housis roun' thar, I didn't keer a durn. I jis' wanted tu git *ni* ole Bullin, onst onsuspected, an' this wer the bes' way tu du hit. I tuk a seat on the side steps ove the pulpit, an' kivvered es much ove my straitch'd face es I could wif my han's, tu prove I wer in yearnis. Hit tuck powerful -- fur I hearn a sorter thankful kine ove buzzin all over the congregashun. Ole Bullin hissef looked down at me, over his ole copper specks, an' hit sed jis' es plain es a look cud say hit:"Yu am thar, ar you -- durn yu, hits well fur yu that yu cum,' I tho't hit wud a been well fur *yu*, ef I hadent a-cum, but I didn't say hit jus then. Thar wer a monstrus crwod in that grove, fur the weather wer fine, an' b'levers wer plenty roun' about Rattilsnaik Springs. Ole Bullin gin out, an' they sung that hyme, yu know:

"Thar will be mournin, mournin yere, an' mournin that,
On that dredful day tu cum."

"Thinks I, ole hoss, kin hit be possibil enybody hes tole yu what's a gwine tu happin; an' then I tho't that nobody know'd hit but me, and I were cumforted. He next tuck hisself a tex pow'fly mixed wif brimstone, an' trim'd wif blue flames, an' then he open'd. He cummenced ontu the sinners; he threaten'd 'em orful, tried tu skeer 'em wif all the wust varmints he cud think ove, an' arter a while he got ontu the idear ove Hell-sarpints, and he dwelt on it sum. He tole 'em how the ole Hell-sarpints wud sarve em if they didn't repent; how cold they'd crawl over thar nakid bodys, an' how like ontu pitch they'd stick tu 'em as they crawled; how they'd rap thar tails roun' that buzzims, an' how tite they tied 'em, an' how sum ove the oldes' an' wus ones wud crawl up thar laigs, an' travil *onder* thar garters, no odds how tight they tied *them*, an' when the two armys ove Hell-sarpents met, then -- -- That las' remark *fotch* 'em. Ove all the screamin, an' hollerin, an' loud cryin, I ever hearn, begun all at onst, all over the hole groun' jus' es he hollered out that word 'then.' He kep on a bellerin,but I got so busy jis' then, that I didn't listen tu him much, fur I saw that my time fur ackshun hed cum. Now yu see, George, I'd cotch seven ur eight big pot-bellied lizzards, an' hed 'em in a littil narrer bag, wha I had made a-purpus. Thar tails all at the bottim, an' so crwodid fur room that they cudent turn roun'. So when he wer a-razvin ontu his tip-toes, an' a-poundin the pulpit wif his fis' -- onbenowenst tu enybody, I ontied my bag ov reptiles, put the mouf ove hit onder the bottim ove his britches-laig, an' sot intu pinchin thar tails. Quick es gunpowder they all tuck up his ba laig, makin a nise like squirrils a-climbin a shell-bark hickory. He stop'd preachin' rite in the middil ove the word 'damnation' an' looked fur a moment like he wer a listenin fur sumthin -- sorter like a ole sow dus, when she hears yu a whistlin' fur the dorgs. The tarifick shape ove his feeters stopp't the shoutin an' screamin; instuntly yu cud hearn a cricket chirp. I gin a long groan, an' hilt my head a-twixt my knees. He gin hisself sum orful open-handed slaps wif fust one han' an' then tuther, about the place whar yu cut the bes' steak outen a beef. Then he'd fetch a vigrus ruff rub whar a hosses tail sprouts; then he'd stomp one foot, then tuther, then bof at onst. Then he run his han' atween his waisbun an' his shut an' reach'd way down, an' roun' wif hit; then he spread his big laigs, an' in his back a good rattlin rub agin the pulpit, like a hog scratches hisself agin a stump, leanin tu hit pow'ful, an' twitchin, an' squirmin all over, es ef he'd slept in a dorg bed, ur ontu a pisant hill. About this time, one ove my lizzards scared an' hurt by all this poundin' an' feelin, an' scratchin, popp'd out his head frum the passun's shut collar, an' his ole brown naik, an' wer a-surveyin the crowd, when ole Bullin struck at 'im jus' too late, fur he'd dodged back agin. The hell desarvin ole raskil's speech now cum tu 'im, an' sez he, 'Pray fur me brethren an' sistern, fur I is a-rastilin wif the great inimy rite now!' an' his voice were the mos' pitiful, trimblin thing I ever hearn. Sum ove the wimmen fotch a painter yell, an' a young docter, wif ramrod laigs, lean'd toward me monstrus knowin like, an' sez he, 'Clar case ove Delishus Tremenjus.' I nodded my head an' sez I, 'Yas, spechuly the tremenjus part, an' Ise feard hit haint at hits worst.' Ole Bullin's eyes wer a-stickin out like ontu two buckeyes flung agin a mud wall, an' he wer a-cuttin up more shines nor a cockroach in a hot skillet. Off went the clawhammer coat, an' he flug hit ahine 'im like he wer a-gwine intu a fight; he hed no jackid tu take off, so he unbuttoned his galluses, an' vigrusly flung the ainds back over his head. He fotch his shut over-handed a durnd site faster nor I got outen my pasted one, an' then flug hit strait up in theair, like he jis' wanted hit tu keep on up furever; but hit lodged ontu a black-jack, an' I seed one ove my lizzards wif his tail up, a-racin about all over the ole ditty shut, skared too bad tu jump. Then he gin a sorter shake, an' a stompin kine ove twis', an' he cum outer his britches. He tuck 'em by the bottim ove the laigs, an' swung 'em roun' his head a time ur two, an' then fotch 'em down cherall-up over the frunt ove the pulpit. You cud a hearn the smash a quarter ove a mile! Ni ontu fifteeen shorten'd biskits, a boiled chicken, wif hits laigs crossed, a big dubbil-bladed knife, a hunk ove terbacker, a cob-pipe, sum copper ore, lots ove broken glass, a cork, a sprinkil ove whisky, a squirt, an' three lizzards flew permiskusly all over that meetin-groun', outen the upper aind ove them big flax britches. One ove the smartes' ove my lizzards lit lit head-fust intu the buzzim ove a fat 'oman, es big es a skin'd hoss, an' ni ontu es ugly, who sot thuty yards off, a fannin herself wif a tucky-tail. Smart tu the las' by golly, he imejuntly commenced runnin down the centre ove her breas'-bone, an' kep on, I speck. She wer jis' boun' tu faint; an' she did hit fust rate -- flung the tucky-tail up in the air, grabbed the lap ove her gown, gin hit a big histin an' fallin shake, rolled down the hill, tangled her laigs an' garters in the top ove a huckilberry bush, wife her head in the branch an' jis' lay still. She were interstin, she wer, ontil a serious-lookin, pale-faced 'oman hung a nankeen ridin skirt over the huckilberry bush. That wer all that wer dun to'ards bringin her too, that I seed. Now ole Bullin hed nuffin left ontu 'im but a par ove heavy, low quarter'd shoes, short wollen socks, an' eel-skin garters tu keep off the cramp. He skeer hed druv him plum crazy, tur he elt roun' in the air, abuv his head, like he wer huntin sumthin in the dark, an' he beller'd out, 'Brethren, brethren, take keer ove yerselves, the Hell-saprints *hes got me!*' When this cum out, yu cud a-hearn the screams tu Halifax. He jis' spit in his han's, an' loped over frunt ove the pulpid *kerdiff!* He lit on top ove, an' rite amung the mos' pius part ove the congregashun. Ole Misses Chaneyberry sot wif her back tu the pulpit, sorter stoopin forrid. He lit a-stradil ove her long naik, a shuttin her up wif a snap, her head atwixt her knees, like shuttin up a jack-knive, an' he sot intu gittin away his levil durndest; he went in a heavy lumberin gallop, like a ole fat waggon hoss, skared at a locomotive. When he jumpt a bainch he shook the yeath. The bonnets, an' fans clar'd the way an' jerked most ove the children wif em, an' the rest he scrunched. He open'd a purfeckly clar track tu the woods, ove every livin thing. He weighed ni ontu three hundred, hed a black stripe down his back, like ontu a ole bridil rein, an' his belly were 'bout the size, an' color ove a beef paunch, an' hit a-swingin out frum side tu side; he leand back frum hit, like a littil feller a-totin a big drum, at a muster, an' I hearn hit plum tu whar I wer. Thar wer cramp-knots on his laigs es big es walnuts, an' mottled splotches on his shins; an' takin him all over, he minded ove a durnd crazy ole elephant, pussessed ove the devil, rared up on hits hind aind, an' jis' *gittin* frum sum imijut danger ur tribulashun. He did the loudest, an' skariest, an' fussiest runnin I ever seed, tu be no faster nur hit wer, since dad tried tu outrun the ho'nets.

"Well, he disapear'd in the thicket jis' bustin -- an' ove all the noises yu ever hearn, wer made thar on that camp groun': sum wimen screamin -- they wer the skeery ones; sum larfin -- they wer the wicked ones; sum cryin -- they wer the fool ones (sorter my stripe yu known); sum trying tu git away wif thar faces red -- they wer the modest ones; sum lookin arter ole Bullin -- they wer the curious ones; sum hangin clost tu thar sweethearts -- they wer the sweet ones; sum on thar knees wif thar eyes shot, but facin the way the ole mud turtil wer a-runnin -- they wer the 'saitful ones; sum duin nuthin -- they wer the waitin ones; an' the mos' dangerus ove all ove em by a durned site.

"I tuck a big skeer myself arter a few rocks, an' sich like fruit, spattered ontu the pulpit ni ontu my head; an' es the Lovingoods, durn em! knows nuffin but tu run, when they gits skeerd, I jis' out fur the swamp on the krick. As I started, a black bottil ove bald-face smashed agin a tree furninst me, after missin the top ove my head 'bout a inch. Sum durn'd fool professor dun this, who hed more zeal nor sence; fur I say that eny man who wud waste a quart ove even mean sperrits, fur the chance ove knockin a poor ornary devil like me down wif the bottil, is a bigger fool nor ole Squire Mackmullen, an' he tried tu shoot hissef wif a onloaded hoe-handle."

"Did they catch you Sut?"

"Ole Barebelly Bullin, es they calls 'im now, never preached ontil yesterday, an' he hadn't the fust durn'd 'oman tu hear 'im; *they hev seed to much ove 'im*. Passuns ginerly hev a pow'ful strong holt on wimen; but, hoss, I tell yu thar ain't meny ove em kin run stark nakid over an' thru a crowd ove three hundred wimen an' not injure thar karacters *sum*. Enyhow, hits a kind ove show they'd ruther see one at a time, an' pick the passun at that. His tex' wer, 'Nakid I cum intu the world, an' nakid I'm a gwine outen hit, ef I'm spard ontil then.' He sed nakidness warnt much ove a sin, purtickerly ove dark nights. That he wer a weak, frail wum ove the dus' an' a heap more sich truck. Then he totch ontu me; sed I wer a livin proof ove the hell-desravin nater ove man, an' that thar warnt grace enuf in the whole 'sociation tu saften my outside rind; that I wer 'a lost ball' forthy years afore I wer born'd, an' the bes' thing they cud du fur the church, wer tu turn out, an' still hunt fur me ontil I wer shot. An' he never said Hell-sarpints onst in the hole preach. I b'leve, George, the durnd fools am at hit.

"Now, I wants yu tu tell ole Barbelly this fur me, ef he'll let me an' Sall alone, I'll let him alone -- a-while; an' ef he don't, ef I don't lizzard him agin, I jis' wish I may be dod durnd! *Skeer him if yu ken*.

"Let's go tu the spring an' take a ho'n.

"Say George, didn't that ar Hell-sarpint sermon ove his'n hev sumthin like a Hell-sarpint aplicashun? -- Hit looks sorter so tu me."

*Bald-face. The same as "Redeye"; new, raw whiskey.

From "Sut Lovingood Yarns Spun By a 'Nat'ral Born Durn'd Fool: Warped and Wove for Public Wear'" by George W. Harris.
Dick & Fitzgerald, 1867. New York

✳ ✳ ✳ ✳ ✳

Back in the late 1800s, the Rev. Moody offered to address the congregation of a friend, but the friend said that wouldn't do because too many members got up and left before or during the sermon. "Don't worry about that," Rev. Moody said. So he spoke to his friend's congregation.

"My friends," said Rev. Moody, "I am going to speak to two sorts of folks today -- saints and sinners. Sinners! I am going to give you your portion first, and would have you give good attention."

When he preached to them as long as he thought best, he paused and said, "There, sinners, I have done with you now; you may take your hats and go out of the meetinghouse as soon as you please." But all tarried and heard him through!

Josh Billings (Henry Wheeler Shaw, 1818-1885) was the last century's most famous, beloved humorist. Friend of mankind, wise and shrewd, his hometown newspaper best described him:

Josh used phonetic spelling to put his humor across -- his readers thought it hilarious. Modern readers need to work at this form of spelling, but once one is accustomed to it, it is great fun.

"In his quaint way, he preached the Ten Commandments; held up the follies of life that men might abandon them and lived wisdom; gave advice marvelously sugar-coated with refined humor; scattered all over the world profound truths in two-line pearly paragraphs. He has done his day and generation good."

Abraham Lincoln loved his humor and considered Josh Billings the wisest man since Shakespeare.

✳ ✳ ✳ ✳ ✳

When a man cums tew the konklusion that he would like tew kill sumboddy at thirty paces, he imagines that he haz bin wronged, and sends hiz best friend a challenge tew fite a dewell; tha meet, and an elegant murder iz committed; the cracks, in this transaktion are puttyed up, and then varnished over, bi being kalled, *"an affair ov honnor."* When a man robs a savings bank, or goes tew urope on the last steamer, with the stolen recipts ov a sanitary kommittee in his pocket, a kommittee ov investigashun are got together tew examine the stait ov affairs and unanimously report *"a diskrepancy in hiz akounts."* 2 ung men hire a hoss and buggy at a livri stable, and go into the kuntry on Sunday. Tha stop at the fust tavern tha meet, and invest in sum ardent speerits. They stop agin pretty soon, and histe in sum more ardent speerts. The more tha histe in, the more tha drive, till bi and bi a devilish bridge tips them over into a devilish gutter that sumboddy haz left bi the side ov the road, and tha are awl killed, including the hoss and buggy. This is kalled a *"Fatal acksident."* A man and hiz wife are living in the middle ov joy and consolashun, tha are surrounded on awl sides bi a yung and interesting familee, their bread iz cut thin, and buttered on both sides and the edges, but the destroyer enters the family, the wife wants a nu silk gown, the man sez he "be d----d if she duz," and she"be d----d if she dont." One word brings on another, till tha fite, both ov them lose awl the hair on their heds, and 2 full sets ov false teeth, the things ends in a divorse, the man runs awa tew Australia bi the overland route, the woman marry's a cirkus rider at 40 Dollars a month, the children are adopted bi sum sunda school, and are brought up on homopathy. This furnishes a collum and a half in the nusepaper, under the hed ov *"Disturbanse ov the marrid relation."* A youth ov 21 summer begins life with 36 thousand dollars. Sevral fast hosses belong tew him, there iz sevral fast wimmin that he belongs tew, awl the tavern keepers are hiz patrons, faro banks are bilt for hiz amuzement, consolidated lotterys are charted on purpiss tew make him happee; nothing iz left undun tew make him feel good. He wakes up about the 25th ov May, without a dollar in his pocket, and a host ov warm friends on hiz hands, without enny visible means ov supporting them. He takes an akount ov stock, he buys a pint ov rum and 4 yards ov bed kord, the one makes him limber, while the other makes him stiff. The putty and varnish in this kase iz, *"Druiven tew desperashun on akount of finanshul preshure."* A rale rode trane stands snorting in front ov the depoe, the last bel iz ringing, the kars are full ov souls that belong tew different incividuals, the konducktor iz full ov Bourbon, that belongs tew the devil, the engineer labors under an attack ov Jamaka for the broketis, the switchmen likes a a leetle good old rey, the kars diskount 45 miles a hour, 2 trains tri tew pass each other on the same track; it kan be did suckcessfully; the mangled and ded are kounted bi skores, a searching investigashun takes plase, the community iz satizfied, bekause it waz, *"an unavoidable katastrophe."* The Devil furnishes putty and varnish, free ov expense, tew hide the frauds and guilt ov men. Aul ov which iz respecfully committed Bi

Josh Billings.

* * * * *

I never knu, in all mi life,
    Enny man tew go crazy
Who alwuss took things setting down,
    And cultivated hiz lazy.

Josh Billings

* * * * *

A TRUE FISH STORY FOUNDED ON FAK

In a little town awa out wes whar i used tew liv, thare wast two elders resided. One ov them wast a Babtiss, Gaffit bi name, and the other wast a Methodis, Sturgiss bi name, and both ov them wast as good fellers as ever sarved the Lord. As good luk wud hav it tha both had a revival ov religion in their floks at the same time. Gaffit was a cunning critter, besides being harmless as the duv. Thare was but one pond in the town, and that was used for babtizing by agreement, on wensday ov each week, bi Gaffit, and on saturday bi Sturgiss. One wensday, as Gaffit was engaged in marking his sheep, or in uther wurds, was bi the side ov the little pond ov water administering the rite ov babtism tew a goodla number, whom he had coazed awa from the wiles ov the devil, Sturgiss looked in upon the happy scene, with eys brimful ov luv. Amung the menny who war waiting tew be babtized, Sturgiss diskovered sevral whom he had convikted, and whom he expected tew add tew his flok on the cumming saturda. The next da the two elders met, Sturgiss charged Gaffit with the pious fraud he had detekted bi the side ov the little pond. Gaffit's eyes puckered with delite, ad he listened tew the charge, then seezin the methodis elder bi the hand with an extra pucker in his eye, whispered: "Brother Sturgiss, mi father larnt me when i was but a little fisher-boy, tew string mi fish as fast as i ketched 'em."

Thiz iz good advise. I don't kno who waz auther ov it, if I did, i wud go for rewarding him, either with a sett ov plated ware, or a prize in the art union. No man kould giv better advise, or consolashun; he ought tew have a 2 story monament, when he dize, with an epitaff on it, founded on fack; he ought tew hav at leaste fifteen hundred little children named after him each year; he ought tew be nussed in men's memorys like a plesant dreme, that afterwards turned out tew be true. He ought to have his fotograph taken bi evry new sky-lite in the land, he ought tew be sett tew musick, and be sung in conneckshun with the docksaloger; he ought tew be stereotyped so that nu edishuns could constantly be worked oph tew meet the pressing demand.

"Giv the Devil hiz due." Yung man, this advise was got up for yu. If yu owe the Devil ennything pay him off at onse, and then discharge him, and don't hire him over agin at enny prise. That's what the author ment. Be honest, pay even the devil, if yu owe him, bu dont owe him agin. If the proprietor ov this most worthy proverb, "Giv the devil hiz due," still lives, altho i haint had the pleasure ov n introducksion tew him, if he ever wants enny thing, *even good advise,* he kan git it in awl natiff purity and innersense, bi dropping a line tu his everlasting well wisher.

Josh Billings.

✳ ✳ ✳ ✳ ✳

The infidel argys just as a
Bull duz chained to a
post, he bellows, and paws,
but he don't git loose from
the post i notiss.--
 ---ot mutch, Josh Billings

* * * * *

Alfred Henry Lewis (1857-1914) was a lawyer who rose to be City Prosecuting Attorney of Columbus, Ohio, where he was born. He quit the profession, the town, and wandered west to be a cowboy and saddle-bum in Kansas. Then he moved to the Texas panhandle and on to Nevada, ending up in Arizona. After his cowboy years, he finally got into the newspaper business and ended his life as chief of the Hearst newspaper chain's Washington office.

His great contributions are the books of cowboy life that he wrote with Arizona as the locale. His mythical town, Wolfville, is really Tombstone and his language, situations, humor -- in short his picture of frontier life -- is unrivaled and wonderfully accurate. In his stories, one learns the truth about our frontier, when the west was wild and woolly.

Wolfville's First Funeral.

"These yere obsequies which I'm about mentionin'," observed the Old Cattleman, "is the first real funeral Wolfville has."

The old fellow had lighted a cob pipe and tilted his chair back in a fashion which proclaimed a plan to be comfortable. He had begun to tolerate -- even encourage -- my society, although it was clear that as a tenderfoot he regarded me with a species of gentle disdain.

I had provoked the subject of funeral ceremonies by a recurrence to the affair of the Yellowhouse Man, and a query as to what would have been the programme of the public-spirited hamlet of Wolfville if that invalid had died instead of yielding to the nursing of Jack Moore and that tariff on draw-poker which the genius of Old Man Enright decreed.

It came in easy illustration, as answer to my question, for the Old Cattleman to recall the funeral of a former leading spirit of Southwestern society. The name of this worthy was Jack King; and with a brief exposition of his more salient traits, my grizzled *raconteur* led down to his burial with the remark before quoted.

"Of course," continued the Old Cattleman, "of course while thar's some like this Yaller-house gent who survives; thar's others of the boys who is downed one time an' another, an' goes shoutin' home to heaven by various trails. But ontil the event I now recalls, the remainders has been freighted east or west every time, an' the camp gets left. It's hard luck, but at last it comes toward us; an' thar we be one day with a corpse all our'n, an' no partnership with nobody nor nothin'.

"'It's the chance of our life,' says Doc Peets, 'an' we plays it. Thar's nothin' too rich for our blood, an' these obsequies is goin' to be spread-eagle, you bet! We'll show Red Dog an' sim'lar villages they ain't sign-camps compared with Wolfville.'

"So we begins to draw in our belts an' get a big ready. Jack King, as I says before, is corpse, emergin' outen a game of poker as sech. Which prior tharto, Jack's been peevish, an' pesterin' an' pervadin' 'round for several days. The camp stands a heap o' trouble with him an' tries to smooth it along by givin' him his whiskey an' his way about as he wants 'em, hopin' for a change. But man is only human, an' when Jack starts in one night to make a flush beat a tray full for seven hundred dollars, he asks too much.

"Thar ain't no ondertakers, so we rounds up the outfit, an' known' he'd take a pride in it, an' do the slam-up thing, we puts in Doc Peets to deal the game unanimous.

"'Gents,' he says, as we-all turns into the Red Light to be refreshed, ''in assoomin' the present pressure I feels the compliments paid me in the seelection. I shall act for the credit of the camp, an' needs your he'p. I desires that these rites be a howlin' vict'ry. I don't want people comin' 'round next week allowin' thar ain't been no funeral, an' I don't reckon much that they will. We've got the corpse, an' if we gets bucked off now it's our fault.'

"So he app'ints Old Monte an' Dan Boggs to go for a box for Jack, an' details a couple of blacks from the corral to dig a tomb.

"'An' mind you-alls,' says Peets, 'I wants that hole at least a mile from camp. In order to make a funeral a success, you needs distance. That's where deceased gets action. It gives the procession a chance to spread an' show up. You can't make no funeral imposin' except you're plumb liberal on distances.'

"It all goes smooth right off the reel. We gets a box an' grave ready, an' Peets sticks up a notice on the stage-station door, settin' the excitement for third-drink time next day. Prompt at the drop of the hat the camp lets go all holds an' turns loose in a body to put Jack through right. He's laid out in splendid shape in the New York Store, with nothin' to complain of if he's asked to make the kick himse'f. He has a new silk necktie, blue shirt an' pearl buttons, trousers, an' boots. Some one -- Benson Annie, I reckons -- has pasted some co't plastern over the hole on his cheek-bone where the bullet gets in, an' all 'round Jack looks better than I ever sees him.

"'Let the congregation remove its hats,' says Peets, a-settin' down on a box up at Jack's head, 'an' as many as can will please get somethin' to camp on. Now, my friends,' he continues, 'thar ain't no need of my puttin' on any frills or gettin' in any scroll work. The objects of this convention is plain an' straight. Mister King, here present, is dead. Deceased is a very headstrong person, an' persists yesterday in entertainin' views touchin' a club flush, queen at the head, which results in life everlastin'. Now, gents this is a racket full of solemnity. We wants nothin' but good words. Don't mind about the trooth; which the same ain't in play at a funeral, nowhow. We all knows Jack; we knows his record. Our information is ample that a-way; how he steals a hoss at Tucson; how he downs a party at Cruces; how that scar on his neck gets from Wells-Fargo's people when he stands up the stage over on the Lordsburgh trail. But we lays it all aside to-day. We don't copper nary bet. Yesterday mornin', accompanied by the report of a Colt's forty-five, Mister King, who lies yere so cool an' easy, leaves us to enter in behind the great white shinin' gates of pearl an' gold, which swings inward to glory eternal. It's a great set back at this time thar ain't no sky-pilot in the camp. This deeficiency in sky-pilots is a hoss onto us, but we does our best. At a time like this I hears that singin' is a good, safe break, an' I tharfore calls on that little girl from Flagstaff to vive us "The Dyin' Ranger."'

"So the little Flagstaff girl cl'ars her valves with a drink, an' gives us the song; an' when the entire congregation draws kyards on the last verse it does everybody good.

'"Far away from his dear old Texas.
        We laid him down to rest;
    With his saddle for a pillow,
        And his gun across his breast.'

"Then Peets gets out the Scriptures. 'I'm goin' to read a chapter outen these yere Testaments,' he says. 'I ain't makin' no claim for it, except it's part of the game an' accordin' to Hoyle. If thar's a preacher yere he'd do it, but bein' thar's no sech brand on tis range I makes it as a forced play myse'f.'

"So he reads us a chapter about the sepulcher, an' Mary Magdalene, an' the resurrection; an' everybody takes it in profound as prairie-dogs, for that's the leas to make, an' we knows it.

"Then Peets allows he'd like to hear from any gent onder the head of 'good of the order.'

"'Mister Ondertaker an' Chairman,' says Jim Hamilton, 'I yields to an inward impulse to say that this yere play weighs on me plumb heavy. As keeper of the dance-hall I sees a heap of the corpse an' knows him well. Mister King is my friend, an' while he's hoverin' near, I loves him. He has his weaknesses, as do we all. A disp'sition to make new rooles as he plays along for sech games of chance as enjoys his notice is perhaps his greatest failin. His givin' way to this habit is primar'ly the cause of his bein' garnered in. I hopes he'll get along thar, an' offers a side bet, even money, up to five hundred dollars, he will. He may alter his system an' stand way up with the angels an' seraphs, an' if words from me could fix it, I'd shorely stack 'em in. I would say further that after consultin' with Billy Burns, who keeps the Red Light, we has, in honor of the dead an' to mark the occasion of his cashin' in, agreed upon a business departure of interest to all. This departure Mister Burns will state. I mournfully gives way to him for said purpose.'

"'Mister Peets, an' ladies an' gents,' says Burns, 'like Mister Hamilton, who I'm proud to meet yere as gent, citizen, an' friend, I knows deceased. He's a good man, an' a dead-game sport from 'way back. A protracted wrastle with the remorseless drinks of the frontier had begun to tell on him, an' for a year or so he's been liable to have spells. Referrin' to the remarks of Mister Hamilton, I states that by agreement between us an' in honor to departed, the quotations on whiskey in this yere camp, from now on, will be two drinks for two bits, instead of one as previous. We don't want to onsettle trade, an' we don't believe this will. We makes it as a ray of light in the darkness an' gloom of the hour.'

"After this yere utterance, which is well received, we forms the procession. Doc Peets, with two buglers from the Fort, takes the lead, with Jack an' his box in one of the stage coaches comin' next. Enright, Tutt, Boggs, Short Creek Dave, Texas Thompson, an' me, bein' the six pall-bearers, is on hosses next in line; an' Jack Moore commandin' of the rest of the outfit, lines out permiscus.

"'This is a great day for Wolfville,' says Peets, as he rides up an' down the line. 'Thar auin't no camp this side of St. Looey could turn this trick. Which I only wishes Jack could see it himse'f. It's more calculated to bring this outfit into fav'rable notice than a lynchin'.'

"At the grave we turns in an' gives three cheers for King, an' three for Doc Peets; an' last we gives three more an' a tier for the camp. The buglers cut loose everythin' they knows, from the 'water-call' to the 'retreat,' an' while the blacks is a-shovelin' in the sand we bangs away with our six-shooters for general results delightful. You can gamble thar ain't been no funeral like it before or since.

"At the last Peets hauls outen the stage we uses for Jack, a headboard. When it's set up it looks like if Jack ain't satisfied, he's shorely hard to suit. On it in big letters is:

> ## JaCK KInG
> LIfE AiN'T
> IN
> HOLDiNG A GooD HAND
> BUT
> In pLAyiNG a PoRE HANd
> WeLL.

"'You sees, we has to work in a little sentiment,' says Doc Peets.
"Then we details the blacks to stand watch-an'-watch every night till further orders. No; we ain't afraid Jack'll get out none, but the coyotes is shore due to come an' dig for him, so the blacks has to stand gyard. We don't allow to find spec'mens of Jack spread 'round loose after all the trouble we takes."

From the "Cowboy Humor of Alfred Henry Lewis," R. D. Myers, editor. 1988. Lincoln-Herndon Press, Springfield, Illinois.

✳ ✳ ✳ ✳ ✳

There ain't no better way to fight old age than by actin' like you ain't.

✳ ✳ ✳ ✳ ✳

GLORIOUS MOMENT
I am twenty-five cents.
I am not on speaking terms with the butcher.
I am too small to buy a quart of ice-cream.
I am not large enough to purchase a box of candy.
I am too small to buy a ticket to a movie.
I am hardly fit for a tip but -- believe me, when I got to church on Sunday, I am considered some money!

Christian Evangelist. 1930

HOT STUFF
by
FAMOUS FUNNY MEN
Melville D. Landon, A.M.
The Reilly & Britton Co., Chicago, IL 1883

The Original Collection Story.

Eli Perkins.

I'll tell an old story, which I wrote out once to illustrate my Uncle Consider's piety in time of danger. The newspapers got hold of it and it is now going the rounds, but it is my story and I'm going to tell it now.

One day Uncle Consider and I were sailing up the Sound in a yacht. As we passed Rye beach there arose a great storm. The waves blew a hurricane, and the wind rolled mountain high. We all rushed frantically about from the main top gib to the low hen-coop -- but everywhere death stared us in the face.

In utter despair I said, "pray, dear Uncle, pray!" but he said he couldn't.

Sez I, "Uncle Consider" -- sez I, "Uncle -- if you can't pray please do something religious."

"I will Eli!" he said, wildly, ketchin' hold of hisself -- and what do you think he did?

Why he took up a collection!

❊ ❊ ❊ ❊ ❊

"May I leave a few tracts?" asked a medical missionary of a lady who responded to his knock.

"Leave some tracks? Certainly you may," said she, looking at him most benignly over her specs. "Leave them with the heels towards the house, if you please."

❊ ❊ ❊ ❊ ❊

Two little girls were comparing progress in catechism study:
"I've got to original sin," said one. "How far have you got?"
"Me? Oh, I'm way beyond redemption," said the other.

❊ ❊ ❊ ❊ ❊

"Man," said the clergyman, "is the first animal in creation; he springs up like sparrow-grass, hops about like a hopper-grass, and dies just like a jack-ass!"

235

On the Wrong Road to Heaven

"Where are you going?" said a young gentleman to an elderly one in a white cravat, whom he overtook a few miles from Little Rock.

"I am going to heaven, my son. I have been on the way eighteen years."

"We, good-bye, old fellow; if you have been traveling towards heaven eighteen years, and got no nearer to it than Arkansas, I'll take another route. Why, you are traveling right away from it."

* * * * *

A Baptist and Congregational minister were riding together one day, when there was a strong manifestation of a coming shower. The former suggested to the latter, who was driving, that he had better quicken the speed of the horse. The Congregationalist replied:

"Why, brother? Are you afraid of *water*?"

"Oh, no!" said the Baptist; "I am not afraid of water; it's the *sprinkling* I wish to avoid."

* * * * *

Disliked New Acquaintances.

A Jerseyman was very sick and not expected to recover.
His friends got around the bed, and one of them said:
"John, do you feel willing to die?"
John made an effort to give his views on the subject, and answered with a feeble voice, "I think I'd rather stay here in Newark where I am better acquainted."

* * * * *

Thare may cum a time, when the lion, and the lam will lie down together, -- i shall be az glad to see it az enny boddy. -- but i am still betting on the lion.

Josh Billings

* * * * *

And here are a few jokes from *"Books of Anecdotes and Jokers Knapsack,"* a best seller back in 1866, a year after the end of our Civil War.

AN AGREEABLE DISAPPOINTMENT.

Mr. Lincoln, as the highest public officer of the nation, was necessarily very much bored by all sorts of people calling upon him.

An officer of the government called one day at the White House, and introduced a clerical friend. "Mr. President," said he, "allow to present to you my friend, the Rev. Mr. F., of _____. Mr. F. has expressed a desire to see you and have some conversation with you, and I am happy to be the means of introducing him."

The President shook hands with Mr. F., and desiring him to be seated, took a seat himself. Then -- his countenance having assumed an expression of patient waiting -- he said: "I am now ready to hear what you have to say." "Oh, bless you, sir," said Mr. F., "I have nothing especially to say. I merely called to pay my respects to you, and, as one of the million, to assure you of my hearty sympathy and support."

"My dear sir," said the President, rising promptly -- his face showing instant relief, and with both hands grasping that of his visitor -- "I am veery glad to see you; I am very glad to see you, indeed. I thought you had come to preach to me."

✳ ✳ ✳ ✳ ✳

I sometimes think that God, in creating man, over-estimated His ability.
Oscar Wilde

✳ ✳ ✳ ✳ ✳

THE OLD WOMAN'S SENTIMENTS
A squad of Indiana volunteers, out scouting, came across a female in a log cabin in the mountains. After the usual salutations, one of them asked her --

"Well, old lady, are you a secesh[1]?"

"No," was the answer.

"Are you Union?"

"No."

"What are you, then?"

"A Baptist, an' always have been." The Hoosiers let down.

1. Secessionist -- a Confederacy sympathizer.

✳ ✳ ✳ ✳ ✳

GENTLEMEN AND THEIR DEBTS
The late Rev. Dr. Sutton, Vicar of Sheffield, once said to the late Mr. Peach, a veterinary surgeon, "Mr. Peach, how is it you have not called upon me for your account?"

"Oh," said Mr. Peach, "I never ask a gentleman for money."

"Indeed!" said the Vicar, "then how do you get on if he don't pay?"

"Why," replied Mr. Peach, "After a certain time I conclude that he is not a gentleman, and then I ask him."

A CHRISTIAN PRECEPT

A physician seeing old Bannister about to drink a glass of brandy, said, "Don't drink that poisonous stuff! Brandy is the worst enemy you have." "I know that," answered Charles, "but we are commanded *to love our enemies.*"

✳ ✳ ✳ ✳ ✳

IMPRESSIVE DISCOURSE

It is stated that the Rev. George Trask, of Pittsburgh, lectured so powerfully in Wesbster, a few days ago, against the use of tobacco, that several of his audience went home and burned their cigars -- holding one end of them in their mouths.

✳ ✳ ✳ ✳ ✳

Experience is a good teacher, but she sends in terrific bills.
Minna Antrim, 1861

✳ ✳ ✳ ✳ ✳

GOOD PRAYER

A witty lawyer once jocosely asked a boarding-house keeper the following question:

"Mr. _____, if a man gives you five hundred dollars to keep for him, and he dies, what do you do? Do you pray for him?"

"No, sir," replied _____, "I pray for another like him."

✳ ✳ ✳ ✳ ✳

If yu trade horses with a jockey yu kant git cheated but once -- but if yu trade with a deakon, yu may git cheated twice, -- once in the horse and once in the deakon.
Josh Billings

✳ ✳ ✳ ✳ ✳

A SUFFICIENT REASON

There was once a clergyman in New Hampshire, noted for his long sermons and indolent habits. "How is it," said a man to his neighbour, "Parson _____, the laziest man living, writes these interminable sermons?" "Why," said the other, "he probably gets to writing and he is too lazy to stop."

There has been a lot of controversy as to who actually wrote this popular example of early American wit. But evidence seems to give the title to William Penn Warren, an itinerant portrait painter and journalist from Cincinnati. The tale is included in every historical collection of American humor from the 1850s until today.

THE HARP OF A THOUSAND STRINGS
by William Penn Brannan

"I may say to you, my brethering, that I am not an educated man, an I am not one o' them that beleeves education is necessary for a gospel minister, fur I beleeve the Lord edecates his preachers jest as he wants em to be educated; and although I say it that oughtn't to say it, yet in the State of Indianny, whar I live, thar's no man as gits a bigger congregation nor what I gits.

"Thar may be some here today, my brethering, as don't know what persuasion I am uv. Well, I may say to you, my brethering, that I am a Hard Shell Baptist. Thar's some folks as don't like the Hard Shell Baptists, but I'd rather hev a hard shell as no shell at all. You see me here today, my brethering, dressed up in fine close; you mout think I was proud, but I am not proud, my brethering; and although I've been a preacher uv the gospel for twenty years and although I'm capting uv that flatboat that lies at your landing, I'm not proud, my brethering.

"I'm not gwine ter tell you *edzackly* whar my tex may be found; suffice it tu say, it's in the leds of the Bible, and you'll find it somewhar 'tween the fust chapter of the book of Generation and the last chapter of the book of Revolutions, and if you'll go and sarch the Scriptures, you'll not only find my tex thar but a great many other texes will do you good to read; and my tex, when you shill find it, you shill find it to read thus:
And he played on a harp uv a thousand strings -- sperits of just men made perfect.

"My tex, brethern, leads me to speak uv sperits. Now thar's a great many kinds of sperits in the world. In the furst place, thar's the sperit as som folks call ghosts; then thar's the sperits uv turpen*time;* and then thar's the sperits as some folks call liquor, and I've got as good artikel uv them kind uv sperits on my flatboat as ever was fotched down the Mississippi River; but thar's a great many other kinds of sperits, for the tex says: 'He played on a harp uv a thou-*sand* strings -- sperits uf just men made perfeck.'

"But I'll tell you the kind of fire as is ment in the tex, my brethering -- it's *hell-fire!* an that's the kind of fire as a great many of you'll come to, ef you don't do better nor what you have bin doin -- for 'He played on a harp uv a *thou*-sand strings -- sperits of just men made perfeck.'

"And then, thar's the Methodis, and they may be likened unto the squirrel runnin up into a tree, for the Methodis believes in gwine on from one degree uv grace to another and finally on to perfecshun; and the squirrel goes up and up, and he jumps from lim to lim, and branch to branch, and the fust thing you know, he falls, and down he comes kerflummux; and that's like the Methodis, for they is allers fallin from grace, ah! And 'He played on a harp of a *thousand* strings -- sperits of just men made perfeck.'

"And then, my brethering, thar's the Baptists, ah! and they hev bin likened unto a possum on a 'simmon tree, and the thunders may roll, and then the earth may quake, but that possum clings there still, ah! And you may shake one foot loose, and the other's thar; and you may shake all feet loose, and he laps his tail around the lim, and he clings furever -- for 'He played ona harp of a *thousand* strings -- sperits of just men made perfeck.'"

✳ ✳ ✳ ✳ ✳

George Peck was a man of many parts who gave the title, "Peck's Bad Boy" to every recalcitrant American mischievous boy. His several books listing the incorrigible doings of young Peck were best sellers on the American market. Here is one of his wonderful stories.

PECK'S BAD BOY AND HIS PA
(His Pa Has Got Religious)

"Well, that beats the devil," said the groceryman, as he stood in front of his grocery and saw the bad boy coming along on the way home from Sunday school, with a clean shirt on, and a testament and some dime novels under his arm. "What got into you, and what has come over your Pa. I see he has braced up and looks pale and solemn. You haven't converted him have you?"

"No, Pa has not got religion enough to hurt yet, but he has got the symptoms. He joined the church on prowbation, and is trying to be good so he can get in the church for keeps. He said it was hell living the way he did, and he has got me to promise to go to Sunday school. He said if I didn't he wuld maul me so my skin wouldn't hold water. You see, Ma said Pa had got to be on trial for six months before he could get in the church, and if he could get along without swearing and doing anything bad, he was all right, and we must try him and see if we could cause him to swear. She said she thought a person, when they was on a prowbation, ought to be a martyr, and try and overcome all temptations to do evil, and if Pa could go through six months of our home life, and not cuss the hinges off the door, he was sure of a glorious immortality beyond the grave. She said it wouldn't be wrong for me to continue to play innocent jokes on Pa, and if he took it allright he was a Christian, but if he got a hot box and flew around mad, he was better out of church than in it.

"There he comes now," said the boy as he got behind a sign, "and he is pretty hot for a Christian. He is looking for me. You ought to have seen him in church this morning. You see, I commenced the exercises at home after breakfast by putting a piece of ice in each of Pa's boots, and when he pulled on the boots he yelled that his feet were all on fire, and we told him that it was nothing but symptoms of gout, so he left the ice in his boots to melt, and he said all the morning that he felt as though he had sweat his boots full. But that was not the worst. You know Pa wears a liver-pad.

"Well, on Saturday my chum and me was out on the lake shore and we found a nest of ants, these little red ants, and I got a pop bottle half full of the ants and took them home. I didn't know what I would do with the ants, but ants are always handy to have in the house. This morning, when Pa was dressing for church, I saw his liver-pad on a chair, and noticed a hole in it, and I thought what a good place it would be for the ants. I don't know what possessed me, but I took the liver pad into my room, and opened the bottle and put the hole over the mouth of the bottle and I guess the ants thought there was something to eat in the liver pad, cause they all went into it, and they crawled around in the bran and condition powders inside of it, and I took it back to Pa and he put it on under his shirt, and dressed himself and we went to church.

"Pa squirmed a little when the minister was praying, and I guess some of the ants had come out to view the landscape o'er. When we got up to sing the hymn Pa kept kicking, as though he was nervous, and he felt down his neck and looked sort of wild, the way he did when he had the jim-jams. When we sat down Pa couldn't keep still, and I like to dide when I saw some of the ants come out of his shirt bosom and go racing around his white vest. Pa tried to look pious and resigned, but he couldn't keep his legs still, an he sweat mor'n a pail full. When the minister preached about 'the worm that never dieth,' Pa reached into his vest and scratched his ribs, and he looked as though he would give ten dollars if the minister would get through. Ma she looked at Pa as though she though she would bit his head off, but Pa he just squirmed and acted as though his soul was on fire. Say, does ants bite, or just crawl around? Well, when the minister said amen, and prayed the second round, and then said a brother who was a misionary to the heathen would like to make a few remarks about the work of the Missionaries in Bengal, and took up a collection, Pa told Ma they would have to excuse *him,* and he lit out for home, slapping himself on the legs and on the arms and on the back, and he acted crazy. Ma and me went home, after the heathen got through, and found Pa in his bed room with part of his clothes off, and the liver-pad was on the floor, and Pa was stamping on it with his boots, talking offul.

"'What is the matter,' says Ma. 'Don't your religion agree with you?'

"'Religion be dashed' says Pa, as he kicked the liver-pad. 'I would give ten dollars to know how a pint of red ants got into my liver pad. Religion is one thing, and a million ants walking all over a man, playing tag, is another. I didn't know the liver pad was loaded. How in Gehenna did they get in there?' and Pa scowled at Ma as though he would kill her.

"'Don't swear dear,' says Ma, as she threw down her hymn book, and took off her bonnet. 'You should be patient. Remember Job was patient, and he was afflicted with sore boils.'

"'I don't care,' says Pa, as he chased the ants out of his drawers, 'Job never had any ants in his liver-pad. If he had he would have swore the shingles off a barn. Here you,' says Pa, speaking to me, 'you head off them ants running under the bureau. If the truth was known, I believe you would be responsible for this outrage.' And Pa looked at me kind of hard.

"'O, Pa,' says I, with tears in my eyes, 'Do you think your little Sunday school boy would catch ants in a pop bottle on the lake shore, and bring them home, and put them in the hole of your liver-pad, just before you put it on to go to church? You are too bad.' And I shed some tears. I can shed tears now any time I want to, but it didn't do any good this time. Pa knew it was me, and while he was looking for the shawl strap I went to Sunday school, and now I guess he is after me, and I will go and take a walk down to Bay View."

The boy moved off as his Pa turned a corner, and the grocery man said, "Well, that boy beats all I ever saw. If he was mine I would give him away."

* * * * *

A guilty conscience is the mother of invention.

* * * * *

Well Timed

"That certainly was a fine sermon," said an enthusiastic church member who was an ardent admirer of the minister. "A fine sermon, and well-timed too."

"Yes," answered his unadmiring neighbor, "It certainly was well-timed. Fully half the congregation had their watches out."

The Brakeman at Church

One bright winter morning, the twenty-ninth day of December, Anno Domini 1879, I was journeying from Lebanon, Indiana, where I had sojourned Sunday to Indianapolis. I did not see the famous cedars, and I supposed they had been used up for lead-pencils, and moth-proof chests, and relics, and souvenirs; for Lebanon is right in the heart of the holy land. That part of Indiana was settled by Second Adventists, and they have sprinkled goodly names all over their heritage. As the train clattered along, stopping at every station to trade off some people who were tired of traveling for some other people who were tired of staying home, I got out my writing-pad, pointed a pencil, and wondered what manner of breakfast I would be able to serve for the ever hungry "Hawkeye" next morning.

I was beginning to think I would have to disguise some "left-overs" under a new name, as the thrifty house-keepers know how to do, when my colleague, my faithful yoke-fellow, who has many a time found for me a spring of water in the desert place -- the Brakeman, came down the aisle of the car. He glanced at the tablet and pencil as I would look at his lantern, put my right hand into a cordial compress that abode with my fingers for ten minutes after he went away, and seating himself easily on the arm of the seat, put the semaphore all right for me by saying:

"Say, I went to church yesterday."

"Good boy," I said, "and what church did you attend?"

"Guess," was his reply.

"Some Union Mission chapel?" I ventured.

"N-no," he said, "I don't care to run on these branch roads very much. I don't get a chance to go to church every Sunday, and when I can go, I like to run on the main line, where your trip is regular, and you make a schedule time, and don't have to wait on connections. I don't care to run on a branch. Good enough, I reckon, but I don't like it."

"Episcopal?" I guessed.

"Limited express!" he said, "all parlor cars, vestibuled, and two dollars extra for a seat; fast time, and only stop at the big stations. Elegant line, but too rich for a brakeman. All the trainmen in uniform; conductor's punch and lanterns silver-plated; train-boys fenced up by themselves and not allowed to offer anything but music. Passengers talk back at the conductor. Trips scheduled through the whole year, so when you get aboard you know just where you're going and how long it will take you. Most systematic road in the country and has a mighty nice class of travel. Never hear of a receiver appointed on that line. But I didn't ride in the parlor car yesterday."

"Universalist?" I suggested.

"Broad gauge," the Brakeman chuckled; "does too much

complimentary business to be prosperous. Everybody travels on a pass. Conductor doesn't get a cash fare once in fifty miles. Stops at all way-stations and won't run into anything but a union depot. No smoking-car allowed on the train because the company doesn't own enough brimstone to head a match. Train orders are rather vague, though; and I've noticed the trainmen don't get along very well with the passengers. No, I didn't go on the broad gauge, though I have some good friends on that road who are the best people in the world. Been running on it all their lives."

"Presbyterian?" I hinted.

"Narrow gauge, eh?" said the Brakeman; "pretty track; straight as a rule; tunnel right through the heart of a mountain rather than go around it; spirit level grade, strict rules, too; passengers have to show their ticket before they get on the train; cars a little bit narrow for sleepers; have to sit one in a seat and no room in the aisle to dance. No stop-over tickets allowed; passenger must go straight through to the station he's ticketed for, or stays off the car. When the car's full, gates are shut; cars built at the shops to hold just so many, and no more allowed on. That road is run right up to the rules and you don't often hear of an accident on it. Had a head-on collision at Schenectady union station and run over a weak bridge at Cincinnati, not many years ago, but nobody hurt, and no passengers lost. Great road."

"May be you rode with the Agnostics?" I tried.

The Brakeman shook his head emphatically.

"Scrub road," he said, "dirt road-bed and no ballast; no time-card, and no train dispatcher. All trains run wild and every engineer makes his own time, just as he pleases. A sort of 'smoke-if-you-want-to' road. Too many side tracks; every switch wide open all the time, switchman sound asleep and the target-lamp dead out. Get on where you please and get off when you want. Don't have to show your tickets, and the conductor has no authority to collect fare. No, sir; I was offered a pass, but I don't like the line. I don't care to travel over a road that has no terminus.

"Do you know, I asked a division superintendent where his road run to, and he said he hoped to die if he knew. I asked him who he reported to, and he said 'Nobody.' I asked a conductor who he got his orders from, and he said he didn't take no orders from any living man or dead ghost. And when I asked the engineer who gave him orders, he said he'd just like to see any man on this planet try to give him orders, black-and-white or verbal; he said he'd run that train to suit himself and he'd run it into the ditch. Now, you see, I'm not much of a theologian, but I'm a good deal of a railroad man, and I don't want to run on a road that has no schedule, makes no time, has no connections, starts anywhere and runs nowhere, and has neither signal man, train dispatcher or superintendent. Might be all right, but I've railroaded too long to understand it."

"Did you try the Methodist?"

"Now you're shoutin'!" he cried with enthusiasm; "that's the hummer! Fast time and crowds of passengers! Engines carry a power of steam, and don't you forget it. Steam-gauge shows a hundred and enough all the time. Lively train crews, too. When the conductor shouts 'All a-b-o-a-r-d!' you can hear him to the next hallelujah station. Every train lamp shines like a head-light. Stop-over privileges on all tickets; passenger can drop off the train any time he pleases, do the station a couple of days and hop on to the next revival train that comes thundering along with an evangelist at the throttle. Good, whole-souled, companionable conductors; ain't a road on earth that makes the passengers feel more at home. No passes issued on any account; everybody pays full traffic rate for his own ticket. Safe road, too; well equipped; Wesleyanhouse air brakes on every train. It's a road I'm fond of, but I didn't begin this week's run with it."

I began to feel that I was running ashore; I tried one more lead:

"May be you went with the Baptists?"

"Ah, ha!" he shouted, "Now you're on the Shore line! River Road, eh? Beautiful curves, lines of grace at every bend and sweep of the river; all steel rail and rock ballast; single track, and not a siding from the round-house to the terminus. Takes a heap of water to run it, though; double tanks at every station, and there isn't an engine in the shops that can run a mile or pull a pound with less than two gauges. Runs through a lovely country -- river on one side and the hills on the other; and it's a steady climb, up grade all the way until the run ends where the river begins, at the fountain head. Yes, sir I'll take the River Road every time for a safe trip, sure connections, good time, and no dust blowing in when you open a window. And yesterday morning, when the conductor came around taking up fares with a little basket punch, I didn't ask him to pass me; I paid my fare like a little Jonah -- twenty-five cents for a ninety-minute run, with a concert by the passengers thrown in. I tell you what it is, Pilgrim, never mind your baggage, you just secure your passage on the River Road if you want to go to --"

But just here the long whistle announced a station, and the Brakeman hurried to the door, shouting --

"Zions-VILLE! ZIONS-ville! All out for Zionsville! This train makes no stops between here and Indianapolis!"

"The Brakeman at Church," Chapter XV from *"Chimes from a Jester's Bells ...,"* by Robert J. Burdette, pp. 197-205. Indianapolis and Kansas City: The Bowen-Merrill Company, 1897. [First printed in the Burlington (Iowa) *Hawkeye*, 1879.]

POETRY MACHINE. -- That Zeke of ours is a dangerous customer. He is quite a moral youth, and is quite seldom absent from the church when opportunity offers. A few evenings since, his devotional feels were assailed by an attack on his olfactories by a very disagreeable scent of unclean feet, and returning home in a fit of anger, he got hold of our Machine, and ground out the following, in revenge upon the assailant for his filthiness:

> There is a youth in our town
> Whose foot's so might large
> His shoe, seen floating down the stream,
> Was taken for a barge.
>
> A stranger, seeing, hastened on,
> T'examine keel and hull,
> But smelling strong the stench which rose,
> Cried, "Contagion, it is *dreadful.*"
>
> Now warning take, who go to church
> And by him get a seat,
> For I can tell, you're sure to smell
> A pair of stinking feet.

March 5, 1842

✳ ✳ ✳ ✳ ✳

Lorenzo Dow (1777-1834) was an old time preacher with a sharp tongue and keen wit. He once described Aaron Burr in this way. "Aaron Burr mean? Why I could take the little end of nothing, whittle it down to a point, punch out the pith of hair and put in forty thousand such souls as his, shake 'em hard and they'd rattle!"

He was an itinerant preacher born in Connecticut. He was a spellbinder, so successful with American congregations that he was called to Iceland and England to spellbind the people there. He introduced the camp meeting to the British Isles and was rumored to be able to make the Devil appear! He was one...strong... exhorter!

LORENZO DOW RAISES THE DEVIL

At one time when Lorenzo Dow was traveling in the South, he asked permission to remain overnight. The woman of the house informed him that her husband being from home, he could not stay. He told her he was a preacher, and would sleep in the stable if he could do no better. This information, together with his long beard, at once suggested to her who he was, and she accordingly inquired if he was Lorenzo Dow. Being answered in the affirmative, she concluded that he might stay -- probably more out of fear that evil might befall her if she turned him off, than out of a wish to have him in the house.

Accordingly Mr. Dow put up; and about the usual hour retired to bed in a back room, where he had not lain long until he heard a man arrive, who soon discovered was not the woman's husband. A series of jokes commenced between the woman and the man, which continued with a good deal of pleasantry till about midnight, when, all of a sudden, their pleasures were disturbed by a rap at the door, which announced that the husband had returned.

Alarm and consternation followed. There was but one door, and at it stood the husband. To escape seemed impossible. At this critical juncture, when the ingenuity of man had failed, the quick perception of woman, as in most cases of emergency, found an expedient. At the foot of the bed stood a large gum full of raw cotton, in which she concealed the visitor. Then turning round very composedly, she opened the door and received her husband. But his lordship had been at the grogshop, and was in what the Irish schoolmaster called an "uproarious mood." "Hush, hush," said the wife, as the husband blundered in, and roared out, "Thunder and potatoes, Mag, and why didn't you open the door?" "Hush, my dear, hush! Lorenzo Dow, is in the house." "O blood and tobacco! And is it Lorenzo Dow, the man who raises the Devil?" "Sure it is, and why don't you be still?" "Oh, by Saint Patrick, he shall come forth, and you shall see the Devil before you sleep." So Mr. Dow was compelled to come forth, and nothing would satisfy the husband but that Lorenzo must raise the devil.

Mr. Dow protested and urged his inability to perform such wonders; but no excuse would satisfy the uncompromising husband. At length, said Mr. Dow, "If you stand in the door and give him a few thumps as he passes, but not so hard as to break his bones, I will see if I can raise him." So saying he took the candle in his hand, and walking up and down the room, Lorenzo touched the candle to the cotton, and said, "Come forth, old boy." Out jumped the hidden gentleman all in a blaze, and breaking for the door like a mass of living fire made good his escape, but not without first receiving a good rap over the shoulder from the husband's cudgel as he passed the threshold.

The job was now done, Lorenzo had raised the Devil, and the husband thought it was a real wonder performed by the Yankee preacher.

✳ ✳ ✳ ✳ ✳

WIT AND HUMOR
A Choice Collection by
Marshall Brown
S. C. Griggs & Co. 1879 Chicago, IL

A thick-headed squire, being worsted by the Rev. Sydney Smith in an argument, took his revenge by exclaiming: "If I had a son that was an idiot, by Jove, I'd make him a parson!"

"Very probable," replied Sydney, "but I see your father was of a very different mind."

✳ ✳ ✳

A Stingy Congregation

The hat was passed around a certain congregation for the purpose of taking up a collection. After it had made the circuit of the church, it was handed to the minister -- who, by the way, had exchanged pulpits with the regular preacher -- and he found not a penny in it. He inverted the hat over the pulpit cushion and shook it, that its emptiness might be known; then raising his eyes to the ceiling, he exclaimed with great fervor:

"I thank God that I got back my hat from this congregation."

✳ ✳ ✳

"It isn't loud praying which counts with the Lord so much as giving four full quarts of whisky for every gallon," says an Arkansas circuit rider.

✳ ✳ ✳

The Minister Jokes His Wife

Eli Perkins

The Rev. George Hepworth, who likes to tell a good joke on his wife, says that he had complained many times that his wife's mince and apple pies looked just alike.

"I can't tell your apple from your mince, my dear," he said, "without tasting them."

"I'll fix that," said Mrs. Hepworth, "I'll have the cook mark them."

The next day when the pies came on Mrs. Hepworth said in triumph, "Now you can tell the mince from the apple. I've had this one marked T.M., 'tis mince, and this one T.M., taint mince!"

A good old lady at a Tennessee camp meeting, appearing to be greatly distressed, attracted the sympathy of one of the brethren, who went to her, and, in kindly tones, asked if he could do anything for her.

"Oh, I don't know," she groaned.

"Do you think you've got religion?"

"O, I don't know; *mebbe it's religion -- mebbe it's worms.*"

Cold or Hot

Chas. A. Dana

An Irishman had a dream which taught him the danger of delay: "I dreamed," said he, "I was wid the Pope, who was as great a jintleman as any one in the district, an' he axed me wad I drink. Thinks I, wad a duck swim, an' seein' the whisky an' the lemon an' sugar on the sideboard, I told him I didn't care if I tuk a wee dhrap of punch. 'Cowled or hot?' axed the Pope. 'Hot, your Holiness,' I replied; an' be that he stepped down to the kitchen for the bilin' water, but before he got back I woke straight up. And now it's distressin' me I didn't take it cowld."

❊ ❊ ❊ ❊ ❊

My private opinyun uiz...that when a man haint got any thing to say, then is the best time not to say it.

Josh Billings

❊ ❊ ❊ ❊ ❊

COUSIN FREEBODY'S LAST PRAYING

When it come to praying, Cousin Freebody Tillman just couldn't be beat -- or stopped, neither, till he'd prayed his self out. When he got up to pray, everybody at Pilgrim Beauty Church House knowed they was in for a spell of squirming, because Cousin Freebody cried aloud and spared none.

He had a special kind of slow solemn way to et down on his knees. He'd turn around red face up towards the rafters and give a sweet smile in the Lord's direction. Then he'd pull at his white chinbrush two or three times and sail in. "Oh Looord, oh Looord," he'd say, each time a mite louder. "Oh Looord, this is Freebody Tillman asking you to send the Holy Spirit down upon them whiskey-making Barfieldses! Oh Looord, drive out the demons from the heart of pore Della Creasy, for she's been galavanting around and got herself in a fix.

"Oh Looord," he'd beller, "who is beknowing to all things, clean with them holy hands of yores the vile hands of them that charges two prices for brought-on goods that they got half price at the county seat. You know who I mean." And he'd open one eye look at Store-keeper Boshears.

That's why they all called him Cousin Freebody, when he wasn't nobody's cousin at all. Cousin-like, he knowed everybody's business and was just dying to tell it around. Yes, when he got warmed up praying, Cousin Freebody would run right through the community, naming names and telling what they'd done against the teaching of the Book since last meeting night.

Cousin Freebody left his own self to the tag end. "Oh Looord," he says, "bless thy humble servant that calls yore attention to these here sinners. Send yore holy lamb to bless his mission of righteousness, oh Looord, *Amen!*" Then he'd get off his knees, looking mighty satisfied and proud of his self.

Some said it wasn't right the way Cousin Freebody taken on his self to tell the Lord all such things in public. But some claimed it was a genuwine service to the community. Both sides argued back and forth and Cousin Freebody kept right on pointing the sinners out every chance he got to pray.

Old Hub Peegrum lived joining farms to Cousin Freebody an knowed him might near as well as anybody, or maybe better. "You know," he says, "it's a queer thing to me that when Freebody Tillmanses will eat possum, come any season, and any fool knowing possum ain't good until from frost till Easter. Why I've seen the meat on the platter, and it don't have that greasy look that possum meat does. It's sort of pink and all lean like -- well, it just *couldn't* be sheep meat, because Cousin Freebody don't raise sheep. But I will say it's the sheepiest-looking possum meat ever I seen!"

You could take it or leave it. Old Hub Peegrum hadn't put his self on no limb, but it did set folks to thinking. They got to thinking about the way the farmers had been missing lambs and couldn't figger what was going with them.

The Main Course

Far and near the folks begun talking about Cousin Freebody's sheepy-looking meat. Some of them says to him, "What kind of possum is that you folks eat, Cousin Freebody?"

"Regular old simmon tree possum, brother," says Cousin Freebody. "Eats good, too. I've eat so much possum, reckon you might say I'm half a possum my own self."

It didn't take the wind out of *his* sails none at all. If anything, he prayed louder and spilled other people's sins out in public harder than ever. His "Oh Looords" got to be so long that some said he counted up to ten in his mind before he'd turn one aloose.

One reason Cousin Freebody got away with all he did was the way he could pray up a rain. Just let it come a drouth and there'd be a special prayer service for rain. By the time Cousin Freebody had got thrugh his prayer, wasn't no need of nobody else trying. Wasn't nothing else left to promise the Lord if he sent rain. So the meeting would break up and the crowd go home. Most usually by that time the sun would be gone behind a cloud. All the womenfolks would go home and get the rain barrels and tubs out, for they knowed that rain was sure coming.

Some that read their almanacs said they noticed Cousin Freebody seemed to pick out the days to pray for rain when the signs were right for it. Some said so to his face.

But Cousin Freebody just laughed. "Well, anyhow," says he, "it *did* rain, didn't it? Almanac or no almanac, you don't see it raining after anybody else prays, do you?"

He had them *there*.

Cousin Freebody not only prayed, but he was likewise visited by visions.

"Didn't a white dog come sneaking out from under Malinda's bed one night and didn't I try to kick it out the door, because Malinda wouldn't have no such truck as a dog in the house, let alone under a body's bed, and didn't my foot go clearn through that hut, and didn't it just sort of fade away without going out the door nor nothing? And, of course, it wasn't no time till Malinda taken with pneumonia fever and died.

"That was a warning for certain," Cousin Freebody would say. "And furthermore than that, I see visions the times I pray for sinners. Yes, the Lord send me signs, and the sinners almost always get converted."

The way Cousin Freebody got warnings and had his prayers answered gave lots of people the all-overs and brought heaps of them to the mourners' bench. But there was one time when Cousin Freebody's vision wasn't just what he bargained for.

The regular Wednesday night prayer meeting was being held over at the Edwardses away across the ridge, and Cousin Freebody and Old Hub Peegrum went over together. On the way, Cousin Freebody said it would be weathering before long, because he had heard a hoot owl hooting that day.

"It's not a sign of weathering," says Hub Peegrum, "to hear a hoot owl, but just them whiskey-making Barfieldses signaling somebody's coming towards their still. Some day," he says, "you'll find out all them signs you go by don't hold water, Cousin Freebody."

Now that didn't set well with Cousin Freebody -- Old Hub's belittling his signs and visions. She he just puffed and blowed, mad as a hornet, all the rest of the way to the meeting.

The womenfolks were there in the parlor and each one had their Bible and songbook and fan. The menfolks were chewing tobacco and smoking out in the yard till Cousin Freebody came in. Then they followed him inside to begin the meeting.

"Cousin Freebody must have a powerful good speaking or something on his mind tonight," everybody says. "He never stopped to swap gossip with the men outside like always. Just come right on in."

"Pears to me," somebody says, "he looks sort of unusually pious too, or else something's troubling his mind a plenty. Maybe another one of them visions he talks about."

The song services ended with them all joining in on "When I Shall See Him Face to Face," and Cousin Freebody got ready to pray. Down on both knees, face lifted to high heaven, hands folded.

"Oh Looord! Oh Lord Almighty God! You who are beknowing to our every need. Oh Looord, send a vision to these sinful people. Something as a token, Lord, to thy faithful servant for telling you all these things these folks been doing all these years. Oh, Loooord, one of our deacons don't believe in warnings from the holy hand. Lord, just a little vision to them as need it most is all I'm asking."

Somebody giggled from over next to the wall where the young bucks was setting with their girls. Cousin Freebody cocked one eye open to see how Old Hub's face was looking. Everybody was bound to know the prayer for a vision was aimed at Hub, the doubting deacon.

And that was the downfall of Cousin Freebody, opening that one eye. If he hadn't done it, likely nothing would have happened. But he did.

He sprung up with both eyes wild and he threw his arms out in front of him like he was trying to push the devil his self.

"Almighty God, remove this evil vision from me!" he howled. "I'll pay Tom Edwards and Hub Peegrum for every last lamb of theirs I et and told it was possum. Almighty God, this ain't the little lamb I et today, you done made a mistake, Lord, it was a young ewe I et today. Oh God Almighty, stop the pitiful bleating of that poor little stolen lamb of Hub's I et lst week! Oh, Loooooord --!"

And there it was, out before God and everybody else what he'd been doing.

Everybody was laughing so hard, and Cousin Freebody howling so loud that Tom Edwards' house near shaken down.

"It ain't no vision, Cousin Freebody!" Tom kept yelling at him. "It's a little pet lamb of Nancy's. A lamb that's been raised up in the house and taken a notion to stroll in. It ain't no vision, Cousin Freebody."

Well, when Cousin Freebody seen what he'd done to his self, he lost his religion. He waved his arms and raved, "You ornery razor-backed, throat-cutting, whisky-drinking bastards can have all the meetings you want to from now on, but I won't be there to help you. Anybody that would make a poor old man think he was getting such a bushwhacking from the Holy Spirit is worthless as frog spit!"

He stomped towards the door, but stopped long enough to say, "and as for you, Tom Edwards, anybody that'd stoop to raising

252

sheep in the house ain't fitten for even a sheep thief to associate with."

And Cousin Freebody never went to another meeting and never prayed again.

Reprinted from "God Bless the Devil!: Liars' Bench Tales," edited by James R. Aswell. © 1940 by The University of North Carolina. Used by permission of the publisher.

✳ ✳ ✳ ✳ ✳

THE FABLE OF THE PREACHER WHO FLEW HIS KITE...

A certain Preacher became wise to the Fact that he was not making a Hit with his Congregation. The Parishioners did not seem inclined to seek him out after Services and tell him he was a Pansy. He suspected that they were Rapping him on the Quiet.

The Preacher knew there must be something wrong with his Talk. He had been trying to Expound in a clear and straightforward Manner, omitting Foreign Quotations, setting up for illustration of his Points such Historical Characters as were familiar to his Hearers, putting the stubby Old English words ahead of the Latin, and rather flying low along the Intellectual Plane of the Aggregation that chipped in to pay his Salary.

But the Pew-Holders were not tickled. They could Understand everything he said, and they began to think he was Common.

So he studied the Situation and decided that if he wanted to Win them and make everybody believe he was a Nobby and Boss Minister he would have to hand out a little Guff. He fixed it up Good and Plenty.

On the following Sunday Morning he got up in the Lookout and read a Text that didn't mean anything, read from either Direction, and then he sized up his Flock with a Dreamy Eye and said: "We cannot more adequately voice the Poetry and Mysticism of our Text than in those familiar Lines of the great Icelandic Poet, Ikon Navrojk:

"To hold is not to have --
Under the seared Firmament,
Where Chaos sweeps, and Vast Futurity
Sneers at these puny Aspirations --
There is the full Reprisal."

When the preacher concluded this extract from the Well-Known Icelandic Poet he paused and looked downward, breathing heavily through his Nose, like Camille in the Third Act.

A Stout Woman in the Front Row put on her Eye-Glasses and leaned forward so as not to miss Anything. A Venerable Harness Dealer over at the Right nodded his Head solemnly. He seemed to

253

recognize the Quotation. Members of the Congregation glanced at one another as if to say: "This is certainly Hot Stuff!"

The Preacher wiped his Brow and said he had no Doubt that every one within the Sound of his Voice remembered what Quarolius had said, following the same Line of Thought. It was Quarolius who disputed the Contention of the great Persian Theologian Ramtazuk, that the Soul in its reaching out after the Unknowable was guided by the Spiritual Genesis of Motive rather than by mere Impulse of Mentality. The Preacher didn't know what all This meant, and he didn't care, but you can rest easy that the Pew-Holders were On in a minute. He talked it off in just the Way that Cyrano talks when he gets Roxane so Dizzy that she nearly falls off the Piazza.

The Parishioners bit their Lower Lips and hungered for more First-Class Language. They had paid their Money for Tall Talk and were prepared to solve any and all Styles of Delivery. They held on to the Cushions and seemed to be having a Nice Time.

The Preacher quoted copiously from the Great Poet Amebius. He recited 18 lines of Greek and then said: "How true this is!" And not a Parishioner batted an Eye.

It was Amebius whose Immortal Lines he recited in order to prove the Extreme Error of the Position assumed in the Controversy by the Famous Italian, Polenta.

He had them Going, and there wasn't a Think to it. When he would get tired of faking Philosophy he would quote from a Celebrated Poet of Ecuador or Tasmania or some other Seaport Town. Compared with this Verse, all of which was of the same School as the Icelandic Masterpiece, the most obscure and clouded Passage in Robert Browning was like a Plate-Glass Front in a State Street Candy Store just after the colored boy gets through using the Chamois.

After that he became Eloquent, and began to get rid of long Boston Words that hadn't been used before that Season. He grabbed a rhetorical Roman Candle in each Hand and you couldn't see him for the Sparks.

After which he sunk his Voice to a Whisper and talked abut the Birds and the Flowers. Then, although there was no Cue for him to Weep, he shed a few real Tears. And there wasn't a dry Glove in the Church.

After he sat down he could tell by the Scared Look of the People in Front that he had made a Ten-Strike.

Did they give him the Joyous Palm that Day? Sure!

The Stout Lady could not control her Feelings when she told how much the Sermon had helped her. The venerable Harness Dealer said he wished to indorse the Able and Scholarly Criticism of Polenta.

In fact, every one said the Sermon was Superfine and Dandy. The only thing that worried the Congregation was the Fear that if it wished to retains such a Whale it might have to Boost his Salary.

In the Meantime the Preacher waited for some one to come and ask about Polenta, Amebius, Ramtazuk, Quarolius and the great Icelandic Poet, Navrojk. But no one had the Face to step up and confess his Ignorance of these Celebrities. The Pew-Holders didn't even admit among themselves that the Preacher had rung in some New Ones. They stood Pat, and merely said it was an Elegant Sermon.

Perceiving that they would stand for Anything, the Preacher knew what to do after that.

Moral: *Give the People what they think they want.*

From "Fables In Slang," by George Ade. 1899. Herbert S. Stone & Co., Publishers. New York.

✳ ✳ ✳ ✳ ✳

Most people repent ov their sins bi thanking God they aint so wicked az their nabors.

Josh Billings

✳ ✳ ✳ ✳ ✳

Lifers Preferred

Even amenities between pastors and their flocks sometimes become somewhat strained. Recently, in a Baptist church in a Western State, the pastor, who was on very bad terms with his congregation, received the appointment of chaplain at the State prison.

Elated at this lucky opportunity of getting rid of him, the congregation came in full numbers to hear his farewell sermon, but whether to compliment or annoy him with their presence, the pastor was not sure. But, any way, it was his chance for getting even, so he chose for his text, "I go to prepare a place for you...that where I am, there ye may be also."

✳ ✳ ✳ ✳ ✳

Mark Twain's Nevada Funeral -- Scotty Briggs and the Clergyman

Scotty Briggs choked and even shed tears; but with an effort he mastered his voice and said in lugubrious tones to the clergyman:

"Are you the duck that runs the gospel-mill next door?"

"Am I the -- pardon me, I believe I do not understand?"

With another sigh, and half-sob, Scotty rejoined:

"Why you see we are in a bit of trouble, and the boys thought maybe you would give us a lift, if we'd tackle you -- that is, if I've got the rights of it and you are the head clerk of the doxology-works next door."

"I am the shepherd in charge of the flock whose fold is next door."

"The which?"

"The spiritual adviser of the little company of believers whose sanctuary adjoins these premises."

Scotty scratched his head, reflected a moment, and then said:

"You ruther hold over me, pard. I reckon I can't call that hand. Ante and pass the buck."

"How? I beg pardon. What did I understand you to say?"

"Well, you've ruther got the bulge on me. Or maybe we've both got the bulge somehow. You don't smoke me and I don't smoke you. You see, one of the boys has passed in his checks and we want to give him a good send-off, and so the thing I'm on now is to roust out somebody to jerk a little chin music for us and waltz him through handsome."

"My friend, I seem to grow more and more bewildered. Your observations are wholly incomprehensible to me. Cannot you simplify them in some way? At first I thought perhaps I understood you, but I grope now. Would it not expedite matters if you restricted yourself to categorical statements of fact, unencumbered with obstructing accumulations of metaphor and allegory?"

Another pause and more reflection. Then, said Scotty:

"I'll have to pass, I judge."

"How?"

"You have raised me out, pard."

"I still fail to catch your meaning."

"Why, that last lead of yourn is too many for me --that's the idea. I can't neither trump nor follow suit."

The clergyman sank back in his chair perplexed. Scotty leaned his head on his hand and gave himself up to thought. Presently his face came up, sorrowful but confident.

"I've got it now, so's you can savvy," he said. "What we want is a gospel-sharp. See?"

"A what?"

"Gospel-sharp. Parson."

"Oh! Why did you not say so before? I am a clergyman -- a parson."

"Now you talk! You see my blind and straddle it like a man. Put it there!"-- extending a brawny paw, which closed over the minister's small hand and gave it a shake indicative of fraternal sympathy and fervent gratification.

"Now we're all right, pard. Let's start fresh. Don't you mind my snuffling a little -- becuz we're in a power of trouble. You see one of the boys has gone up the flume --"

"Gone where?"

"Up the flume -- throwed up the sponge, you understand."

"Throw'd up the sponge?"

"Yes -- kicked the bucket --"

"Ah! -- has departed to that mysterious country from whose bourne no traveler returns."

"Return! I reckon not. Why pard, he's *dead!*"

"Yes, I understand."

"Oh, you do? Well I thought maybe you might be getting tangled some more. Yes, you see he's dead again --"

"*Again!* Why, has he ever been dead before?"

"Dead before? No! Do you reckon a man has got as many lives as a cat? but you bet you he's awful dead now, poor old boy, and I wish I'd never seen this day. I don't want no better friend than Buck Fanshaw. I knowed him but the back; and when I know a man and like him, I freeze to him -- you hear *me.* Take him all round, pard, there never was a bullier man in the mines. No man ever knowed Buck Fanshaw to go back on a friend. But it's all up, you know, it's all up. It ain't no use. They've scooped him."

"Scooped him?"

"Yes -- death has. Well, well, well, we've got to give him up. Yes, indeed. it's kind of a hard world, after all, *ain't* it? But Pard was a rustler. You ought to see him get started once. He was a bully boy with a glass eye! Just spit in his face and give him room according to his strength, and it was just beautiful to see him peel and go in. He was the worst son of a thief that ever drawed breath. Pard, he was *on* it! He was on it bigger than an Injun!"

"On it? On what?"

"On the shoot. On the shoulder. On the fight, you understand. *He* didn't give a continental for *anybody. Beg* yur pardon, friend, for coming so near saying a cuss-word -- but you see I'm on an awful strain, in this palaver, on account of having to camp down and draw everything so mild. But we've got to give him up. There ain't any getting around that I don't reckon. Now if we can get you to help plant him --"

"Preach the funeral discourse? Assist at the obsequies?"

"Obs'quies is good. Yes. That's it -- that's our little game. We are going to get the thing up regardless, you know. He was always nifty himself, and so you bet you his funeral ain't going to be no slouch -- solid silver door-plate on his coffin, six plumes on the hearse, and a black man on the box in a biled shirt and a plug hat

-- how's that for high? And we'll take care of *you*, pard. We'll fix you all right. There'll be a kerridge for you; and whatever you want, you just 'scape out and we'll tend to it. We've got a shebang fixed up for you to stand behind, in No. 1's house, and don't you be afraid. Just go in and toot your horn, if you don't sell a claim. Put Buck through as bully as you can, pard, for anybody that knowed him will tell you that he was one of the whitest men that was ever in the mines. You can't draw it too strong. He never could stand it to see things going wrong. He's done more to make this town quiet and peaceable than any man in it. I've seen him lick four Greasers in eleven minutes, myself. If a thing wanted regulating, *he* warn't a man to go browsing around after somebody to do it, but he would prance in and regulate it himself. He warn't a Catholic. Scasely. He was down on 'me. His words was, 'No Irish need apply!' But it didn't make no difference about that when it came down to what a man's rights was -- and so, when some roughs jumped the Catholic bone-yard and started in to stake out town lots in it he *went* for 'em! And he *cleaned* 'em too! I was there, pard, and I seen it myself."

"That was very well, indeed -- at least the impulse was -- whether the act was strictly defensible or not. Had deceased any religious convictions? That is to say, did he feel a dependence upon, or acknowledge allegiance to a higher power?"

More reflection.

"I reckon you stumped me again, pard. Could you say it over once more, and say it slow?"

"Well, to simplify it somewhat, was he, or rather had he ever been connected with any organization sequestered from secular concerns and devoted to self-sacrifice in the interests of morality?"

"All down but nine -- set 'em up on the other alley, pard."

"What did I understand you to say?"

"Why, you're most too many for me, you know. When you get in with your left I hunt grass every time. Every time you draw you fill; but I don't seem to have any luck. Let's have a new deal."

"How? Begin again?"

"That's it."

"Very well. Was he a good man, and --"

"There -- I see that; don't put up another chip till I look at my hand. A good man, says you? Pard, it ain't no name for it. He was the best man that ever -- pard, you would have doted on that man. He was always for peace, and he would *have* peace -- he cold not stand disturbances. Pard, he was a great loss to this town. It would please the boys if you could chip in something like that and do him justice. Here once when the Micks got to throwing stones through the Methodis' Sunday school windows, Buck Fanshaw, all of his own notion, shut up his saloon and took a couple of six-shooters, and mounted guard over the Sunday school. Says he, 'No Irish need apply!' And they didn't. He was the bulliest man in the mountains, pard! He could run faster, jump higher, hit harder, and hold more tangle-foot whisky without spilling it than any man in seventeen counties. Put that in, pard -- it'll please the boys more than anything you could say. And you can say, pard, that he never shook his mother."

"Never shook his mother?"

"That's it -- any of the boys will tell you so."

"Well, but why *should* he shake her?"

"That's what *I* say -- but some people does."

"Not people of any repute."

"Well, some that averages pretty so-so."

"In my opinion the man that would offer personal violence to his own mother ought to --"

"Cheese it, pard; you've banked your ball clean outside the string. What I was drivin' at was that he never *throwed off* on his mother -- don't you see? No, indeedy! He gave her a house to live in, and town lots, and plenty of money; and when she was down with the small-pox, I'm d---d if he didn't set up nights and nuss her himself! *Beg* your pardon for saying it, but it hopped out too quick for yours truly. You've treated me like a gentleman, pard, and I ain't the man to hurt your feelings intentional. I think you're white. I think you're a square man, pard. I like you, and I'll lick any man that don't. I'll lick him till he can't tell himself from a last year's corpse! Pu it *there!*" [Another fraternal hand-shake -- and exit.]

✳ ✳ ✳ ✳ ✳

"The wicked flee when no man pursueth," quoted the deacon to the minister.

"Yes," said the minister, who believed in aggressive Christianity, "that is true, but they make much better time when somebody is after them."

✳ ✳ ✳ ✳ ✳

NOAH AN' JONAH AN' CAP'N JOHN SMITH
by Don Marquis

Noah an' Jonah an' Cap'n John Smith,
Mariners, travelers, magazines of myth,
Settin' up in Heaven, chewin' and a-chawin',

Eatin' their terbaccy, talkin' and a-hawin';
Settin' by a crick, spittin' in the worter,
Talkin' tall an' tactless, as saints hadn't orter,
Talkin' tall an' tactless, as saints hadn't orter,
Lollin' in the shade, baitin' hooks and anglin'.
Occasionally friendly, occasionally wranglin'.

Noah took his halo from his old bald head
An' swatted of a hoppergrass an' knocked it dead,
An' he baited of his hook, an' he spoke an' said:
"When I was the skipper of the tight leetle Ark
I useter fish fer porpus, useter fish fer shark,
Often I have ketched in a single hour on Monday
Sharks enough to feed the fambly until Sunday --
To feed all the sarpints, the tigers an' donkeys,
To feed all the zebras, the insects an' monkeys,
To feed all the varmints, bears an' gorillars,
To feed all the camels, cats an' armadillers,
To give all the pelicans stews fer their gizzards,
To feed all the owls an' contamounts an' lizards,
To feed all the humans, their babies an' their nusses,
To feed all the houn'dawgs an' hippopotamusses,
To feed all the oxens, feed all the asses,
Feed all the bison an' leetle hoppergrasses --
Always I ketched in half an hour on Monday
All that the fambly could gormandize till Sunday!"

Jonah took his harp, to strum an' to string her,
An' Cap'n John Smith tetched his nose with his finger.
Cap'n John Smith, he hemmed some and hawed some,
An' he bit off a chaw, an' he chewed some an' chawed some: --
"When I was to China, when I was to Guinea,
When I was to Javy, an' also in Verginny,
I teached all the natives how to be ambitious,
I learned 'em my trick of ketchin' devilfishes.
I've fitten tigers, I've fitten bears,
I have fitten sarpints an' wolves in their lairs,
I have fit with wild men an' hippopotamusses,
But the periloussest varmints is the bloody octopusses!
I'd rub my forehead with phosphorescent light
An' plunge into the ocean an' seek 'em out at night!
I ketched 'em in the grottoes, I ketched 'em in caves,
I used fer to strangle 'em underneath the waves!
When they seen the bright light blazin' on my forehead
They used fer to rush at me, screamin' something horrid!
Tentacles wavin', teeth white an' gnashin',

Hollerin' an' bellern', wallerin' an' splashin'!
I useter grab 'em as they rushed from their grots,
Ketch all their legs an' tie 'em into knots!"

Noah looked at Jonah an' said not a word,
But if winks made noises, a wink had been heard.
Jonah took the hook from a mudcat's middle
An' strummed on the strings of his hallelujah fiddle;
Jonah gave his whiskers a backhand wipe
An' cut some plug terbaccer an' crammed it in his pipe!
-- (Noah an' Jonah an' Cap'n John Smith,
Fisherman an' travellers, narratin' myth,
Settin' up in Heaven all eternity,
Fishin' in the shade, contented as could be!
Spittin' their terbaccer in the little shaded creek,
Stoppin' of their yarns fer ter hear the ripples speak!
I hope fer Heaven, when I think of this --
You folks bound hellward, a lot of fun you'll miss!)
Jonah, he decapitates that mudcat's head,
An' gets his pipe ter drawin'; an' this is what he said:
"Excuse me if yer stories don't excite me much!
Excuse me if I seldom agitate fer such!
You think yer fishermen! I won't argue none!
I won't even tell yer the half o' what I done!
You has careers dangerous an' checkered!
All as I will say is: Go an' read my record!
You think yer fisherman! You think yer great!
All I ask is this: Has one of ye been *bait*?
Cap'n Noah, Cap'n John, I heerd when ye hollered:
What I asks is this: Has one of ye been *swallered*?
It's might easy fishin' with little rods and creels,
It's might pleasant ketchin mudcats fer yer dinners,
But here is my challenge fer saints an' fer sinners,
Which one of ye has v'yaged in a varmin's inners?
When I see a big fish, tough as Mathooslum,
I used fer to dive into his oozy-goozlum!
When I see a strong fish, wallopin' like a lummicks,
I uster foller 'em, dive into their stummicks!
I could v'yage an' steer 'em, I could understand 'em,
I uster navigate 'em, I useter land 'em!
Don't you pester *me* with any more narration!
Go git famous! Git a reputation!"

Cap'n John he grinned his hat brim beneath,
Clicked his tongue of silver on his golden teeth;
Noah an' Jonah an' Cap'n John Smith,

Strummin' golden harps, narratin' myth!
Settin' by the shallows forever an' forever,
Swappin' yarns an' fishin' in a little River!

From "Noah An' Jonah An' Cpn. John Smith"
by Don Marquis. © 1921 by D. Appleton & Company.
Used by permission of Doubleday, a division of Bantam
Doubleday Dell Publishing Group, Inc.

✳ ✳ ✳ ✳ ✳

BIBLE STORIES

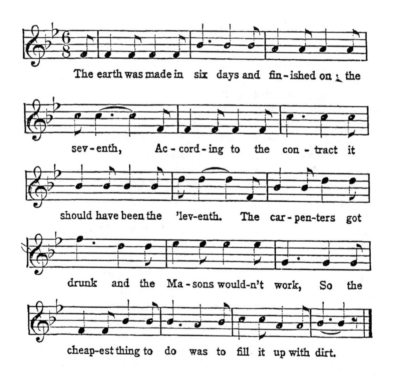

The earth was made in six days and fin-ished on the sev-enth, Ac-cord-ing to the con-tract it should have been the 'lev-enth. The car-pen-ters got drunk and the Ma-sons would-n't work, So the cheap-est thing to do was to fill it up with dirt.

Chorus

Old folks, young folks, everybody come,
Join the kiddie's Sunday scholl and make yourselves at home.
Kindly check your chewing gum, and razors at the door,
And we'll tell you Bible stories that you never heard before.

Adam was the first man and Eve she was his spouse;
They lost their job for stealing fruit and went to keeping house.
All was very peaceful and quiet on the main
Until a little baby came and they started raising Cain.

Chorus

The Lord made the devil, and the devil made sin;
The Lord made a cubbyhole to put the devil in.
The devil got sore and said he wouldn't stay;
The Lord said he had to, 'cause he couldn't get away.

Chorus

Cain he raised potatoes and he peddled them in town.
Abel called him hayseed every time he came around
Cain he laid a stick of wood on brother Abel's head,
And when he took that stick away, he found poor Abel dead.

Chorus

Noah was the keeper of the Asiatic zoo;
He built an ocean liner when he hadn't much to do;
One day he got excited when the sky was getting dark,
So he gathered all his animals and put them in the ark.

Chorus

It rained for forty days and it rained for forty nights,
The water washed the land completely out of sight!
But when Noah was a-wondering as to what he'd better do,
The ark hit Mount Ararat and stuck as tight as glue!

Chorus

Methusaleh is famous, because he couldn't croak,
Although he finally grew to be an old and seedy bloke.
He had so many whiskers that you couldn't see his head;
If he'd lived a little longer, he'd have used them for his bed.

Chorus

Elijah was an aeronaut, or else I am a liar,
He ascened up to heaven in a chariot of fire;
His eccentric disappearance gave the Israelites a shock,
They said he beat the Wright brothers by fully half a block.

Abraham was a patriarch, the father of his set;
He took his little Ikey out to kill him on a bet.
And he'd have met his finish if it wasn't for a lamb,
For papa had his razor out and didn't give a damn!

> *"More Pious Friends and Drinking Companions"*
> *by Frank Shay. The Macauley Company. 1926*

✳ ✳ ✳ ✳ ✳

"Now I know why Solomon took 13 years to build his house,"
growled the muchly married young man to his pastor.
"Why, son?"
"He had 1000 wives making suggestions."

✳ ✳ ✳ ✳ ✳

WARM BABIES

Shadrach, Meshach, Abednego,
Walked in the furnace to an' fro,
Hay foot, straw foot, fro an' to,
An' the flame an' the smoke flared up the flue.
Nebuchadnezzar he listen some,
An' he hear 'em talk, an' he say "How so?
Dem babies was hawg tied a hour ago!"

Then Shadrach call, in an uppity way,
"A little mo' heat or we ain' gwine stay!"
An' Shadrach bawl so dat de furnace shake:
"Lan'lawd, heat! fo' de good Lawd's sake!"
Abednego yell, wid a loud "Kerchoo!"
"Is you out to freeze us, an' kill us, too?"

Nebuchadnezzar, he rare an' ramp,
An' call to his janitor, "You big old scamp!
Shake dem clinkers an' spend dat coal!
I'll bake dem birds, ef I goes in de hole!"
So he puts on de draf' an' he shuts de door
Till de furnace glow an' de chimbly roar.

Ol' Nebuchadnezzar gives up de fight;
He open dat door an' he bow perlite.
He shade his eyes from the glare infernal

An' say to Abednego, "Step out, Colonel."
An' he add, "Massa shadrach, I hopes you all
Won't be huffy at me at all."

Then Shadrach, Meshach, Abednego,
Hay foot, straw foot, three in a row,
Stepped right smart from dat oven door
Jes' as good as they wux before,
An' far as Nebuchadnezzar could find,
Jes' as good as they wuz behind.

(Keith Preston -- 1884-1927)

7
EPITAPHS

Epitaphs were common for burials in the 18th and 19th centuries and books have been written about them. From these books the following epitaphs were selected because of what they reveal about attitudes toward death and dying. Many are intentionally funny (or so it seems), and many are inadvertently so.

Epitaph, meaning to celebrate in words, is the end of life of God's creature. What more fitting way to end this book than with words celebrating life now...and then.

* * * * *

When you are dressed in all your best,
    In fashion most complete.
Think how like me you soon will be,
    Dressed in your winding sheet.
        Berkshire Center, Vermont.

* * * * *

Here is an epitaph erected to the memory of Brigham Young, the primary leader of the Church of the Latter Day Saints (Mormon).
    Brigham Young
    Born
    On this spot
    1801
    A man of much courage
    And superb equipment.
        Whitingham, Vermont.

* * * * *

He was man of invention great,
Above all that lived nigh.
But he could not invent to live,
When God called him to die.
        Jonathan Kilbor, d. Oct. 14, 1785, Colchester, CT

* * * * *

Here lies one Wood enclosed in wood,
One Wood within another.
The outer wood is very good,
We cannot praise the other.
        Maine

* * * * *

Jane, wife of James Graham,
Died Oct. 29, 1863, aged 30 y's 5 m's.
James was holding in his hand,
    The likeness of his wife --
Fresh as if touched by fairy wand,
    With beauty, grace and life.
He almost tho't it spoke, he gazed
    Upon the treasure still,
Absorbed, delighted and amazed,
    To view the artist's skill.

This picture is yourself, Dear Jane,
    'Tis drawn to nature true:
I've kissed it o'er and o'er again,
    It is so much like you.
"And has it kissed you back, my dear,
    "Why-no-my love!" said he.
"Then James, it is very clear
    "Tis not at all like me!"

Here lyes interred ye Body of
Mrs. Elizabeth Phillips; Who
was Born in Westminister, in Great
Britain and was commissioned by John
Lord Bishop of London, in ye year
1718 to ye office of a Midwife; came
to this country in ye year 1719 & by
ye Blessing of God has brought into
this world above 130,000 children.
Died May 6, 1761, Aged 76 years.

* * * * *

The little hero that lies here
Was conquered by the diarhoea.
                    Portland, Maine

* * * * *

We can but mourn our loss,
Though wretched was his life.
Death took him from the cross,
Erected by his wife.
                    Kittery, Maine 1803

* * * * *

JOHN PHILLIPS
Accidentally shot as a mark of affection by his brother.

* * * * *

Here lies Cynthia, Steven's wife.
She lived six years in calm and strife.
Death came at last and set her free.
I was glad and so was she.
                    Hollis, New Hampshire

* * * * *

Here lies old Caleb Ham,
By trade a bum.
When he died the devil cried,
Come, Caleb, come.
                    Hollis, New Hampshire

HERE LIES
JAKE,
HIT THE GAS
INSTEAD OF THE
BRAKE!

* * * * *

Our little Jacob has been taken away to bloom in a superior flower pot.

Vermont

* * * * *

My wife lies here.
All my tears cannot bring her back;
Therefore, I weep.

Vermont

* * * * *

Beneath this stone our baby lays,
He neither crys or hollers.
He lived just one and twenty days,
And cost us forty dollars.

Charity wife of Gideon Bligh
Underneath this stone doth lie
Naught was she ever known to do
That which her husband told her to.
                Burlington, VT

* * * * *

Here lies the wife of brother Thomas,
Whom tyrant death has torn from us,
Her husband never shed a tear,
Until his wife was buried here,
And then he made a fearful rout,
For fear she might find her way out.
                Burlington, VT

* * * * *

She lived with her husband fifty years
And died in the confident hope of a better life.
                Burlington, VT

* * * * *

Here lies the body of Uncle David,
Who died in the hope of being sa-ved.
Where he's gone and how he fares,
Nobody knows and nobody cares.
                Stowe, VT

* * * * *

Stay, reader, drop upon this stone
One pitying tear and then be gone.
A handsome pile of flesh and blood
Is here sunk down in its first mud.
                Stowe, VT

* * * * *

A rum cough carried him off.
                Stowe, VT

* * * * *

Sacred to the memory of three twins.
                Stowe, VT

"By the time we got the child-proof cap off his medicine bottle he was gone!"

* * * * *

Here lies the body of Samuel Proctor,
Who lived and died without a doctor.
                Wendell, MA

* * * * *

Here lies the bones of Richard Lawton,
Whose death alas! was strangely brought on.
Trying his corns one day to mow off,
His toe or rather what it grew to,
An inflammation quickly flew to.
Which took alas! to mortifying,
And was the cause of Richard's dying.
                Plymouth, MA

* * * * *

Here I lie bereft of breath,
Because a cough carried me off;
Then a coffin they carried me off in.
                Boston, MA

This world's a city, full of crooked streets;
And Death the market place where all men meets.
If Life were merchandise that we could buy,
The rich would live and none but poor would die.
Dorchester, MA

✳ ✳ ✳ ✳ ✳

Here is a blacksmith's epitaph, written by myself:
My sledge and hammer lie reclined,
My bellows too have lost their wind,
My fire's extinct, my forge decayed,
And in the dust my vice is laid.
My iron is spent, my coal is gone,
My nails are drove -- my work is done.
Norton, MA

✳ ✳ ✳ ✳ ✳

Peggy Dow shared the vicissitudes of Lorenzo fifteen years and
died at age 39.
Hebron, CT

✳ ✳ ✳ ✳ ✳

Epitaph on a baby who died at only four days old:
Since I so very soon was done for
I wonder what I was begun for.
New Haven, CT

✳ ✳ ✳ ✳ ✳

God works a wonder now and then,
He thought a lawyer was an honest man.
New Haven, CT

✳ ✳ ✳ ✳ ✳

Underneath this pile of stones,
Lies all that's left of Sally Jones.
Her name was Lord, it was not Jones,
'But Jones was used to rhyme with stones.
Skaneateles, NY

✳ ✳ ✳ ✳ ✳

He's done a catching cod
And gone to meet his God.

* * * * *

While on earth my knee was lame,
I had to nurse and heed it.
But now I'm in a better place,
Where I don't even need it.
Ithaca, NY

* * * * *

Tabitha, wife of Moses Fledger
Aged 55
We shall miss thee, mother
(Job printing neatly done.)

* * * * *

Stranger pause my tale attend,
And learn the cause of Hannah's end.
Across the world the wind did blow,
She ketched a cold that laid her low.
We shed a lot of tears 'tis true,
But life is short -- aged 82.
Bayfield, MS

Here lies my wife in earthly ould,
Who when she lived did naught but scold.
Peace! Wake her not, for now she's still,
She had, but now I have my will.
               Bayfield, MS

* * * * *

(Epitaph on the grave of a railroad engineer.)
Until the brakes are turned on time,
Life' throttle-value shut down.
He works to pilot in the crew,
That wears the martyr's crown.
On schedule time, on upper grade,
Along the homeward section,
He land his train in God's roundhouse,
The morning of resurrection.
His name on God's pay roll,
And transportation through to Heaven,
A free pass for his soul.
               Alexandria, VA

* * * * *

Beneath this stone, a lump of clay,
    Lies Arabella Young,
Who on the twenty first of May
    Began to hold her tongue.

* * * * *

Within this grave do lie,
    Back to back my wife and I.
When the last trump the air shall fill,
    If she gets up, I'll just lie still.

* * * * *

Mammy and I together lived,
Just three years and a half.
She went first, I followed next,
The cow before the calf.

* * * * *

Sacred to the remains of Jonathan Thompson a pious Christian
and an affectionate husband.
    His disconsolate widow still continues to carry on his business at
the old place since his bereavement.

* * * * *

Here lies the body of Mary Ford,
We hope her soul is with the Lord.
But if for now she's changed this life,
Better there than J. Ford's wife.

* * * * *

Here lies interred Prisilla Bird,
Who sang on earth till sixty two.
Now up on high above the sky,
No doubt she sings like sixty-too.

* * * * *

Here lies Jane Smith
Wife of Thomas Smith, Marble Cutter
This monument was erected by her husband as a tribute to her
memory and a specimen of his work.
Monuments of this same style are two hundred and fifty dollars.

Alpha White
Weight 309 lbs.
Open wide ye gold gates
That lead to the heavenly shore
Our father suffered in passing through
And mother weighs much more.

* * * * *

(Epitaph to a dentist)
View this gravestone with gravity
He's filling his last cavity.

* * * * *

(This was on the tombstone of a nasty old man.)
"deeply regretted by all who never knew him."

* * * * *

Here lies my wife a slatterned shrew,
If I said I regretted her I should lie too.

* * * * *

To all my friends I bid adieu;
A more sudden death you never knew;
As I was leading the mare to drink
She kicked and killed me quicker 'n a wink.
Oxford, NH c. 1800

* * * * *

DR. ISAAC BARTHOLOMEW
He that was sweet to my Repose
Now is become a stink under my nose.
This is said of me
So will it be said of thee.
Cheshire, CT 1710

* * * * *

DANIEL EMERSON
The land cleared is now my grave.
Think well my friends how you behave.
Marlboro, NH 1829

* * * * *

MRS. SHUTE
    Here lies, cut down like unripe fruit,
        The wife of Deacon Amos Shute.
    She died of drinking too much coffee,
        Anny dominy eighteen forty.
           Windsor, CT 1840

* * * * *

Lansman or sailors,
For a moment avast,
    Poor Jack's topsail
    Is laid to the mast.
The worms gnaw his timbers,
    His vessel's a wreck.
When the last whistle sounds,
    He'll be up on deck.
        East Hampton, CT 1883

CHIEF ORONO OF THE PENOBSCOT INDIANS
Safe lodged within his blanket here below,
Lies the last relics of Old Orono.
Wore down with care, he in a trice.
Exchanged his wigwam for a Paradise.
Old Town, ME 1801

* * * * *

WILLIAM BARY
Opened my eyes, took a peep,
Didn't like it, went to sleep.
Petersborough, NH 1823

* * * * *

Sacred to the memory of Jared Bates, who died August the 6th, 1880. His widow aged 24 who mourns as one who can be comforted lives at 7 Elm Street, this village and possesses every qualification for a good wife.
Lincoln, ME 1800

* * * * *

Here lies the remains of H.P. Nichols' wife,
Who mourned away her natural life.
She mourned herself to death for her man,
While he was in the service of Uncle Sam.
Fletcher, VT 1863

* * * * *

Five times five years, I lived a virgin's life.
Nine times five years, I lived a virtuous wife;
Wearied of this mortal life, I rest.
Plainfield, VT 1888

* * * * *

NATHANIEL PARKE
In Memory of
Mr. Nathaniel Parke
At 19, who on
21st March 1794
Being out hunting
And concealed in a ditch
Was casually shot by
Mr. Luther Frink.
Holyoke, MA 1794

Here lies the body of Mary Ann Lowder
Who burst while drinking a seidlitz powder;
Called forth from this earth to her Heavenly rest
She should have waited till it effervesced.
                Burleigh, NJ 1880

* * * * *

LESTER MOORE
    HERE LIES
    Lester Moore
    Four slugs
    from a 44
    no less
    no more.
            Tombstone, AZ c. 1880

* * * * *

ANONYMOUS
    HE CALLED
    BILL SMITH
    A LIAR
            Cripple Creek, CO 1875

* * * * *

ANONYMOUS
    Cold is my bed, but ah I love it,
    For colder are my friends above it.
            Chicago, IL 1859

* * * * *

Here lies the body of Mrs. Mary, wife
of Dea. John Buel ESQ. She died
Nov. 4 1768 Aeat.90
Having had 13 children
101 grand-children
274 great-grand-children
49 great-great-grand-children
410 Total. 336 survived her.
            Litchfield, CT 1768

* * * * *

PHINEAS G. WRIGHT
    Going. But know not where.
    Putnam, CT 1918

WILLIAM P. ROTHWELL, M.D.
This is on me.
Pawtucket, RI 1939

* * * * *

PHILLIP SIDNEY
P.S. The Old Nuisance
East Calais, VT c. 1800

* * * * *

ROBERT HALLENBECK FAMILY
The Family of Robert T. Hallenbeck
None of us ever voted for
Roosevelt or Truman
Elgin, MN c. 1950

* * * * *

Epitaph: A belated advertisement for a line of goods that has been permanently discontinued.

Irving Cobb

* * * * *

Here lies the body of Robert Gordin,
Mouth almighty and teeth accordin';
Stranger, tread lightly over this wonder,
If he opens his mouth, you are gone, by
thunder.
South Carolina

* * * * *

Here lies the corpse of Dr. Chard
Who filled the half of this churchyard.

* * * * *

This is the grave of Mike O'Day
Who died maintaining his right of way.
His right was clear and his will was strong
But he's just as dead as if he'd been wrong.

* * * * *

If you want a free headstone when you die, just leave word to bury you up to your neck.

BIBLIOGRAPHY

America's Phunniest Phellow -- Josh Billings. Edited by James E. Myers. 1986. Lincoln-Herndon Press, Inc., Springfield, IL

Book of Anecdotes & Jokers Knapsack. 1866. John E. Potter & Company, Publishers. Philadelphia, PA

Burlington Liar's Club. Phillip Strandvold. 1964. Burlington, WI

Carolina Chats. Carl Goerch. 1944. Edwards & Broughton Company, Raleigh, NC. Permission granted by the Estate of Carl Goerch.

Cartoons by Steve Delmonte, Buffalo, NY

Cartoons by John Hayes, Overland Park, KS

Cartoons by Lo Linkert, Mission, B.C. Canada

Cartoons by Masters Agency, Hollister, CA

Cartoons by Eldon Pletcher, Slidell, LA

Cartoons by Dan Rosandich, Chassell, MI

Cartoons by Harley Schwadran, Ann Arbor, MI

Chimes From a Jester's Bells. Robert J. Burdette. 1897. The Bowen-Merrill Co., Indianapolis, IN and Kansas City, MO

Cover -- Capper's Farmer. July 1934. Reprinted with permission of Stauffer Magazine Group, Topeka, KS

The Cowboy Humor of Alfred Henry Lewis. Edited by R. D. Myers. 1989. Lincoln-Herndon Press, Inc., Springfield, IL

Down Home. Carl Goerch. 1943. Edwards & Broughton Company, Raleigh, NC. Permission granted by Estate of Carl Goerch.

Fables in Slang. George Ade. 1899. Herbert S. Stone & Company, Publishers, New York

God Bless the Devil! Liar's Bench Tales. Edited by James R. Aswell. 1940. The University of North Carolina Press, Chapel Hill, NC

Hot Stuff by Famous Funny Men. Melville D. Landon, A.M. 1883. The Reilly & Britton Company, Chicago, IL

Irish Stew. 1994. The State Journal-Register, Springfield, IL

It is to Laugh. Eric Frey. 1907. Dodge Publishing Co., NY

Just For the Fun of It. Carl Goerch. 1954. Edwards & Broughton Company, Raleigh, NC. Permission granted by the Estate of Carl Goerch.

Kids Say the Darndest Things. Art Linkletter. 1957. Prentice Hall, Div. of Simon & Schuster, Englewood, NJ

Life As It's Lived. Jack Boyd. 1989. Texas Tech University Press, Lubbock, TX

More Pious Friends and Drinking Companions. Frank Shay. 1926. The Macauley Company, NY

Noah an' Jonah an' Cpn. John Smith. Don Marquis. 1921. D. Appleton & Company, Publishers. Used by permission of Doubleday, a Div. of Bantam Doubleday Dell Publishing Group, Inc., New York, NY

Nothing Ain't No Good. E.P. Holmes. 1955. Permission granted by John Wesley Clay, Winston-Salem, NC

On a Slow Train Through Arkansaw. 1903. Thomas W. Jackson, Publishers

Remarks. Bill Nye. 1886.

A Snake in the Bathtub. Curt Brummett. 1990. August House, Inc., Little Rock, AR

Steve! Is Mama Home? Josh Sarasohn. Pennfield Press. 1933.

Sut Lovingood Yarns Spun by a "Nat'ral Born Durn'd Fool: Warped and Wove for Public Wear." George W. Harris. 1867. Dick & Fitzgerald, New York, NY

Tar Heel Laughter. Edited by Richard Walser. The University of North Carolina Press, Chapel Hill, NC

That Darned Minister's Son. Haydn S. Pearson. 1950. Doubleday & Company, New York, NY

<u>Tone the Bell Easy</u>. J. Mason Brewer. 1932. Texas Folklore Society No. X, Nacogdoches, TX

<u>Wit and Humor, A Choice Collection</u>. Marshall Brown. 1879. S.C. Griggs & Company, Chicago, IL